100 Film Musicals

100 FILM MUSICALS

BFI SCREEN GUIDES

Jim Hillier & Douglas Pye

A BFI book published by Palgrave Macmillan

First published in 2011 by
PALGRAVE MACMILLAN

on behalf of the

BRITISH FILM INSTITUTE
21 Stephen Street, London W1T 1LN
www.bfi.org.uk

There's more to discover about film and television through the BFI. Our world-renowned archive, cinemas, festivals, films, publications and learning resources are here to inspire you.

Palgrave Macmillan in the UK is an imprint of Macmillan Publishers Limited, registered in England, company number 785998, of Houndmills, Basingstoke, Hampshire RG21 6XS. Palgrave Macmillan in the US is a division of St Martin's Press LLC, 175 Fifth Avenue, New York, NY 10010. Palgrave Macmillan is the global academic imprint of the above companies and has companies and representatives throughout the world. Palgrave® and Macmillan® are registered trademarks in the United States, the United Kingdom, Europe and other countries.

Series cover design: Paul Wright
Cover image: *On the Town* (Gene Kelly, 1949), © Loew's Incorporated
Series design: Ketchup/couch
Set by Cambrian Typesetters, Camberley, Surrey
Printed in China

This book is printed on paper suitable for recycling and made from fully managed and sustained forest sources. Logging, pulping and manufacturing processes are expected to conform to the environmental regulations of the country of origin.

British Library Cataloguing-in-Publication Data
A catalogue record for this book is available from the British Library
A catalog record for this book is available from the Library of Congress
10 9 8 7 6 5 4 3 2 1
20 19 18 17 16 15 14 13 12 11

ISBN 978–1–84457–378–3 (pbk)
ISBN 978–1–84457–379–0 (hbk)

Contents

Acknowledgments

Our thanks go to Rebecca Barden for commissioning this book and for her tact and patience, and to Sophia Contento for her technical support. We are also grateful, in a variety of ways, for the support and advice of the following: Chris Bacon, Susie and John Bates, Joachim Hillier, Fiona and Martha Morey, Alastair Phillips, Liz Pye, Michael Raine, Mike Stevenson, students in the Department of Film, Theatre & Television at the University of Reading, and members of the Department's informal close analysis seminar, The Sewing Circle. Aaron Morey generously shared his knowledge of contemporary popular culture.

Introduction

For thirty years from the coming of sound in the late 1920s, the musical was at the heart of the Hollywood studio system. One of the most popular of all the popular genres on which Hollywood production was based, for many people its combination of music, sophisticated production values, song and dance epitomised the glamour and appeal of Hollywood. Musicals showcased, in ways few other films could rival, the remarkable resources and depth of talent in the major studios. As other film industries across the world developed and converted to sound, musicals, with their direct emotional and sensuous appeal, became a feature of more and more national cinemas, sometimes beginning in imitation of Hollywood but developing into diverse cultural forms. In the US, the production of musicals declined markedly from the 1960s; the genre has frequently seemed on the point of extinction (rather like the Western, which underwent a parallel decline). But among the smaller number of musicals produced, there have been enormous hits from time to time, as though the appeal of what they can offer remains there to be tapped. At the same time, the affection for musicals of the studio period – available for home viewing now as never before – appears undimmed.

What the musical is, how it works, what it does, have been the subject of considerable debate in the last thirty years or so, and studies of the genre, as well as reference books and varied celebrations of musicals, their studios, makers and stars, continue to proliferate. This introduction touches on some of the analytical approaches that have marked out the critical terrain, and reference to critical approaches recur in the entries on individual films. We hope that the 100 films we have selected for this *BFI Screen Guide* will also provide insights into the development and variety of the genre, both in Hollywood, its dominant tradition, but also in perhaps less familiar forms of the film musical that evolved in other national cinemas.

Like all the major film genres, the film musical had a rich prehistory in other cultural forms. In the US, for instance, almost all types of musical performance – including opera, ballet, operetta, vaudeville, revue, the minstrel show, the musical play – ultimately fed the emergence of what became a multifaceted genre. For its first thirty years, however, cinema was 'silent'. Although screenings were generally accompanied by live music and, from the earliest days of 'moving pictures', repeated attempts were made to link picture with recorded sound, there could be no true equivalent on film of these performance traditions. Many films based on musical theatre and performance were produced and famous performers filmed during the 'silent' period but the film musical could emerge only when technology enabled the reliable synchronisation of sound and image.

As soon as movies could 'talk', they also sang. In the tangled evolution of competing technologies for synchronising sound and image and the gradual investment in sound equipment for exhibition venues that characterised the early years of the sound era, the new medium might have been named 'the talkies' but music was just as central to its appeal. As Hollywood prepared itself for sound, studios facilitated the complex process by investing in the recording and radio industries as well as in music publishing, which brought them the rights to swathes of popular music. Musical shorts of well-known singers were produced in large numbers from 1926, as well as others featuring bands, orchestras and dance. The film often regarded as the great breakthrough for sound cinema, the hybrid 1927 Warner Bros. feature, *The Jazz Singer** – over 60 per cent of which is 'silent' – is more notable for Al Jolson's singing than for its dialogue (though it is salutary to remember that many more people watched its first release as an entirely silent film than saw it in theatres equipped for sound). A good deal of the experimentation – both technological and aesthetic – that Hollywood film-makers undertook as they worked out how sound films could be made was devoted to finding various ways of incorporating music and musical performance into feature films.

Narrative had become massively the focus of film production in the US, as well as in most film industries internationally, well before the feature-length film became its dominant form. In the early years of sound, some films were made that followed the structure of theatrical revue – a series of more or less unconnected star performances and musical spectacles – and this remained an intermittent feature of the Hollywood musical, less in the form of revue (though see *Ziegfeld Follies**) than in the form of films in which narrative was tangential to, or a pretext for, varied musical numbers (see, for instance, *Anchors Aweigh**, *Stormy Weather**, *The Girl Can't Help It**). But in line with the industry mainstream, the emergent film musical became predominantly a narrative genre in which the main characters (and often many of the minor ones) sang and danced, and varied relationships between narrative action and musical number came to characterise different forms of the musical.

In 'backstage' or (to use Rick Altman's term) 'show' musicals, numbers tended to be confined to the theatrical venues in which the characters earned their livings (see, for instance, *42nd Street**, *Gold Diggers of 1933**, *Footlight Parade**). In the 'integrated' musical, there was no rigid demarcation between the two realms of performance and narrative action: characters could break into song and dance in their apartments, in the street, or anywhere that the impulse struck them, as though it was the most natural thing in the world, usually accompanied by full orchestra (see *Top Hat**, *Meet Me in St. Louis**, *Seven Brides for Seven Brothers** and many more in this book). Some films mixed the integrated format with numbers performed on stage (*The Band Wagon** or *Easter Parade**, for instance) and/or on camera (*Anchors Aweigh**, *Singin' in the Rain**). Negotiating the relationships between narrative and number and between various levels of artifice became second nature to the musical.

The show musical and the many other films set wholly or partly in the varied worlds of live entertainment point to one of many ways in which the Hollywood musical remained marked by its theatrical inheritance. Paradoxically, for a medium defined by recording and mechanical reproduction of both sound and image and therefore the separation of performer and spectator, the image and associations of live performance (performers in the presence of an audience) remained crucial to many musicals. It is as though, in Jane Feuer's words, 'The Hollywood musical becomes a mass art which aspires to the condition of a folk art …' (1982), drawing sustenance from an experience that cinema inherently denies. Celebration of the show by an audience in the film's world is invariably the climax of a backstage story; even in non-showbiz settings, numbers will often be staged in such a way as to facilitate or mimic immediate connection with the spectator via direct address to the camera, in ways that were anathema to most other narrative films.

Some integrated musicals drew directly on the conventions of theatrical operetta, in which score and story are intertwined. A number of operettas were adapted for the screen (see *The Merry Widow**, *Naughty Marietta**), while the elegant European settings and the musical styles of operetta were adopted by a range of other musicals, especially in the early years of the genre (see, among others, *The Love Parade**, *Love Me Tonight**). But the development of musical comedy and of the indigenous Broadway musical became increasingly influential. In the 1920s and 30s, George Gershwin, Cole Porter, Jerome Kern, Richard Rodgers, Lorenz Hart and others developed the styles that came to dominate American popular song and the Hollywood musical from the mid-30s on. The hugely successful RKO films starring Fred Astaire and Ginger Rogers (see *Flying Down to Rio**, *The Gay Divorcee**, *Top Hat**, *Swing Time**) draw some of their settings from the elegant world of operetta but are basically musical comedies with predominantly American characters singing and dancing to the music of Porter, Berlin, Kern and Gershwin. *Show Boat* (1927), with Kern's music and Oscar Hammerstein II's adaptation of Edna Ferber's novel, was a key moment in the development of the musical play – 'book' (i.e. story), score and numbers integrated into a dramatic whole – and also on the eventual direction of the film musical. Rodgers and Hammerstein's *Oklahoma!* (1942) completed the process of integrating all the elements of musical theatre, songs and also dances written and designed to advance the story and develop the characters. Although it was twelve years before a screen version of *Oklahoma!* appeared, the show's integrated approach and Agnes de Mille's choreography, with its dream ballet and ensemble numbers that drew on folk and modern dance styles, were major influences on Hollywood musicals of the 1940s and 50s. In the mid-1950s, in fact, as the number of original film musicals declined, Hollywood began to rely more and more on adaptations of successful Broadway book musicals (see, for example, *Oklahoma!**, *Carousel**, *The Pajama Game**, *The Sound of Music**).

In the US and Great Britain, until well into the second half of the twentieth century, cultural status often seemed in inverse proportion to mass appeal. In an extreme version of the disdain accorded to most Hollywood films by critics and theorists, musicals were largely taken at face value, their frothy concoctions of song, dance, extravagant design and inconsequential stories – the very epitome of trivial light entertainment – self-evidently unworthy of serious study. As a result, systematic critical analysis of the musical began relatively late. Even when, in the 1960s – partly inspired by French critical journals like *Cahiers du cinéma* and *Positif* – new writers began seriously to analyse and evaluate the achievements of Hollywood directors and genres, the musical remained initially on the sidelines. Male action genres – especially the Western – were the focus of attention in the first wave of English-language genre theory in the 1960s and early 70s. The assumptions – and their gendered basis – underpinning these choices and wider questions of taste and value only began to be challenged as the 1970s progressed.

Scattered essays that began to look systematically at musicals appeared in the 1970s, but it was the 80s before the formative book-length studies of the Hollywood musical by Rick Altman (1981, 1987),

Jane Feuer (1982), and Bruce Babington and Peter Evans (1985) appeared. In this respect, the musical shares something of the critical history of melodrama, another central tendency in Hollywood cinema that became visible to film criticism and theory in the 1970s, particularly through approaches to the development and ideological significance of cultural forms and approaches to representation informed by feminism. Perhaps the most influential of the 1970s essays, Richard Dyer's 'Entertainment and Utopia' (1977), focused directly on the concept of entertainment itself, challenging its self-evident status and asking how and why entertainment works: in specific cultural and historical contexts, what is it in us and in the culture that leads us to take pleasure in 'showbiz' forms? Responding to the sensuous and affective appeal of the musical, Dyer analysed the genre in terms both of its 'representational' and its 'non-representational' dimensions – not just its stars, stories, situations but also 'colour, texture, movement, rhythm, melody, camerawork', qualities fundamental to musicals but particularly difficult to discuss. Dyer therefore tackled head-on the very characteristics of the musical that had made it so resistant to analysis and so inimical to cultural commentators (as well as so popular).

In 1976, Robin Wood – reflecting new currents in film and cultural theory – wrote that the Hollywood genres can be seen as 'different strategies for dealing with the same ideological tensions' (Wood, 1989). The writers who opened up the musical to considered analysis took similar positions on the function of genres in dramatising the conflicting needs, anxieties and values that are deeply embedded in our culture, more often than not appearing to 'deal with' them by resolving contradictions in an affirmative ending. For Dyer, the 'escapism' or 'wish fulfilment' often attributed to entertainment points to its central function – to offer 'utopian' solutions to lacks and needs in people's lives. In dramatising qualities of 'energy, abundance, intensity, transparency, community', musicals enable us to sense what utopian solutions to exhaustion, scarcity, dreariness, manipulation, isolation, might *feel* like. Dyer is very aware of the social complexities of race, class and gender that his categories do not directly address, but the strength of his approach was that it offered one explanation of 'why entertainment *works*'. Films, he argued, work through contradictions in various ways, including in the varied relationships between narrative and numbers, which also indicated contrasting approaches to utopian dreams. Some musicals separate them rigidly so that numbers represent a utopian escape from the realities of the characters' problems (*Gold Diggers of 1933**); in others (Dyer cites *Funny Face**), numbers integrated into the narrative represent temporary escapes from or potential solutions to the conflicts experienced by the characters; and in his final, less common, category, the film suggests that 'utopia is implicit in the world of the narrative as well as in the world of the numbers' (his example is *On the Town**).

For Jane Feuer, too, 'community' becomes an ideal in her thesis about the musical's attempt to compensate for the alienation of mass communication. In ways that we touched on earlier, she ingeniously unpicked the varied and sometimes contradictory strategies musicals used both to tap into the potent associations of live entertainment and yet to exploit the freedoms that only film can offer. Rick Altman, in what remains the seminal study of the American film musical (1987), is also committed to an ideological analysis of musicals: in his case, as a form of ritual, 'a cultural problem-solving device', which works through 'problematic dichotomies for society' and brings about 'a more workable configuration, a concordance of opposites'. In particular, Altman identifies in the Hollywood musical not the familiar linear development of 'classical narrative', but a 'dual-focus' structure in which scenes featuring the man and woman who will form the romantic couple appear in alternation, setting up a process of comparison and contrast which leads ultimately to the dichotomies being resolved through the promise of marriage.

These influential writers also have in common a commitment to analysing musicals as a whole, identifying their characteristic structures, approaches and concerns and how their various features interact to produce meaning and affect. Character, narrative, fictional world and the ways in which these are realised become not mere frameworks for musical spectacle but the centre of attention, in relation to which musical numbers take on their significance. Altman's study, in particular, offers sophisticated and detailed analysis of the syntactical and semantic features of the American musical, which he divides into three traditions, the 'fairy tale', 'folk' and 'show' musicals – categories that have become essential reference points in writing about the musical (and that appear throughout this book).

Altman's argument for the centrality of a dual-focus narrative and of the romantic couple in the history of the Hollywood musical have been challenged by a number of writers (see, for instance, Steve Neale, 2000) as too exclusive and tending to marginalise certain kinds of musical (like *The Wizard of Oz**, or *Ziegfeld Follies**). With such doubts in mind, it is a rewarding exercise to see how far the dual-focus approach works in particular cases. But the place of heterosexual romance in the musical can hardly be exaggerated and a good deal of writing since the 1980s has focused wholly or in part on representations of gender in the genre (see Babington and Evans, 1985; Steven Cohan, 2002), as it has on the parallel traditions of romantic comedy (see, for example, Kathrina Glitre, 2006). In the excellent analysis of *Easter Parade** with which Babington and Evans open their detailed study of individual musicals, for instance, they make the modest but significant claim that 'While it may not, at a deep level, seriously question, as *Viridiana* emphatically does, the roles men and women are expected to play both in private and in public, *Easter Parade* frequently shows the struggles of characters fitting into their ideological roles.' Many musicals take the form of romantic comedy, and the central motif of the making of a heterosexual couple allows for all sorts of variations in the way in which images of masculinity and femininity are played out in relation to traditional assumptions about gender. The re-education Fred Astaire's character undergoes in *Easter Parade** is far from unique, and some musicals (see, for example, *The Pirate**) go further in probing the possibility of equality within the couple.

As the 1950s progressed, these issues – always potentially fraught but generally contained within the conventions of comedy – appeared in more openly problematic forms in Hollywood musicals that veered into the terrain of melodrama (see, for instance, *Carousel**, *A Star Is Born**, *Love Me or Leave Me**).

While contested gender roles and patterns of representation became central to analysis of a number of Hollywood genres from the 1970s – associated with discussions of how far Hollywood movies might be seen to question ideological norms – race remained much less examined until the 1990s and beyond. The deep-rooted racism that produced demeaning and stereotypical representations of African-Americans and other ethnic groups across the whole of Hollywood cinema affected the musical as much as other genres. The marginalisation of African-Americans in the musical was all the more striking given the vital contributions of minstrelsy and jazz to the emergence of the standard popular song forms which constituted the mainstay of Broadway and movie musicals. In recent years, significant studies have appeared, looking, for instance, at the use of blackface in performance traditions and in musicals (see *The Jazz Singer** and *Show Boat** among others), at the place of black performers such as Bill 'Bojangles' Robinson (see *The Littlest Rebel**, *Swing Time**) and the appropriation of African-American musical forms. Writers such as Arthur Knight (2002) and Susan Smith (2005) have looked in detail at traditions represented in this book by a number of 'black cast' Hollywood musicals, including *Hallelujah!**, *Cabin in the Sky**, *Stormy Weather** and *Carmen Jones**. This is a growing area of work that examines what is on the whole a disreputable history but also probes some of what Smith calls 'strains of resistance' and 'strategies of subversion'. Since the 1960s, Hollywood musicals have become more racially integrated. Curiously, the 1970s produced several all- (or mostly) black musicals, such as *Car Wash** and *The Wiz* (1978), though in a very different social context.

By the mid-1950s, the Hollywood studio musical was clearly in decline. Broadway adaptations were becoming more common; the studio system in which production, distribution and exhibition had been integrated was breaking up, with the consequent decline in its large contracted labour forces; rock and roll burst onto the scene in 1956; in 1957, Fred Astaire and Gene Kelly starred in their last major musicals. Threading through this period were also the darker currents just referred to. Michael Wood (1975), writing about a change of mood in MGM musicals that he located especially in *It's Always Fair Weather**, argued that 'By the mid-fifties in America, it seemed impossible to break into song and dance, even metaphorically …', that the confidence that had sustained the earlier MGM musical had evaporated and that '… when your confidence is gone, the musical goes too. You can't like yourself, and it's never fair weather.'

The forms of the Hollywood musical dominated much of the production of musicals in other countries. In the 1930s, for example, Britain and Germany both made movies designed to compete in international markets with the Hollywood product (see, for example, *Evergreen**, *Der Kongress tanzt**) while at the same time making films aimed much more obviously at home markets (see, for example, *Sing as We Go**, *Come on George!**). Other national cinemas, in India, Egypt, Mexico and Japan, for example, though clearly influenced by Hollywood in their taste for spectacle, developed more independently, drawing on their own traditions of music, song and dance (see *Afrita Hanem**, *Ansiedad**, *Janken musume**). In Indian cinema, western generic distinctions – Western, gangster, comedy, musical – applied much less and Indian popular films tended to mix together different kinds of 'generic' material within individual films, virtually all of which incorporated song and dance (see, for example, *Shree 420**, *Pyaasa**, *Pakeezah**, *Sholay**, *Dil se …**). In addition, Indian cinema adopted the convention by which star actors mimed to 'playback singers', whose celebrity could match that of the stars.

Indian popular cinema continued to thrive from the 1960s onwards as Hollywood production (and notably the production of musicals) declined, without ever disappearing. Though 'old style' musicals continued to be made occasionally, and could be very successful (see, for instance, *Mary Poppins**, *The Sound of Music**), other Hollywood musicals became more reflective, consciously acknowledging the classic musicals of the past (see, for example, *Nashville**, *New York, New York**, *One from the Heart**, or later co-productions like *Moulin Rouge!**). At the same time, Hollywood became more responsive to changing trends in popular music, as the major audience for movies got younger (see, for instance, *Saturday Night Fever**, *Grease**).

The decline of the classic Hollywood musical also had the effect of stimulating experimentation with musical conventions outside Hollywood: in Europe, Jacques Demy essayed a modern operetta form in the wholly sung *Les Parapluies de Cherbourg**, though many denied it the status of 'musical' for its lack of distinction between narrative and 'numbers'. Films like Demy's later *Les Demoiselles de Rochefort**, Chantal Akerman's *Golden Eighties**, François Ozon's *8 femmes**, Alain Resnais's *Pas sur la bouche** and Lars von Trier's *Dancer in the Dark** more consciously referenced the classical Hollywood musical.

This is a book about *film* musicals – musicals made for theatrical distribution (although, of course, since the 1960s, television broadcasts have provided important revenue streams for all theatrical features). However, it would be as much a mistake not to take account of the relationship of television to the musical as it would be to ignore the relationships between film musicals and the theatre. The ending of the Hollywood studio system coincided roughly with the rise of television in the US (and, of course, many have seen in that a causal connection). In the 1930s and 40s, radio made extensive use of Broadway and vaudeville artists and songs, as well as adapting popular films, and it was always likely that television would take on some of the functions and formats established by the Hollywood studios as well as developing its own emphases. In terms of its relationship to 'the musical', television has occupied a slightly uncertain space somewhere between Broadway and Hollywood, but it has certainly played a major role in preserving the musical as a significant genre.

As film musicals became less frequent in the 1950s, so television began to expand its own production, in several distinct ways. As well as tribute shows to Broadway composers and lyricists, television utilised their talents to produce original musicals, favouring particularly musicals based on fairy tales, such as CBS's *Cinderella* (1957), with songs by Richard Rodgers and Oscar Hammerstein and starring Julie Andrews; ABC's *The Dangerous Christmas of Red Riding Hood* (1965), with songs by Jule Styne and Robert Merrill and starring Liza Minnelli; and NBC's *Jack and the Beanstalk* (1967), directed by and starring Gene Kelly, with songs by Sammy Cahn and Jimmy Van Heusen. The operetta tradition was continued in productions like *Naughty Marietta* (NBC, 1955), *The Merry Widow* (NBC, 1955) and Gilbert and Sullivan productions. More important were television adaptations of Broadway shows and (occasionally) Hollywood musicals: *Anything Goes* (ABC, 1954), *Annie Get Your Gun* (NBC, 1957), *Kiss Me Kate* (NBC, 1958), *Meet Me in St. Louis* (CBS, 1959), *The Jazz Singer* (NBC, 1959), *Brigadoon* (ABC, 1966), *Carousel* (ABC, 1967), *George M!* (CBS, 1972), and many more. One of the effects of such shows was to provide big Broadway stars like Ethel Merman, Mary Martin and Carol Burnett with some of the widespread exposure which had eluded them in movies. In more recent years, with the fragmentation of broadcasting and cable, PBS has taken a major role in presenting Broadway adaptations, such as *Show Boat* (1989), *Cats* (1998) and productions of Stephen Sondheim's Broadway shows.

More originally, television has tried out, though without much success in most cases, episodic musical television series, several of which grew out of successful theatrical movies: *That's Life* (ABC) ran for a single season in 1968–9; *Seven Brides for Seven Brothers* (CBS) ran for twenty-two episodes in 1982–3; *Dirty Dancing* (CBS) ran for just a few episodes in 1988–9; Steven Bochco's *Cop Rock* (ABC) lasted only eleven episodes and *Hull High* (NBC) (see *High School Musical**) only eight in 1990. The only significantly successful show was *Fame* (MGM Television for NBC), based on the 1980 film, which ran from 1982 to 1987. Alongside such experiments, a tradition emerged in which successful non-musical sitcoms and other shows featured the occasional musical episode, from *I Love Lucy* (1956) and the *Dick Van Dyke Show* (1963) to *Happy Days* (1971, 1981) to *Chicago Hope* (1997), *Xena: Warrior Princess* (2000), *Ally McBeal* (2000), *Buffy the Vampire Slayer* (2001) and *Oz* (2005).

Just as Disney has maintained since the 1930s (see *Snow White and the Seven Dwarfs**) a special commitment to the theatrical animated musical, spectacularly so in the string of 1990s hits like *Beauty and the Beast* (1991), *Aladdin* (1992), *The Lion King* (1994) and *The Hunchback of Notre Dame* (1996), so it has mined a vein of live-action juvenile musical television films, like *The Cheetah Girls* (2003) (and its sequels) and the *Hannah Montana* series (starting in 2006, feature film 2009). Though very popular, none achieved the phenomenal success of the 2006 Disney Channel television movie *High School Musical** and its three sequels, which in turn spawned more challenging and innovative musical series like 20th Century-Fox Television's *Glee* (first broadcast in 2009).

Steven Bochco, the creator of *Cop Rock*, acknowledged the influence of Dennis Potter's BBC television mini-series *Pennies from Heaven* (1978) and *The Singing Detective* (1986). Potter opened up new possibilities for the musical form by having characters mime to 1930s/40s recordings of popular songs and used the same format, with recordings of 50s popular songs, in *Lipstick on Your Collar* (made for Channel 4, 1993). Like Potter's work, Peter Bowker's mini-series *Blackpool* (2004) and *Viva Blackpool* (2006), made for BBC Television, also used characters miming to popular records. Although *Pennies from Heaven* was adapted as a Hollywood feature (directed by Herbert Ross, 1981), few Hollywood or British film musicals have followed Potter's lead, though his influence is evident in films like Alain Resnais's *On connaît la chanson* (1997) and forms part of a wider pattern of experimentation with musical conventions.

Last, but certainly not least, we should note the pervasive influence since the 1980s of MTV and musical television as a whole on the visual presentation of popular music, an influence already apparent in movie musicals as early as *Flashdance* (1983) and *Footloose** and a major context for more recent films like *Moulin Rouge!**.

About the book

Given the history of the musical and the nature of the debates that have circulated about it, it was perhaps inevitable that just over half of our entries are products of the major Hollywood studios and were made in the years between the coming of sound and 1960, generally regarded as the core period for the production of musicals. Though these films form the cornerstone of the book, a third of the entries come from the period after 1960 and almost a third were made outside the US. No doubt many of our titles would find their way onto numerous lists of 'best' musicals, but the intention has been to give prominence not only to 'classics' but also to films which represent different tendencies within the genre and those made outside the Hollywood studio norms.

Availability on DVD (in one region or another) and/or regular circulation on terrestrial or cable television was an additional criterion for choice: reading about films that one is unable to see can be frustrating. At the same time, there remain a few titles here that are not readily available to see or buy or rent. Perhaps this volume will encourage distributors to make some of these titles available.

Each entry aims to identify what is distinctive about a particular film and relate it to some of the major debates about the musical genre. In addition, entries try to provide some historical context – for example, the film's relationship with Broadway shows – and relate it to other films, whether included as entries in the book or not. References to other entries in the book are marked with an asterisk to allow ease of cross-reference (although there are certainly more relationships to be made between films than those we highlight).

As non-English-language entry titles often have several different official or unofficial English translations, we have entered them under their original titles – which in many cases are the titles they are best known under anyway. Translations are provided within the entry and appear in the index as well as the original title.

At the end of each entry we provide a list of production credits. For reasons of space, these credits are selective, but our selection is slightly different from those in other volumes in the series. It seemed to us that for a book on musicals, credits for songs, music, art direction and choreography were vital. Credits have been adapted in several cases to take some account of different modes of production. We follow the Screen Guide convention of including the director's name immediately under the entry title. However, this should not be taken to imply that we necessarily consider the director of a particular film to be the major, or only significant, influence on the way it turns out, as a number of our entries make clear.

The book includes two appendices:

References

This lists all books and essays that we refer to in the Introduction and the individual entries. For the sake of readability, we decided against a formal academic annotation system, but this list of references should enable readers to readily locate all sources.

Further Reading

This overlaps with References, but offers a more extensive listing of important English-language books on the film musical.

Afrita Hanem
Egypt, 1949 – 112 mins
Henri Barakat

Egypt, like India, had a busy movie industry from the 1930s and functioned as a sort of Arab Hollywood (or perhaps Bollywood), providing films for the Arabic Middle East and North Africa. The movie industries in 'less developed' countries like Egypt, India and Mexico experienced their 'golden ages' from the mid-1940s to the mid-60s, a little later than Hollywood, due partly to the later advent of television (though in each case, as everywhere, old movies provided essential television programming). Musicals of one kind or another were a – perhaps *the* – staple genre in industries dominated, like Hollywood, by studios and stars (see, for example, *Shree 420**, *Pyaasa**, *Ansiedad**). Stars, in Egypt, often meant singing stars like Farid Al Atrache (the 'sad singer' and 'King of the *Oud*' [a lute-like instrument]) and Abdel Halim Hafez, established radio and recording stars, and dancers like Samia Gamal (declared by King Farouk in 1949 as Egypt's 'national dancer'), and many films were essentially vehicles for their performances (as they often were in Hollywood). Singing stars provided their own voices, as they did in Mexican cinema (in contrast to the 'playback' tradition in Indian cinema).

Afrita Hanem (known in English variously as *The Genie Lady*, *Lady Genie*, *Little Miss Devil*), a lively, somewhat screwball musical comedy, makes ample space for songs by star/producer/singer/composer Al Atrache and dances by Gamal, whether as stage performances or spontaneous song and dance. Humble stage singer Asfour (Al Atrache) pines after gold-digging dancer Aleya (Lola Sedki), who plans to marry a wealthy man to finance her theatre-owner father. Asfour discovers a magic lamp whose genie, Kahramana (Gamal), visible only to him, claims they were lovers a millennium earlier. Bound to grant his wishes, she is nevertheless determined to thwart his pursuit of Aleya. Granted his wish for a theatre of his own, Asfour auditions the dancer Semsema, identical to the genie but very much flesh and blood and visible to everyone. After various comic misadventures, Asfour 'summons up' Kahramana/ Semsema and, after passing through an expressionist netherworld (which may or may not be part of a stage show) whose lugubrious 'sultan'/Lucifer grants the couple their freedom, love reigns supreme.

Farid Al Atrache performs some celebrated poetic songs (in the – to western ears – rather mournful, recitative Arab style) and Samia Gamal's *raqs sharqi* (Oriental dance) routines (misleadingly known in the West as 'belly dance') are captivatingly sexy, but perhaps the chief pleasure is Gamal's infectious comic performance, as Kahramana uninhibitedly enjoys the chaotic fun she unleashes. Certainly, Gamal seems more at ease here than in high melodramas like *A Glass and a Cigarette* (1955) (though, as in many Indian films, the melodrama is paralleled by a comic plotline). Many Egyptian 'musicals' were (like Indian films) essentially melodramas, like *Days and Nights* (1955), a vehicle for young heart-throb singer Abdel Halim Hafez. Running through all these films (as through so many Indian films), exploring moral dilemmas in bourgeois family settings, is a discourse in which western modernity – cars, clothes, manners – is viewed negatively in relation to traditional values. The sage who presides over the genie in *Afrita Hanem* pops up from time to time to deliver homilies about materialistic greed and selfishness.

Samia Gamal also played in international films: she was an exotic dancer (of course) in the Hollywood film *Valley of the Kings* (1954), shot partly in Egypt, and co-starred with Fernandel in Jacques Becker's Moroccan-shot *Ali Baba et les quarante voleurs* (1954). JH

Dir: Henri Barakat; **Prod**: Farid Al Atrache; **Scr**: Henri Barakat, Abul Soud Al Ibyari; **DOP**: Julio de Luca (with Ahmed Adley, Umberto Lanzano) (b&w); **Song Music/Lyrics**: Farid Al Atrache, *et al*.; **Art**: Anton Bulizwis; **Main Cast**: Farid Al Atrache, Samia Gamal, Lola Sedki, Ismail Yassin, Abdel Salam Al Nabulsy; **Prod Co**: Ahmed Darwich Film.

An American in Paris
USA, 1951 – 115 mins
Vincente Minnelli

It is one of the marks of Arthur Freed's ambitions for *An American in Paris* that from the outset he intended to conclude his film with a ballet set to the whole of George Gershwin's 1928 tone poem from which the musical took its name. Ballets invariably offered opportunities to display the star dancers' virtuosity, but their stylised nature also enabled them to enact disturbed dreams or fantasies. The 'American in Paris' ballet begins with a desolate Jerry (Gene Kelly) thinking he has lost Lise (Leslie Caron in her first film) after their parting at the black-and-white ball, and its several episodes present a parallel version of their relationship in which Lise is lost, found and lost again. What is unique, however, is its combination of length (almost 17 minutes), its position at the end of the film and, most markedly, the ostentatious brilliance of its design and execution. Famously, the Parisian settings are each presented in the style of a different painter (Dufy, Renoir, Utrillo, Rousseau, Van Gogh, Toulouse-Lautrec), but the ballet as a whole is characterised by Minnelli's dazzling integration of the self-consciously sophisticated designs with Gershwin's music, Kelly's elaborately varied choreography and John Alton's unorthodox use of limited lighting.

The ballet is a fitting climax to a musical that was emphatically designed to impress. Perhaps as a result, *An American in Paris* is a film of mixed pleasures. Some of the most elaborate numbers are in effect, like the ballet, splendid set pieces, tied only minimally to the narrative: Adam (Oscar Levant)'s ingeniously created fantasy in which he becomes pianist, conductor, the whole orchestra and the audience in Gershwin's Concerto in F; the Folies Bergère-inspired staging of Henri Bourel (Georges Guétary) singing 'I'll Build a Stairway to Paradise'; even 'I've Got Rhythm', Jerry's English lesson for a crowd of kids, although set in the street, has something of this quality. On the other hand, some of the most delightful numbers arise unaffectedly from situation and setting in the lovely studio-built recreation of Paris (the film's opening evokes the famous introduction to Paris in *Love Me Tonight**). 'Melody by Strauss' begins with Adam casually playing the piano and leads to Jerry dancing with the elderly ladies of the neighbourhood café; much later, Jerry and Henri, unwittingly both in love with Lise, burst into ''S Wonderful' and a dance double act in the same location; on the banks of the Seine, Jerry sings 'Our Love Is Here to Stay' to Lise and they dance tentatively together for the first time.

Their romance, however, like much of the plot, seems largely taken for granted. There is no significant development in the relationship from the moment that Lise's initial resistance to Jerry abruptly crumbles. Strangely enough, more fully developed – and distinctly uncomfortable – is Jerry's relationship with the needy but vulnerable Milo Roberts (Nina Foch), the American heiress who is fostering (and funding) his painting. The insensitivity and opportunism of his treatment of Milo are fascinating disturbances in the film's presentation of Jerry that her withdrawal from the scene and the film's romantic resolution cannot entirely erase.

An American in Paris was a triumph for the studio: it not only grossed over $6 million more than its very considerable $2.7 million budget but it won six Academy Awards, including Best Picture. At the same ceremony, both Arthur Freed and Gene Kelly were also honoured individually, Kelly with an Honorary Oscar and Freed with the Irving Thalberg Award for 'his extraordinary accomplishment in the making of musical pictures' (Fordin, 1975). DP

Dir: Vincente Minnelli; **Prod**: Arthur Freed; **Scr**: Alan Jay Lerner; **DOP**: Alfred Gilks, John Alton (colour); **Song Music/Lyrics**: George Gershwin/Ira Gershwin; **Musical Dir**: Johnny Green, Saul Chaplin; **Choreog**: Gene Kelly; **Art**: Cedric Gibbons, Preston Ames; **Main Cast**: Gene Kelly, Leslie Caron, Oscar Levant, Georges Guétary, Nina Foch; **Prod Co**: Metro-Goldwyn-Mayer.

Anchors Aweigh
USA, 1945 – 141 mins
George Sidney

Before moving to MGM in 1941, Joe Pasternak produced the extremely popular Deanna Durbin musicals at Universal (see *100 Men and a Girl**). MGM musicals of the 1940s are now associated particularly with the production unit headed by Arthur Freed (see, among others, *An American in Paris**, *Easter Parade**, *Meet Me in St. Louis**, *On the Town**, *Summer Holiday**) but Pasternak became a key producer, contributing some of the biggest hits of the decade to the studio's large and profitable output of musicals. In particular, his work with Deanna Durbin made him the obvious person to work with the young soprano Kathryn Grayson, and he became central to the continuing strand of Hollywood musicals featuring operatic voices (he later worked with Mario Lanza on such films as *The Toast of New Orleans*, 1950, and *The Great Caruso*, 1951).

Anchors Aweigh feels now like an interesting hybrid. Its story of two sailors (Gene Kelly and Frank Sinatra in the first of their buddy double acts) on a brief shore leave, meeting girls and falling in love, looks forward to *On the Town*. (In fact, the waitress from Brooklyn [Pamela Britton] that Clarence [Sinatra] eventually falls for even seems to anticipate Betty Garrett's much more developed role as Hildy in that film.) When their leave is derailed by a little boy (Dean Stockwell) who wants to join the navy and whom they have to escort home, they meet his Aunt Susie (Grayson), a movie extra and aspiring singer. First Clarence and then Joe (Kelly) fall for Susie, and much of the plot turns on their attempts (in echoes of *100 Men and a Girl*) to get her an audition with José Iturbi, the pianist and conductor who appeared as himself in several MGM films of this period. With performers split between popular and more classical musical styles, the film has to accommodate widely different numbers.

Perhaps inevitably, then, the pleasures of the film come less from the integration of number and narrative that characterises many of the great

Freed unit musicals, than from its separate parts. Many of the sixteen numbers are presented with minimal narrative motivation. Most famous is Kelly's remarkable song and dance ('The Worry Song') with Jerry the mouse, a seamless mixture of live action and animation. This springs from a story Joe is telling a group of school kids, and one of Kelly's later numbers ('The Mexican Hat Dance') is performed to and with a little girl (Sharon McManus). Susie amazes Joe and Clarence (and us) with the range and power of her voice when she performs 'Jealousy' in the restaurant where she works, and much later, in her screen test, sings to the waltz from Tchaikovsky's Serenade for Strings, a number staged to reveal much of the technology and many of the personnel of the sound stage. As Clarence, Sinatra has what are in effect three reflective soliloquies, the Jule Styne and Sammy Cahn songs 'What Makes the Sunset', 'The Charm of You' and 'I Fall in Love Too Easily'. Iturbi, too, has his own musical interludes, including a performance of Liszt's Hungarian Rhapsody No. 2 with a mass of young pianists in the Hollywood Bowl. Yet the film's level of energy seems perceptibly to rise in the numbers Sinatra and Kelly share: 'We Hate to Leave', performed to Joe and Clarence's jealous shipmates as the friends prepare to go on leave; 'I Begged Her', their boastful account to fellow navy men of their fictitious romantic adventures; and their frenetic 'improvisation' of 'If You Knew Susie' to frighten off Susie's dinner date. DP

Dir: George Sidney; **Prod**: Joe Pasternak; **Scr**: Isabel Lennart, from a story by Natalie Marcin; **DOP**: Robert Planck, Charles Boyle (colour); *Tom and Jerry* cartoon by MGM Cartoon Studio; **Song Music/Lyrics**: Jule Styne/Sammy Cahn; Joseph Meyer/Buddy de Sylva, *et al*.; **Musical Dir**: George Stoll; **Choreog**: Gene Kelly, Stanley Donen; **Art**: Cedric Gibbons, Randall Duell; **Main Cast**: Gene Kelly, Frank Sinatra, Kathryn Grayson, José Iturbi, Dean Stockwell, Pamela Britton; **Prod Co**: Metro-Goldwyn-Mayer.

Ansiedad
Mexico, 1953 – 110 mins
Miguel Zacarias

The Mexican film industry, like those in India and Egypt (see, for example, *Shree 420**, *Pyaasa**, *Afrita Hanem**), experienced a 'golden age' from the mid-1930s to around 1960, when it was the pre-eminent Spanish-language cinema, distributed widely in Central and Latin America. During this period, a number of Mexican stars, such as Dolores del Rio, Cantinflas, María Félix, Pedro Armendiaz and Ricardo Montalban, appeared in Hollywood movies and elsewhere. Like Indian, Egyptian and Hollywood cinemas, Mexican cinema relied on genres and stars, with the musical and its stars among the most popular. None were more celebrated than Pedro Infante and Jorge Negrete, both also massively popular recording and radio artists, though neither achieved much fame outside Mexico. *Ansiedad* (*Anxiety*), a relatively typical musical from the time, is one of several in which Infante co-starred with 'Sweetheart of the Americas' Libertad Lamarque (Argentinian, though most of her films were made in Mexico), also a prolific recording artist.

   Ansiedad combines the familiar melodrama narrative of twins separated at or near birth and growing up apart until their paths cross dramatically with the familiar musical narrative of singers' rise to fame and celebrity. Infante plays no fewer than three roles. An unemployed singer, he finds an abandoned baby which falls ill and dies, forcing him, via various complications, to give up one of his own twin baby sons; soon after, he is shot dead. Infante also plays both grown-up sons – Rafael, who has been raised by his singer mother María (Lamarque), and Carlos, who has grown up in a wealthy family. Both Rafael and María rise to fame as singers. Mother and son are exceptionally close, almost like lovers when they sing duets, despite tension caused by María's big secret about Rafael's twin. Inevitably, the paths of the mother and the twins cross, and the wealthy, powerful son, taking exception to their humble origins, stands in the way of Rafael's and María's careers and private lives.

Finally, of course, when the mother is almost fatally shot, the truth comes out and the brothers are reconciled. The film trades heavily on traditional values of family, maternal love, humility and hard work.

All the songs except one (Rafael's drunken duet with María, 'Ando muy boracho' ['I'm Very Drunk']) are performances of one kind or another. Lamarque gives fine renditions of her trademark tangos, 'Sus ojos se cerraron' ('His Eyes Closed') and 'Cuesta abajo' ('Downhill'), both by Carlos Gardel. Rafael's rise to fame allows Infante to sing in several different styles, whether popular *ranchera*-type songs set to *mariachi* music ('Tu recuerdo y yo' ['Your Memory and Me'], 'Amor de mis amores' ['Love of All My Loves']) or more romantic songs like Agustin Lara's 'Mujer' ('Woman'), which he sings on radio. The film charts Rafael's and María's rise to fame in terms of the venues they perform in, from small, humble theatres to larger, more elegant ones, society soirées and television. The extended television studio sequences ('Farolito' ['Little Streetlight'] and 'Marimba'), involving more 'American'-style elaborate sets, ballet-style dancers and mobile cameras, are a far cry from Rafael's simply shot *ranchera*-style debut in a small, basic theatre.

The film was photographed by Gabriel Figueroa, who shot numerous mainstream Mexican pictures as well as John Ford's 1947 *The Fugitive* and many of Luis Buñuel's 1950s/60s Mexican films; Figueroa's talent for moody, shadowy lighting is put to good use in the film's night-time exteriors. JH

Dir/Prod: Miguel Zacarias; **Scr**: Edmundo Baez, Miguel Zacarias; **DOP**: Gabriel Figueroa (b&w); **Song Music/Lyrics**: Agustin Lara, Carlos Gardel, Jose Alfredo Jimenez, *et al*.; **Music**: Manuel Esperón; **Art**: Javier Torres Torija; **Main Cast**: Pedro Infante, Libertad Lamarque, Irma Dorantes, Arturo Soto Rangel; **Prod Co**: Producciones Zacarias S.A.

Applause
USA, 1929 – 79 mins
Rouben Mamoulian

Applause is not quite a fully-fledged musical like Rouben Mamoulian's later *Love Me Tonight**, *Summer Holiday** and *Silk Stockings**, but it affords an arresting representation of the backstage world of vaudeville and burlesque. It also features 1920s cabaret and Broadway torch singer Helen Morgan (most celebrated for playing Julie LaVerne in the 1927 Broadway and 1936 movie versions of *Show Boat**), who sings 'What Wouldn't I Do for That Man'. *Applause* is a classic maternal melodrama, almost in the class of *Stella Dallas* (1937): Kitty Darling (Morgan), a fading burlesque star, sends her daughter away from the vaudeville world to be educated in a convent but is pressured by her two-timing partner Hitch (Fuller Mellish Jr) to bring her now grown-up daughter April (Joan Peers) into the business. Repulsed by burlesque and the sexual attentions of Hitch, April nevertheless tries to support her mother, taking her place on stage as the abandoned and abused Kitty kills herself. Kitty's death frees April to leave the business and marry the nice sailor she has met, the couple framed before a Kitty Darling burlesque show poster as the film ends.

Mamoulian carried the stylishness and innovation of his work in opera, operetta and Broadway shows through to his movie debut at the coming of sound: 'Here I had been recruited as a stage expert on dialogue, and all I could think of was the marvellous things one could do with the camera and the exciting new potential of sound recording' (Sarris, 1971). *Applause* does give a strong sense of a newcomer experimenting with styles and techniques, some of which work admirably and some of which do not. The opening sequences evoke burlesque's false glamour and rancid sex appeal: the camera dollies and pans to follow a handbill for Kitty's show as it is blown along a rundown street; cuts show people rushing as the sound of distant ragtime music grows louder, and then we are in the parade itself; from this sequence, we cut to the show in progress via shots of the hard-working band and a lateral track along the ungainly legs of the dancers and their no longer young upper halves. The sentiments of this sequence are strongly amplified later when April, fresh from the convent, is brutally introduced to the world of burlesque, recoiling in disgust amid a rapid montage of grotesque sweaty close-ups of leering male spectators and dancers' faces, legs and thighs. Mamoulian pushed for innovative uses of sound, insisting, for example, on two microphones (and subsequent track mixing) for a scene in which April quietly prays while her mother hums a lullaby. Less successful are some poorly motivated overhead shots and unduly expressionist uses of shadow and frame composition.

While Mamoulian established himself in the 1930s and 40s as an in-demand Hollywood movie director (though *Applause* was shot at New York's Astoria Studios), he remained active in Broadway theatre, directing a number of important shows, including the all-black *Porgy and Bess* (1935) and *St Louis Woman* (1946), as well as the first productions of *Oklahoma!* (1943) and *Carousel* (1945). The successful 1970 Betty Comden–Adolph Green Broadway musical *Applause* (Lauren Bacall's singing-dancing stage debut) was an adaptation of the 1950 film *All About Eve* and had nothing to do with the 1929 film. JH

Dir: Rouben Mamoulian; **Prod**: Monta Bell, Jesse L. Lasky, Walter Wanger; **Scr**: Garrett Fort, from a novel by Beth Brown; **DOP**: George Folsey (b&w); **Song Music/Lyrics**: Jay Gorney/ E. Y. Harburg; Joe Burke/Dolly Morse; Fats Waller, Harry Link/Billy Rose; **Art**: not known; **Main Cast**: Helen Morgan, Joan Peers, Fuller Mellish Jr, Henry Wadsworth, Jack Cameron, Dorothy Cumming; **Prod Co**: Paramount.

The Band Wagon
USA, 1953 – 112 mins
Vincente Minnelli

The Band Wagon took its name from a 1931 Broadway revue in which Fred Astaire starred with his sister Adele. Twenty-two years later, the song catalogue of Arthur Schwartz and Howard Dietz, who wrote the numbers for the original revue, became the basis for a film in which Astaire's age and image are invoked even more overtly than in *Easter Parade**. Astaire's long history is the heart of *The Band Wagon*'s highly self-conscious reassertion of traditional entertainment values in a time of change.

The identification of Tony Hunter (Astaire) with Fred Astaire himself could not be clearer. In the auction of Hollywood memorabilia that opens the film, the iconic top hat and cane of movie song and dance man Hunter fail to sell. Firmly associated with the past, when his train pulls into New York (where Ava Gardner takes all the press attention), Tony's first number is the introverted 'By Myself'. In contrast, his second ('A Shine on Your Shoes'), inspired by an amusement arcade on 42nd Street that has replaced one of the theatres he used to know, is an explosion of spontaneous song and dance that all but takes over the arcade and demonstrates to the film audience how far from finished Tony is.

Before that can be made clear in the world of the film, such intrinsically American popular forms are submerged by the transformation of the musical comedy written by Lily and Lester Marton (Nanette Fabray and Oscar Levant), into 'a modern version of Faust', by the imperious (and British) theatrical superstar, Jeffrey Cordova (Jack Buchanan). Challenged by Cordova to change, Tony is half persuaded by the film's first version of 'That's Entertainment' that on stage 'anything can go'. As rehearsals begin, however, Tony is intimidated by dancing with the ballet star Gabrielle Gerard (Cyd Charisse) and increasingly undermined by Cordova's grandiloquent vision, until finally, in a petulant but painful outburst ('I'm Mrs Hunter's little boy, Tony – a song and

Fred Astaire, Cyd Charisse, 'Girl Hunt Ballet'

dance man'), he quits. When he and Gaby discover (in one of the genre's
most romantic numbers, 'Dancing in the Dark', set in Central Park) that
they can actually dance together, Tony returns, but the overpowering
artifice of the show lumbers on. After the New Haven opening, the
buoyant backers of Cordova's Faustian folly are transformed into haggard
individuals who creep silently out of the theatre.

   At the 'wake' later that night, the forms of entertainment and the
communal energy that have been suppressed burst out again in 'I Love

Louisa', the comic number Lester, Tony and Lily perform to cheer the
assembled company. When Tony determines to save the show and artistic
pretension is banished, success is suddenly effortless. We see no more
rehearsals, as though true entertainment needs no labour – only a
succession of vibrant numbers, one for each city on the out-of-town
tour: 'I See a New Sun' (Gaby), 'I Guess I'll Have to Change My Plan'
(Tony and Jeff in top hat and tails), 'Louisiana Hayride' (Lily leading the
company), and Tony, Lily and Jeff dressed as babies in 'Triplets'.
Finally, on New York opening night, it is the 'Girl Hunt Ballet', a parody
of a hard-boiled detective story in dance, featuring Tony and Gaby.
Apparently abandoned after the show, Tony begins to sing 'By Myself'
again, only to find the whole company waiting for him on the stage.
Gaby declares her love and the film ends with all the principals,
backed by the whole company, reprising 'That's Entertainment', but this
time as the film's wholehearted endorsement of American popular song
and dance. DP

Dir: Vincente Minnelli; **Prod**: Arthur Freed; **Scr**: Betty Comden, Adolph Green; **DOP**: Harry
Jackson (George Folsey) (colour); **Song Music/Lyrics**: Arthur Schwartz/Howard Dietz;
Musical Dir: Adolph Deutsch; **Choreog**: Michael Kidd (Fred Astaire uncredited); **Art**:
Cedric Gibbons, Preston Ames; **Main Cast**: Fred Astaire, Cyd Charisse, Oscar Levant,
Nanette Fabray, Jack Buchanan, James Mitchell; **Prod Co**: Metro-Goldwyn-Mayer.

Cabaret
USA, 1972 – 124 mins
Bob Fosse

Bob Fosse was the most distinctive American choreographer/director of stage musicals in the decades following his first Broadway shows as choreographer in 1954–5 (see *The Pajama Game**). Among several award-winning musicals, he directed such shows as *Sweet Charity* (1966) and *Chicago* (1975), before adapting *Sweet Charity* for his 1969 film debut. *Cabaret*, his second film, based on the 1966 musical play (itself derived from the play *I Am a Camera* and Christopher Isherwood's stories of 1930s Berlin), was a prodigious success: among its eight Academy Awards, Fosse won Best Director and Liza Minnelli Best Actress for her remarkable first starring role in a musical.

Fosse and scriptwriter Jay Presson Allen made extensive changes to the stage musical. A whole subplot was cut and a new relationship – between Jewish heiress Natalia Landauer (Marisa Berenson) and fortune-hunter Fritz Wendel (Fritz Wepper) – introduced. With the casting of Liza Minnelli, Sally Bowles became American; the show's American Cliff Bradshaw became unworldly British academic Brian Roberts (Michael York), whose bisexuality is pivotal to the uncertainties of gender and sexual relationships the film introduces in its portrait of cultural confusion and political disorder in 1931 Berlin. The musical structure of the show was radically changed, abandoning the conventions of the integrated musical, in which characters can burst spontaneously into song and dance, for a version of the backstage or show musical: all but one of the film's numbers are confined to the cabaret of the seedy and transgressive Kit-Kat Klub. Several songs from the show were dropped and new ones introduced, together with an earlier John Kander–Fred Ebb composition, 'Maybe This Time'.

One of the film's most striking inventions is the intercutting between the club and events outside, so that the numbers, guided by the leering cynicism of the Master of Ceremonies (Joel Grey, reprising his Broadway role), parallel and comment on the action. 'Maybe This Time', Sally's passionate solo to a largely empty club, is intercut with Brian and Sally after they have first made love. The thigh-slapping lederhosen dance is cut against the club-owner being savagely beaten by Nazis.

'Money, Money, Money' comes immediately after Sally's meeting with the immensely wealthy Maximilian (Helmut Griem). The Master of Ceremonies' 'Two Ladies' anticipates the three-way relationship between Sally, Brian and Max; his 'If You Could See Her with My Eyes' ('… she wouldn't seem Jewish at all'), sung to a gorilla-suited partner, occurs just as Fritz, now in love with Natalia, confesses that he is in fact Jewish too. The club itself becomes the central image of a culture in chaos, a George Grosz-inspired purgatorial vision, vividly created in Fosse's montage-based style of rapidly juxtaposed angles and scales of shot. By contrast, there is a ringing clarity in the chilling 'Tomorrow Belongs to Me', the film's most lyrical song, sung in the open air by a blond, fresh-faced member of the Hitler Youth.

What does the film want us to make of all this? Natalia and Fritz, their love consecrated in their synagogue wedding, appear doomed, yet there is no liberation in the sexual freedom of the other characters. Sally is a role-playing, damaged young woman, endearing but oblivious to what is happening around her; only Brian tries, ineffectually, to take a political stand, though he retreats to his scholarly life in Cambridge. In the final number, 'Cabaret', Sally sings that 'Life is a cabaret, old chum', affirming her own denial of the wider world. In *Cabaret*, the show is a moral dead-end in a society that offers no hope. DP

Dir: Bob Fosse; **Prod**: Cy Feuer; **Scr**: Jay Presson Allen, from the musical play, book by Joe Masteroff, based on John Van Druten's play, *I Am a Camera*; **DOP**: Geoffrey Unsworth (colour); **Song Music/Lyrics**: John Kander/Fred Ebb; **Musical Dir**: Ralph Burns; **Choreog**: Bob Fosse; **Art**: Jurgen Kiebach, Rolf Zehetbauer; **Main Cast**: Liza Minnelli, Michael York, Helmut Griem, Joel Grey, Fritz Wepper, Marisa Berenson; **Prod Co**: Allied Artists/ABC Pictures.

Cabin in the Sky
USA, 1943 – 99 mins
Vincente Minnelli

It may have been, as James Naremore (1993) suggests, because of Minnelli's experience in directing 'sophisticated Broadway reviews featuring black performers' that he was allocated *Cabin in the Sky* for his first film as director. Minnelli (1974) himself tells us that the film, the first Hollywood musical with an all African-American cast since *Hallelujah!**, was a second choice for producer Arthur Freed, made when *Porgy and Bess* proved unavailable, and he expresses his initial reservations about the story, 'which reinforced the naive, childlike stereotype of blacks'. If he was going to make it, he writes, he 'would approach it with great affection and not condescension'.

As a project, *Cabin the Sky* has a good deal in common with *Hallelujah!* (but makes an interesting contrast with *Stormy Weather**). Adapted (with significant changes) from the musical play, the film presents another social world inhabited entirely by black characters and divided between the values of the pious, rural home and the temptations of the town. Again, religious faith is central to the story and the male protagonist is torn between warring impulses, represented by two women who embody opposed paths of virtue and vice. This binary is given emphatic form by the central conceit of *Cabin in the Sky*, the recurrent presence, unobserved by the human characters, of emissaries from Heaven and Hades who battle for the soul of Little Joe (Eddie 'Rochester' Anderson) after he has been shot while gambling, and who agree to give him a further six months of life either to earn salvation or confirm that he belongs in the other place.

The film's comedic register (very different to the intensity of *Hallelujah!*) is central to Minnelli's inflection of the stereotypes that had so concerned him and to the avoidance of condescension. If in the human world faith is dignified and prayer a potent force, the supernatural framework is presented, with a range of comic incident, in

Lena Horne, Eddie 'Rochester' Anderson, Ethel Waters, 'Bubbles' (John W. Sublett)

predominantly light-hearted terms. The film also inflects the symmetry of the story and challenges its accompanying moral oppositions.
Church and saloon are each introduced through sustained camera movements that show us both the individual and communal vitality of the opposed milieus. Church is certainly not too solemn and saloon more celebratory than sinful. In the Paradise saloon, after all, Duke Ellington provides the music and the wonderful Lena Horne plays Georgia Brown, the temptress regarded by Lucifer Jr (Rex Ingram) as one of his own.

Although Joe is the focus of the story, his wife Petunia (Ethel Waters) is the heart of the film. Petunia's prayers call down the forces of Heaven, though her piety is leavened both by her love for the weak-willed Joe and a generous humanity that makes her determination to save him for God remarkably un-repressive. Waters gives one of the great performances in a musical, taking Petunia from modestly dressed traditional housewife, via the initially tentative, then increasingly confident romantic feeling rekindled in 'Taking a Chance on Love', to her transformation into the glamorously attired woman, secure in her own sexuality, who arrives in the saloon, sings the song ('Honey in the Honeycomb') earlier performed by Georgia Brown and follows it with an improvised dance of free and uninhibited energy.

When at the end of the film Joe wakes, thoroughly alarmed and repentant, and it turns out that most of what we have witnessed has been his delirious dream, it is not the adoration of 'Happiness Is Just a Thing Called Joe' to which the overjoyed Petunia returns, but the hope of a new start in 'Taking a Chance on Love'. DP

Dir: Vincente Minnelli; **Prod**: Arthur Freed; **Scr**: Joseph Schrank, from the musical play by Lynn Root, John Latouche, Vernon Duke; **DOP**: Sydney Wagner (b&w); **Song Music/Lyrics**: Vernon Duke/John Latouche; Harold Arlen/E. Y. Harburg; Duke Ellington; **Musical Dir**: Georgie Stoll; **Art**: Cedric Gibbons, Leonid Vasian; **Main Cast**: Ethel Waters, Eddie 'Rochester' Anderson, Lena Horne, Rex Ingram, Kenneth Spencer, Oscar Polk, 'Bubbles' (John W. Sublett), Louis Armstrong, Duke Ellington and His Orchestra; **Prod Co**: Metro-Goldwyn-Mayer.

Calamity Jane
USA, 1953 – 97 mins
David Butler

Calamity Jane was Warner Bros.' unashamedly derivative answer to
Annie Get Your Gun (1950), with Doris Day as another legendary
man-rivalling woman of the Old West but the same co-star, Howard
Keel, as the MGM hit. The film takes very little from the life of Martha
Jane ('Calamity Jane') Cannary Burke but the cross-dressing 'Calamity'
gave Day her meatiest role to date, while several of the Sammy
Fain–Paul Francis Webster songs written for the film (notably 'My Secret
Love', a major hit which won the Academy Award for Best Original
Song) became indelibly associated with her.

At one level, the narrative of *Calamity Jane* seems completely
normative: the buckskin-clad, unsocialised but exuberant figure of the
opening, riding shotgun and singing 'The Deadwood Stage', has been
transformed by the end into an image of bridal loveliness, all in white.
Along the way, Calamity receives lessons in femininity from Katie Brown
(Allyn McLerie) in the horribly prim 'A Woman's Touch', as Calamity's
slovenly cabin becomes a home fit for ladies. And yet, as feminist writers
re-evaluating Doris Day's films in the 1980s perceived, all is not quite so
simple (Merck, 1980). At the end, Calamity hasn't entirely relinquished
her tomboy feistiness – she has a concealed six-gun in her wedding dress
and as the stage leaves she is up on the buckboard as she was at the
beginning, though now with her husband, Wild Bill Hickok (Keel), at the
reins. More significantly, throughout its length the film has had a great
deal of fun with matters of gender and identity.

The whole plot turns on mistaken identities, disguise and misdirected
affections. Its central metaphor – most literally embodied by the stage of
Deadwood's Golden Garter saloon – is performance. The Fran*ces* Farmer
hired as the saloon's star attraction turns out to be Fran*cis* Farmer (Dick
Wesson), who, to his embarrassment, is initially made to perform as a
woman. When Calamity goes to Chicago, she is mistaken for a man; she

then returns to Deadwood not with the great star Adelaid Adams (Gale Robbins) but with her maid Katie, who is pretending to be Miss Adams. Bill Hickok swore he would dress as a squaw and carry a papoose if Calamity managed to bring Adelaid Adams to Deadwood, and does just that on Katie's opening night (the film embodies the casual racism still prevalent in Westerns of the period). In terms of romance, Bill thinks he is in love with Katie ('My Heart Is Higher Than a Hawk'); Calamity thinks she is in love with Lt Danny Gilmartin (Philip Carey); Calamity and Bill are most often at odds with each other ('I Can Live without You'), only to discover that they have been self-deceived. Calamity's 'Secret Love' turns out to have been a secret even to her.

If at the end the principals have achieved the romantic outcomes they really want, the film's playfulness with who and what people are or what they might be gently implies that how identities are ordered is less straightforward than convention allows. Day's terrific performance holds the whole thing together: from raucously exaggerated impersonation of frontier manhood to not entirely feminised bride, she makes Calamity unwittingly the film's boldest actor.

With the end of her Warner Bros. contract in 1954, Doris Day extended her style and dramatic range in films such as *Love Me or Leave Me**, Alfred Hitchcock's *The Man Who Knew Too Much* (1956) and *The Pajama Game**; by the end of the decade, with comedies like *Pillow Talk* (1959), she had become Hollywood's biggest female star. DP

Dir: David Butler; **Prod**: William Jacobs; **Scr**: James O'Hanlon; **DOP**: Wilfrid M. Cline (colour); **Song Music/Lyrics**: Sammy Fain/Paul Francis Webster; **Musical Dir**: Ray Heindorf; **Choreog**: Jack Donohue; **Art**: John Beckman; **Main Cast**: Doris Day, Howard Keel, Allyn McLerie, Philip Carey, Dick Wesson, Paul Harvey, Chubby Johnson, Gale Robbins; **Prod Co**: Warner Bros.

Car Wash
USA, 1976 – 97 mins
Michael Schultz

Car Wash is an ensemble music comedy with a largely black cast which
follows one working day's activities at the Dee-Luxe Car Wash in Los
Angeles. It is a Hollywood film that would have been unimaginable fifteen
or even ten years earlier. The civil rights and black power movements,
along with the wider social and political changes that occurred during the
1960s, provide a necessary context for the emergence of radically
different representations of African-Americans in 70s Hollywood, most
obviously in 'blaxploitation' pictures, aimed at crossover as well as black
audiences: for example, crime pictures like *Shaft* (1971), *Superfly* (1972)
and *Truck Turner* (1974). Vital to the success of such films were their
rhythm and blues/soul soundtracks by artists like Isaac Hayes and Curtis
Mayfield, while black music's growing crossover appeal to mass audiences
during the 1960s is an essential further context for *Car Wash*. The film's
songs, sung mostly by Rose Royce, were written and produced by Norman
Whitfield, composer of 'I Heard It through the Grapevine' and responsible
for many 1960s Tamla Motown hits.

Most of the wall-to-wall music in *Car Wash* is generated by local
radio station KGYS and its DJs rather than by characters in the film,
though, exceptionally, The Pointer Sisters do perform a cameo song ('You
Gotta Believe') when they turn up with the charlatan leader of the
Church of Divine Economic Spirituality, Reverend Daddy Rich (Richard
Pryor); and two of the car-wash workers, Floyd (Darrow Igus) and Lloyd
(Otis Day), budding music and dance artistes, rehearse their material –
very entertainingly – as they work. Music is vital both to the characters
and the rhythm of their work and to the film's energy: when the car
wash's white owner, Mr B (Sully Boyar), tries to change the channel, he is
quickly shouted down.

As an ensemble film, no characters are given noticeably more
prominence than others and all suggest, more or less, their own

narratives, which come together – and sometimes collide – at the car wash. Though the main non-black characters, Mr B, his Mao-spouting son (Richard Brestoff) and the cashier, Marsha (Melanie Mayron), with their lives of quiet desperation, and the young Hispanic and Native American workers are all given their stories, it is the African-American characters who take centre stage. Despite the high-energy, non-stop music and an overall exuberant sense of community and racial tolerance fuelled by repartee, practical jokes and gags, African-American director Michael Schultz offers sobering reflections on the frustration, anger and confusion occasioned by racial inequalities. As Richard Dyer (1993) suggests, the music's repetition and circularity 'suggest spatial and temporal stasis, the impossibility of change for the happier, in oneself or society', in contrast to white musicals. The younger characters are as yet relatively carefree and the snappy TC (Franklyn Ajaye), resplendent in his Afro, just wants to win the radio competition and date the waitress next door. But the older characters are clearly burdened: middle-aged family man and ex-con Lonnie (Ivan Dixon) struggles to preserve his dignity and survive on his meagre earnings; troubled Duane/Abdullah (Bill Duke) seeks identity as a black Muslim; hooker Marlene (Lauren Jones) is totally lost, desolate; Lindy (Antonio Fargas) compulsively plays out his cross-dressing gay identity; Justin (Leon Pinkney) and his girlfriend Mona (Tracy Reed) argue about whether he should go to college or earn a living.

Car Wash's time-limited, multi-character narrative and its radio/DJ soundtrack suggest a strong influence on Spike Lee's *Do the Right Thing* (1989), and Ice Cube has acknowledged the film's influence on *Friday* (1995) and its sequels. JH

Dir: Michael Schultz; **Prod**: Art Linson, Gary Stromberg; **Scr**: Joel Schumacher; **DOP**: Frank Stanley (colour); **Song Music/Lyrics**: Norman Whitfield; **Art**: Robert Clatworthy; **Main Cast**: Franklyn Ajaye, Ivan Dixon, Richard Pryor, Bill Duke, Antonio Fargas, Melanie Mayron, Lauren Jones, Sully Boyar; **Prod Co**: Universal.

Carmen Jones
USA, 1954 – 105 mins
Otto Preminger

Oscar Hammerstein II's updating and relocation of Bizet's opera *Carmen* to World War II and an African-American setting ran for over 500 performances after its 1943 Broadway opening. The opera's tobacco factory became a parachute factory in the Deep South; Don José became Joe, a young soldier; and the bullfighter, Escamillo, became Husky Miller, a champion boxer. In the same year, Hollywood produced *Cabin in the Sky** and *Stormy Weather** – a cluster of all-black musicals produced at a time of increasing pressure from African-American groups about limited opportunities for black performers. Otto Preminger's film appeared in a markedly different context: in 1954, the Supreme Court ruled in 'the Brown Case' that segregation in schooling was unconstitutional, and *Carmen Jones* became one of the last of the black-cast musicals that had long occupied an uneasy place in Hollywood production.

The transposition of Bizet's opera produced a plot with close parallels to the earlier musicals *Hallelujah!** and *Cabin in the Sky* – a weak-willed man pulled between two women, one representing love, security and settlement, the other passion, danger and rootlessness. In *Carmen Jones*, however, religion and home, which were so central to the other two films, are almost wholly absent and instead of the man being saved for settlement, the story, following the original, ends in tragedy. It becomes in effect a drama of displacement: the initial setting is the South but Joe (Harry Belafonte) is in the army; the film begins with his fiancée, Cindy-Lou (Olga James), arriving at the base to be with him; Joe and Carmen (Dorothy Dandridge) drive across country when Joe is ordered to take her to the nearest town; and all the main characters end up in Chicago. A further dislocation and break with the tradition is produced by Bizet's music, the lyrics brilliantly rewritten by Hammerstein, which displaces the blues, jazz and spirituals that inform the earlier films' numbers.

Preminger sets this potentially exotic cross-cultural fantasy in a world of unglamorous landscapes and functional spaces – settings for what he saw as 'a dramatic film with music rather than a conventional film musical' (Fujiwara, 2008) – and directs his cast of relative newcomers to film accordingly. Dandridge and Belafonte, in their first starring roles (though their singing voices were dubbed), are the film's twin centres, but it is Dandridge who dominates. Her Carmen is wonderfully provocative and sensual, constantly disrupting the orderly and restricted spaces – like the dining hall ('Dat's Love') and the jeep ('There's a Café on the Corner') – in which Preminger places her. She is only still for a significant period when she is being faithful to the conventional and stolid Joe, playing no part in Frankie (Pearl Bailey)'s exuberant 'Beat Out That Rhythm on the Drum' in the café or the welcoming crowd around Husky Miller (Joe Adam)'s 'Stan' up and Fight'. Preminger's characteristic long takes and his staging of the action across the CinemaScope frame maintain an observational distance on the characters' various, ultimately forlorn, attempts to escape the constraints of their lives. The collision of Joe's obsessive love and Carmen's refusal to be confined ends in the storage cupboard in which Preminger sets Carmen's death at Joe's hands.

The film enjoyed considerable success at the box office and opened the 1955 Cannes Film Festival. Dorothy Dandridge became the first African-American to be nominated for the Best Actress Academy Award, though she lost to Grace Kelly in *The Country Girl*. A few years later, Preminger directed *Porgy and Bess* (1959) when George Gershwin's 1935 'folk opera' was finally adapted for the screen. DP

Dir/Prod: Otto Preminger; **Scr**: Harry Kleiner, from the musical play by Oscar Hammerstein II, itself adapted from the opera by Georges Bizet; **DOP**: Sam Leavitt (colour); **Song Music/Lyrics**: Georges Bizet/Oscar Hammerstein II; **Musical Dir**: Herschel Burke Gilbert; **Art**: Edward L. Ilou; **Main Cast**: Dorothy Dandridge, Harry Belafonte, Olga James, Pearl Bailey, Diahann Carroll, Joe Adams, Brock Peters; Le Vern Hutcherson (singing voice for Harry Belafonte), Marilynn Horne (singing voice for Dorothy Dandridge); **Prod Co**: Otto Preminger Productions/20th Century-Fox.

Carousel
USA, 1956 – 128 mins
Henry King

The film of *Carousel* somewhat softened Rodgers and Hammerstein's 1945 adaptation of Ferenc Molnar's 1909 play, *Liliom*. Billy (Gordon MacRea) is killed by accident in the film, not by suicide. The original built to the shock of Billy's death and only then introduced the afterlife and his return to earth, whereas the film recalls events in flashback as Billy tells his story to the Star-maker (Gene Lockhart), who will decide whether he can revisit his family for a day. We therefore know that Billy has died and his redemption is strongly implied from the outset. Even so, in the film's otherwise faithful, though rather stolid, adaptation, much of what was disturbing in the show remains: Billy's death and its consequences; Billy himself, who has as much in common with the villainous Jud in *Oklahoma!** as with that show's hero, Curly; and the abusive relationship between Billy and Julie (Shirley Jones). The film is also significant as one of a number of mid-1950s musicals (including *A Star Is Born** and *It's Always Fair Weather**) that in their problematic treatment of relationships have much in common with melodrama.

Characters in *Carousel* are constantly imagining what life *might* become. Julie's friend Carrie (Barbara Ruick) sings '*When* I Marry Mr Snow'; Julie and Billy each sing '*If* I Loved You', as they test their feelings early in the film; after the marriage, Billy reaches for a positive future only when Julie tells him she is pregnant, anticipating in his great 'Soliloquy' what 'My boy Bill' or 'My little girl' may be like. Even the show's famous anthem, 'You'll Never Walk Alone', first sung to Julie by her cousin Hettie (Claramae Turner) after Billy's death, is a stirring appeal to believe in the future: 'At the end of the storm/Is a golden sky/And the sweet silver song of a lark'. From eternity, on the other hand, Billy looks *back* at dreams unfulfilled and at a daughter whose life he has blighted.

Correspondingly, although *Carousel*, like *Oklahoma!*, is set in the American past – here a Maine fishing village in the late nineteenth century – community and romance are more complexly treated. The high-spirited communal number 'June Is Busting Out All Over' celebrates springtime desire, powered by the sexual energy of the young men and women. Yet the only relationships shown are those of Carrie and the stiflingly conventional Mr Snow (Robert Rounseville) and of Julie and Billy – Billy resentful and violent, Julie committed to a vision of love that casts the woman as self-denying, or even self-abasing. She sings 'Oh, what's the use of wond'ring/If he's good or if he's bad?/He's your feller and you love him/That's all there is to that', and chillingly claims to their daughter, Louise, that 'It's possible … for someone to hit you … and it not hurt you at all.'

Julie makes that extraordinary statement when she intuits Billy's spectral presence after his disastrous meeting with Louise, which ended with him hitting her for refusing the star he was offering. As 'You'll Never Walk Alone' is reprised at the school graduation, Billy is able to whisper encouragement to Louise and 'I loved you' finally to Julie; their faces light up and they join optimistically in the singing. As Billy walks away, though, apparently redeemed, we may wonder, through the song's stoical assertion of hope, just what is being affirmed.

This was still dark material for a 1956 musical, which may at least partly account for the film's limited box-office appeal, whereas the cast album sold extremely well. DP

Dir: Henry King; **Prod**: Henry Ephron; **Scr**: Phoebe and Henry Ephron, from the musical play based on Ferenc Molnar's *Liliom*, music by Richard Rodgers, book and lyrics by Oscar Hammerstein II; **DOP**: Charles G. Clarke (colour); **Song Music/Lyrics**: Richard Rodgers/Oscar Hammerstein II; **Musical Dir**: Alfred Newman; **Choreog**: Rod Alexander (ballet derived from Agnes de Mille's original); **Art**: Lyle R. Wheeler, Jack Martin Smith; **Main Cast**: Gordon MacRae, Shirley Jones, Cameron Mitchell, Barbara Ruick, Claramae Turner, Robert Rounseville, Gene Lockhart; **Prod Co**: 20th Century-Fox.

Cavalcade
USA, 1933 – 110 mins
Frank Lloyd

Cavalcade, probably the least-remembered Best Picture and Best Director Oscar winner, was adapted from Noel Coward's spectacular stage show which ran at the Theatre Royal, Drury Lane, from 1931 to 1932, and which Fox Movietone cameramen filmed as a guide for the film version. Given Coward's high profile as a dramatist, his celebrated musical theatre works during the 1920s/30s and the importance of musical theatre as source material for musical films, it is surprising that so little of Coward's output was adapted for cinema.

As the play's title suggests, it adopts a pageant-like approach, as does the film, evoking the years 1899–1933 as experienced by an upper-class English family and their servants. More particularly, it privileges the emotional life of the upper-class wife/mother Jane Marryot (Diana Wynyard) rather than husband/father Robert (Clive Brook in typical stiff-upper-lip mode) or the downstairs servant family, the Bridges. The focus here is very much *English* rather than British, though its genteel Englishness is very different from the robustly down-to-earth comedies being made around the same time by Gracie Fields (see *Sing as We Go**) and George Formby (see *Come on George!**).

The historical pageant moves from 1899 and the Boer War to Queen Victoria's death (1901), the sinking of the *Titanic* (1912), World War I and the Jazz Age (and, unspoken, the Depression). Since it is the story of a family 'sheltered through two generations of Victorian prosperity [awaiting] the headlong cavalcade of the Twentieth Century', it is inevitably also about the nation and the beginning of the end of empire. The Marryots lose one son and daughter-in-law on the *Titanic* (though the film implies they are lucky to be spared what is to come), and receive news of the death of the younger son as the armistice is announced. Tellingly, the younger son had been planning to break class taboos and marry the downstairs servants' daughter Fanny (Ursula Jeans), now a celebrated singer and dancer.

In an uncertain conclusion, Robert toasts England's future, while Jane pines for a past England of gallantry and dignity, but their quiet toasts are displaced by a frantic, chaotic montage of maimed solders, war graves and Jazz Age decadence, itself displaced by crowds singing 'Auld Lang Syne' and 'God Save the King' over an image of St Paul's and the leitmotiv of the ghostly cavalcade of equestrian historical figures.

Though *Cavalcade* is not a traditional musical, music and song are integral to its design. Traditional popular songs like 'It's a Long Way to Tipperary', 'Pack up Your Troubles' and 'Keep the Home Fires Burning', used almost entirely off screen, punctuate the lengthy war montage. Period songs are integrated into on-screen performance: a seaside band performs 'I Do Like to Be Beside the Seaside', for example, while there are theatrical and nightclub performances of new Noel Coward songs like 'Girls of the CIV', 'Mirabelle' and 'Twentieth-Century Blues' (one of his most celebrated), sung by Fanny with syncopated jazz backing, and reprised in the frantic montage at the end of the film. The song's emphasis on 'strange illusion, chaos and confusion' embodies much of what the film and play are about. JH

Dir: Frank Lloyd; **Prod**: Frank Lloyd, Winfield R. Sheehan (uncredited); **Scr**: Reginald Berkeley, from the stage play by Noel Coward; **DOP**: Ernest Palmer (b&w); **Song Music/Lyrics**: Noel Coward, *et al.*; **Music**: Peter Brunelli, Louis De Francesco, Arthur Lange, J. S. Zamecnik; **Art**: William Darling; **Main Cast**: Diana Wynyard, Clive Brook, Una O'Conor, Herbert Mundin, Beryl Mercer, Irene Browne, Frank Lawton, Ursula Jeans; **Prod Co**: Fox Film Corporation.

Chicago
USA, 2002 – 109 mins
Rob Marshall

It took an unusually long time for *Chicago* to be adapted for the screen. Bob Fosse, who co-wrote the show's book and both directed and choreographed the 1975 Broadway production, had been persuaded to work on a film version after years of reluctance, but his death in 1985, just as pre-production was about to begin, put the project in limbo for another fifteen years. It was when Rob Marshall outlined his ideas for reworking the original to producer Martin Richards that the film finally became a reality.

Finding a solution to the relationship between narrative and numbers that would work on film had been a major stumbling block. *Chicago* was subtitled 'A Musical Vaudeville' on Broadway: the numbers, presented in the style of various vaudeville acts and performers, commented on the action but – unlike a conventional book musical – occupied a different level of theatrical reality. Marshall's concept for motivating such theatricality in the film was to suggest that most numbers are in the mind of the wannabe performer and killer of her lover, Roxie Hart (Renée Zellweger). The opening and closing numbers take place on stage in the 'real' world – 'All That Jazz', performed by Velma Kelly (Catherine Zeta-Jones) just before she is arrested for the murder of her unfaithful boyfriend and her sister, and 'Nowadays', in which Roxie and Velma triumphantly celebrate the success of their double act. The others – mainly also presented as theatre performances – become Roxie's fantasies. The film begins by zooming into the pupil of an eye and the title appears as if in its depths. It is a conceit that gave Marshall the flexibility to dissolve between and intercut action and number without having to maintain Roxie's viewpoint slavishly through the film.

Such intercutting, combined with the garish theatricality of the numbers, Marshall's nods to Bob Fosse's Broadway choreography, and John Kander and Fred Ebb's musical echoes of their celebrated previous show, recalls and pays homage to *Cabaret**. Like Fosse's film, too, *Chicago* gains much of its energy from an intensely edited visual style, cut to the rhythms of Kander's music. The method produces exhilarating effects and striking images from its montage of varied angles, close and more distant shots, in numbers like 'Cell Block Tango', with the jailed women celebrating and re-enacting their crimes ('He had it coming'), and 'Razzle Dazzle', attorney Billy Flynn (Richard Gere)'s demonstration to Roxie that the trial is really just a circus. But in also splintering space, time and bodies, it sacrifices continuity of performance for the synthetic continuity created by elaborate editing. By 2002, these were methods long familiar from music video and advertising, and had been widely incorporated into mainstream film style. They may also represent the only way of directing a dance musical with stars who are not professional dancers.

In its satire of celebrity culture, *Chicago* also has something in common with *Nashville**, which opened in the same year as the original Broadway production. Although the show ran for 936 performances, there were mixed critical responses to what was by all accounts its bitter tone and confrontational style. It is possible that the aftermath of the 1995 O. J. Simpson trial gave additional resonance to *Chicago*'s story of the murderess Roxie Hart made into a celebrity by a sensationalised media and found not guilty through the machinations of an unscrupulous defence attorney. Certainly the film was an extraordinary hit, taking over $300 million worldwide and winning six Oscars, including Best Picture. DP

Dir: Rob Marshall; **Prod**: Martin Richards; **Scr**: Bill Condon, from the musical play, book by Bob Fosse, Fred Ebb, music by John Kander, based on the play by Maurine Dallas Watkins; **DOP**: Dion Beebe (colour); **Song Music/Lyrics**: John Kander/Fred Ebb; **Musical Dir**: Paul Bogaev; **Choreog**: Rob Marshall; **Art**: John Myhre, Andrew Stearn; **Main Cast**: Renée Zellweger, Catherine Zeta-Jones, Richard Gere, Queen Latifah, John C. Reilly, Dominic West, Lucy Liu; **Prod Co**: Miramax.

Come on George!
UK, 1939 – 88 mins
Anthony Kimmins

George Formby was Britain's most popular (and highest paid) male film star during the late 1930s and the 1939–45 war years – and second only to Stalin in popularity in the Soviet Union (while fellow Lancastrian performer Gracie Fields, with films like *Sing as We Go**, was Britain's most popular female star during the early and mid-30s). Formby's films are perhaps more 'comedies with music' than 'musical comedies': they could work without songs, but a Formby film without four or five musical numbers with his ukulele was unimaginable. Formby's background was in music hall/variety, and his films – like Fields's – were partially vehicles for an already established comic/musical persona. Both stars' personae were strongly Lancastrian, though they each quickly became popular nationally (while the more subversive Lancashire comic Frank Randle, for example, retained a more regional appeal). Made by a special Formby unit (headed by Anthony Kimmins) at Ealing Studios, Formby's later films were as much a projection of Britain as Michael Balcon's more prestigious Ealing films.

Formby's films were formulaic, their plots shifting over time from Depression themes in the earlier 1930s to wartime themes: his apparently naive, socially awkward character (usually called George, as here) bumbles into some narrative business by accident, but once involved – while remaining at some level clueless – demonstrates both determination and skill. Blessed with good luck, George finally wins through: saves the pub, exposes the counterfeiters, wins the horse or motorcycle race. Formby later embodied the British war spirit, where 'winning' involved unmasking spies (*Let George Do It*, 1940) and fifth columnists (*Spare a Copper*, 1941). His bumbling but persistent 'little man' – very different from Fields's forthright character – led Geoffrey Macnab (2000) to see Formby as 'Lancashire's very own answer to Private Schweyek … the archetypal little man as hero'. 'Winning' also means winning the girl, attracted by George's lack of sophistication and warm-hearted sincerity. George is a sexual innocent, and the overt expression of sexuality (like most other crises) sends him into dithering cries of 'Ooh, Mother ...'

Come on George! is a typical Formby film, more lively than some. George is a racecourse ice-cream seller and aspiring jockey suspected of picking a horse-owner's pocket. In a madcap escape from police, George ends up in a train horsebox with a fiery horse that has a tendency to throw jockeys, but is docile with anyone unaware of its reputation, and he is misled into looking after and training the animal. When George discovers that 'Lamb' is really 'Man Eater', he needs (comic) psychiatric help to ride the horse and, naturally, everything goes wrong: George is kidnapped by rivals, escapes, arrives at the racecourse in the nick of time and wins the race – and, of course, the girl, Mary, the local police sergeant's daughter (played winningly by a young Pat Kirkwood).

Some Formby films feature George as a musician: in *Let George Do It*, for example, he plays the ukulele in a band and the plot revolves around music. More usually, the songs are performed to other characters or frontally to the camera. Big production numbers were not considered appropriate, and the musical sequences are deliberately modest, designed more to add an extra – generally very sentimental – dimension to the Formby persona: in *Come on George!*, he serenades the horse, courts Mary and sings her younger brother to sleep, and sings about not letting the stable down. Typically upbeat and humorous – though with sexual innuendo thrown into the mix – the songs exemplify the optimistic and populist nature of Formby's appeal. JH

Dir: Anthony Kimmins; **Prod**: Jack Kitchin; **Scr**: Leslie Arliss, Anthony Kimmins, Val Valentine; **DOP**: Ronald Neame (b&w); **Song Music/Lyrics**: George Formby, Harry Gifford, Fred E. Cliffe; **Music**: Ernest Irving; **Art**: Wilfrid Shingleton; **Main Cast**: George Formby, Patricia Kirkwood, Joss Ambler, Meriel Forbes, Cyril Raymond, George Hayes, George Carney; **Prod Co**: Associated Talking Pictures.

Cover Girl
USA, 1944 – 105 mins
Charles Vidor

By 1944, Rita Hayworth was already a major star and glamour icon (as well as Columbia studio boss Harry Cohn's special protégée). A cousin of Ginger Rogers, Hayworth was a dancer before making movies; in the early 1940s, Columbia were intent on making her a musical star (although her singing was always dubbed), notably in *You'll Never Get Rich* (1941) and *You Were Never Lovelier* (1942), in both of which she was a very good dancing match for Fred Astaire. Columbia's first colour musical, *Cover Girl*, as the title suggests, was primarily a vehicle for Hayworth, showing off her looks and her dancing, though it also developed the melancholic and vulnerable side of her persona.

Gene Kelly's first lead Broadway role was in late 1940 in *Pal Joey* (directed by George Abbott, choreographed by Robert Alton, with Stanley Donen as a young dancer); Kelly and Donen then choreographed Abbott's 1941 show *Best Foot Forward* before going to Hollywood together. Despite co-starring in MGM's *For Me and My Gal* (1942) (with Judy Garland) and *Thousands Cheer* (1943) (with Kathryn Grayson), Kelly was loaned to Columbia for *Cover Girl*, the first film to fully feature his distinctive dance style and star persona. Donen choreographed the 1943 film version of *Best Foot Forward*, before working (uncredited) on Kelly's *Cover Girl* routines, and later choreographing *Anchors Aweigh**.

Cover Girl draws on familiar (but pleasurable) showbiz narratives. Rusty Parker (Hayworth) and Danny McGuire (Kelly) sing and dance together in Danny's 'honky tonk place' in Brooklyn, along with comic sidekick Genius (Phil Silvers). Rusty upsets the work/romance equilibrium by winning a glamour magazine cover competition and is lured away. Of course, Hollywood, with its millions, sides with Danny's small-scale, cash-strapped but romantic and 'authentic' club rather than with Fifth Avenue and Broadway; Rusty's extravagant Broadway 'Cover Girl' production number, despite its enormous stage ramp and extensive male chorus, is slow and static compared to the energy and inventiveness of the numbers with Danny, among Kelly's best early dance routines. In 'Make Way for Tomorrow', Kelly, Hayworth and Silvers dance exuberantly along a night-time street; in 'Put Me to the Test', Kelly (on stage with Hayworth) combines his athletic ballet style (influenced by Agnes de Mille and new American dance) with accomplished tap; Danny and Rusty are reconciled in the lovely, gently romantic 'Long Ago and Far

Gene Kelly, Rita Hayworth, Phil Silvers, 'Make Way for Tomorrow'

Away', set in the empty nightclub. Several features of *Cover Girl* seem to look forward to *Singin' in the Rain** – the romantic couple plus comic sidekick, the cop who looks on disapprovingly during 'Make Way for Tomorrow' and the 'Cover Girl' number (reminiscent of 'Beautiful Girl').

The film's high point is Kelly's 'Alter Ego Dance', a prototype for the ambitious ballet sequences in later musicals like *Singin' in the Rain*, *On the Town** and *An American in Paris**, and perhaps the first evidence of the Kelly – or, more properly, Kelly–Donen – choreographic style in fully achieved form. Counterpointing the earlier 'Make Way for Tomorrow' (reprised for the happy ending), Kelly's introspective Danny, in turmoil after losing Rusty, is alone in a deserted night-time street when his bitter stream-of-consciousness dialogue conjures up his reflection in a store window. Danny's 'ghost' then leaps into the street, pulling him into an energetic, ballet-type double dance, potently dramatising his conflicted emotions and demonstrating Kelly's characteristic melodramatic physicality and intensity, whether ecstatic or anguished – very different from Fred Astaire's 'weightlessness'. In this fine sequence, remarkable for its virtuoso dance performance and cinematography, Kelly and Donen established their film musical credentials. JH

Dir: Charles Vidor; **Prod**: Arthur Schwartz; **Scr**: Virginia Van Upp, adapted by Marion Parsonnet, Paul Gangelin from a story by Erwin Gelsey; **DOP**: Rudolph Maté, Allen M. Davey (colour); **Song Music/Lyrics**: Jerome Kern/Ira Gershwin; **Musical Dir**: Maurice Stoloff; **Choreog**: Val Raset, Seymour Felix, Stanley Donen (uncredited); **Art Dir**: Lionel Banks, Cary Odell; **Main Cast**: Rita Hayworth, Gene Kelly, Phil Silvers, Jinx Falkenburg, Leslie Brooks, Eve Arden, Otto Kruger; **Prod Co**: Columbia.

Dancer in the Dark

Denmark/Germany/Netherlands/US/UK/France/Sweden/Finland/
Iceland/Norway, 2000 – 134 mins
Lars von Trier

'Dancer in the Dark' would evoke for many something romantic, dreamy, like the lovely Fred Astaire–Cyd Charisse number 'Dancing in the Dark' in *The Band Wagon**. But *Dancer in the Dark*, which Lars von Trier describes as 'a musical melodrama colliding with reality', is a very different beast (though its title is, in fact, very apposite): set in the US in the 1960s, the story involves childlike, desperate single-parent Czech immigrant Selma (Björk), who hides her increasing blindness to work long hours in a factory in order to fund an eye operation for her young son and who, in most bizarre circumstances, murders her cop neighbour, friend and landlord (David Morse), is sentenced to death and hanged. Hardly story material for a musical, but musicals offer Selma escape. *Dancer in the Dark* is a collaboration between two controversial artists, Dogme-inspired Danish director von Trier and idiosyncratic Icelandic pop singer Björk, both acquired tastes. The film's melodramatic plotting combines with unpolished Dogme-style shooting – hand-held camera, available light, colour-drained, slightly sepia image. Its seedy observational naturalism contrasts sharply with energetic, colourful musical numbers shot with a hundred DV cameras and edited together in music video style. The numbers build from the sounds and rhythms around Selma in factory or courtroom: rarely have musical sequences been so integrated with narrative action.

The film won the Palme d'Or and Best Actress awards at Cannes 2000 (and many other awards) but rarely has a film divided critics and audiences so violently, due in part, no doubt, to resentment at what was seen as its assault on musical conventions – or at least the conventions of the Hollywood 'musical comedy'. It is certainly difficult to decide whether *Dancer in the Dark* is a pretentious, gimmicky work, a musical pastiche, trading on Björk's (and von Trier's) celebrity, or a genuinely experimental addition to the film musical canon. *Dancer in the Dark* is nothing if not reflexive, as much *about* the musical form as it *is* a musical, and abounds in film musical references: it begins with a traditional 'overture'; the first scene finds Selma rehearsing a community production of *The Sound of Music*; Selma and her friend Kathy (Catherine Deneuve) enjoy watching black-and-white 1930s musicals; and so on. Shortly before she is hanged, Selma tells her prison guard that 'in a musical nothing dreadful ever happens'.

The musical numbers stitch songs together from everyday reality and transport Selma into a realm of different possibilities, enabling her to 'see' in ways denied her in the physical world. The first number – a third into the film – comes after Selma is asked why characters in musicals suddenly start singing and dancing: after a near accident due to her poor sight and fatigue, the noises of the machine shop form themselves into a rhythm and 'Cvalda' ('Clatter, crash, clack') emerges and gains momentum, drawing the workers into dance; 'I've Seen It All' arises from the rhythm of a train and draws in railway workers and ordinary people in passing backyards. Considerably more oddly and controversially, 'Smith and Wesson' builds from the confused murder; 'In the Musicals' arises from Selma's trial and sentencing; '107 Steps' accompanies her journey to execution and 'Next to Last Song' is sung in a kind of ecstasy as she is prepared for hanging; while 'New World' emerges out of the darkness following her death. As all this implies, *Dancer in the Dark* is bold and challenging, as much an anti-musical as a musical, or perhaps it should be seen as having more in common (despite obvious differences) with Indian musical melodramas like *Dil se …** than with the Hollywood tradition. JH

Dir/Scr: Lars von Trier; **Prod**: Vibeke Windeløv; **DOP**: Robby Müller (colour); **Song Music/Lyric**s: Björk, Mark Bell, Sjón Sigurdsson, Lars von Trier; **Choreog**: Vincent Paterson; **Art**: Karl Juliusson, Peter Grant; **Main Cast**: Björk, Catherine Deneuve, David Morse, Peter Stormare, Joel Grey, Vladica Kostic, Jean-Marc Barr; **Prod Co**: Zentrope Entertainments/Trust Film Svenska/Film I Väst/Liberator Productions/Pain Unlimited GmBH Filmproduktion/Cinematograph A/S/What Else? B.V./Icelandic Film Corporation/Blind Spot Pictures Oy/France 3 Cinéma/Danmarks Radio/arte France Cinéma/SVT Drama/Arte.

Les Demoiselles de Rochefort
France, 1967 – 120 mins
Jacques Demy

Whether the entirely 'en chanté' Les Parapluies de Cherbourg* can be classed as a 'musical' or not, Jacques Demy's follow-up film is a more obviously American-style musical comedy: its characters perform as well as passing from everyday speech and movement to song and dance to celebrate their heightened feelings (though, less characteristically, some of the rhyming dialogue and punning of Les Parapluies recurs here, and passers-by are also inclined to break spontaneously into dance for no more obvious reason than the sheer pleasure of it). Les Demoiselles de Rochefort is a much sunnier film, its Michel Legrand score more upbeat and jazzy and with an emphasis on bright pastels rather than saturated dark colours, although, this being Demy, it incorporates a darker side (soldiers on manoeuvre, a sadistic killer). Demy is attached to port city settings like Rochefort, Cherbourg (and Nantes in Lola, 1961), places of arrival and departure, appropriate for the choreographed chance meetings and missed encounters of whimsical fate or predestination which characterise the Demy world.

The story unfolds over one weekend, during which a travelling show sets up and performs in Rochefort's main square. The film's two demoiselles are sisters Delphine (Catherine Deneuve) and Solange (Françoise Dorléac, Deneuve's actual elder sister, killed in a motor accident shortly before Les Demoiselles premiered); their mother, Yvonne (Danielle Darrieux), runs a glass-sided, aquarium-like café in the square. The film's complex network of characters searching for their ideal lovers – past or future, dreamed-of, perhaps mythical – centres on the café. The male characters include Maxence (Jacques Perrin), a sailor based in Rochefort (about to be demobbed), and a painter, Simon Dame (Michel Piccoli), musician and former partner of Yvonne and (unbeknown to him) father of her son Boubou, Simon's American composer friend Andy (Gene Kelly) and the men running the show (George Chakiris and Grover

Dale). Solange (destined to meet Andy) runs into Maxence (destined to meet Delphine); Delphine runs into Andy; Simon (destined to get back with Yvonne) meets Delphine, sent by Yvonne to collect Boubou; and so on. Teasingly, Demy leaves open until the very last shot the question of whether everyone finds their partner.

Les Demoiselles starts promisingly, as the travellers board the Rochefort–Martrou transporter bridge: the dancers begin to stretch, then move into languorously dreamy dance movements, suspended above the water far below. Some of the other dance sequences, particularly the large group dances, are not so inspired, but the film gets a definite lift when Gene Kelly (then in his mid-fifties) appears: his broad grin announces the Kelly persona and, although no longer quite as athletic as in the 1940s and 50s, his performance wonderfully evokes his own large contribution to the history of the movie musical, particularly, in a scene with children, 'I Got Rhythm' from *An American in Paris** and, dancing with sailors, *On the Town**. Later, Deneuve and Dorléac sing and dance ('Chanson des jumelles') in costumes and a style designed to recall Marilyn Monroe's and Jane Russell's 'Little Girl from Little Rock' from *Gentlemen Prefer Blondes**. The presence of George Chakiris reminds us of *West Side Story** (though he falls rather flat here).

Les Demoiselles is not the masterpiece some (like Jonathan Rosenbaum, 1998) have claimed but it is nevertheless very good, and a fascinating hybrid. If *Les Demoiselles* pays homage to the American musical, then Olivier Ducastel and Jacques Martineau's *Jeanne et le garçon formidable* (*Jeanne and the Perfect Guy*) (1998), centred around romantic love in the AIDS age and starring Virginie Ledoyen and Demy's son (with Agnès Varda) Mathieu Demy, pays homage to Demy's musicals. JH

Dir/**Scr**: Jacques Demy; **Prod**: Mag Bodard, Gilbert De Goldschmidt; **DOP**: Ghislain Cloquet (colour); **Song Music/Lyrics**: Michel Legrand/Michel Legrand, Jacques Demy; **Music**: Michel Legrand; **Choreog**: Norman Maen; **Art**: Bernard Evein; **Main Cast**: Catherine Deneuve, Françoise Dorléac, Michel Piccoli, George Chakiris, Gene Kelly, Danielle Darrieux, Jacques Perrin, Grover Dale; **Prod Co**: Madeleine Films/Parc Film.

Dil se …
India, 1998 – 163 mins
Mani Ratnam

In Indian popular cinema, 'musical' is less a generic choice than a given. With few exceptions, Indian films, strongly influenced by traditional forms as well as by Hollywood, prominently feature song and dance. However, the 'masala film' (Sholay*, for example) mixes up song and dance with the different 'spices' of high melodrama, broad comedy, spectacular action, and so on, in sharp shifts of generic mode that can still make western audiences uncomfortable. Tamil director Mani Ratnam has been crucial in reworking Indian cinema's popular forms. His loose trilogy Roja (1992), Bombay (1995) and Dil se … (From the Heart) aimed to address contemporary Indian issues, just as classic films like Shree 420* and Pyaasa* also did, albeit rather differently.

As its title suggests, Dil se … foregrounds 'romance': in its opening scene, Amar (Shahrukh Khan), an All-India Radio reporter gathering views as India approaches the fiftieth anniversary of independence, awaits a train at a night-time, rain-swept station. He sees a lone woman, Meghna (Manisha Koirala), and, for him, it's 'love at first sight', though she seems troubled, preoccupied. However, their odd 'romance' unfolds against a backdrop of guerrilla activity in India's far north (Assam and Ladakh) and Meghna's involvement with separatists. When Meghna disappears, Amar agrees to a semi-arranged marriage with Preeti (Preity Zinta) but Meghna's mysterious reappearance, with her 'terrorist' associates, as Delhi prepares its independence celebrations, draws Amar back to her. With their sharply different relationships to both 'India' and to 'love', the explosive final scenes embody the impossibility of transcendent union for either the doomed couple or divided India itself – hardly typical material for a 'musical'.

Classic filmi songs, often extravagantly poetic, performed by celebrated 'playback singers' like Lata Mangeshkar, Asha Bhosle and Mohammed Rafi whose popularity could exceed that of the stars – in contrast to Hollywood, where dubbed stars were almost a guilty secret – were always vital to films' commercial success. As Anna Morcom (2008) has shown, with the mass diffusion of audio cassettes from the 1980s and then the advent of MTV, music became ever more vital in marketing: songs, released well in advance, created audiences for the films. The globally successful composer/arranger A. R. Rahman, classically trained and combining Indian and western musical forms and instrumentation, has often collaborated with Ratnam, who sees song 'picturisations' as providing 'a license to transcend dramatic logic' (Ratnam, 2002). Are the song and dance sequences more dissociated from narrative than those of older films? The infectious, driving rhythm of the worldwide hit song 'Chaiya, chaiya' ('Walk in the Shadows') combines with erotic dance movement to give physical expression to Amar's desire.

Set atop a moving train, Amar's feelings for Meghna are displaced onto a gypsy woman whose languorously sexual movements are heightened by some deliciously vulgar phrasing (playback singer: Sapna Awasthi). In the sharply contrasting 'Dil se …', Amar imagines Meghna as delicately feminine and in need of his protection as they dodge soldiers and explosions. Again, the male voice and point of view dominate (strikingly, back in the narrative, Meghna asks him to stop harassing her). Only in the 'Satrangi re' ('Colours of the Rainbow') sequence, set in the mountainous Ladakh desert, are Meghna's conflicted feelings and loyalties foregrounded, in the fractured movement and angular shapes of their dance.

Though these song and dance sequences could be argued to 'transcend dramatic logic' to some degree, they nevertheless feed off and back into the narrative. Only the extravagantly spectacular, strongly sexual 'Jiya jale' ('My Heart Burns'), celebrating Amar's and Preeti's engagement – incongruously shot in lush Kerala settings – strains the relationship between number and narrative. JH

Dir/Scr: Mani Ratnam; **Prod**: Shekhar Kapur, Mani Ratnam, Ram Gopal Varma; **DOP**: Santosh Sivan (colour); **Song Music/Lyrics**: A. R. Rahman/Gulzar; **Playback**: Sapna Awasthi, Lata Mangeshkar, A. R. Rahman, Sukwinder Singh, *et al*.; **Choreog**: Farah Khan; **Art**: Samir Chanda; **Main Cast**: Shahrukh Khan, Manisha Koirala, Preity Zinta; **Prod Co**: India Talkies/Madras Talkies.

Die Dreigroschenoper
Germany, 1931 – 110 mins
G. W. Pabst

Two hundred years after John Gay's English 'ballad opera' *The Beggar's Opera*, the 1928 production of *Die Dreigroschenoper* (*The Threepenny Opera*), with book and lyrics by Bertolt Brecht and music by Kurt Weill, was one of the triumphs of Weimar theatre. Brecht and Weill transposed the action to late-Victorian London but kept Gay's paralleling of the criminal underworld and corrupt bourgeois society. The play's success, during a period of economic and political crisis, led to a film adaptation by G. W. Pabst, one of Germany's most prestigious directors. The film simplified the action, dropped most of the play's songs, turned the episodic structure into a more coherent narrative and made clearer its moral and political message: the opening song tells respectable society to feed the poor before preaching morality, suggesting that people only survive by cheating and mistreating others and by 'forgetting they are members of the human race'. Both Brecht and Weill sued the producers for changing their work, though Brecht himself had originally signed up to help adapt it; Brecht lost his case, but Weill won.

Macheath (Mackie Messer, or Mack the Knife) (Rudolf Forster), a dangerous criminal, runs a gang of thieves, and Peachum (Fritz Rasp) makes a handsome profit from organising London's beggars; both run their activities like legitimate businesses. As we learn from the 'Kanonen-Song' ('Cannon Song', adapted from Kipling), Macheath is protected by his colonial war buddy police chief Tiger Brown (Rheinhold Schünzel). When Mackie courts and 'marries' Peachum's daughter Polly (Carola Neher), Peachum threatens to unleash his beggars to disrupt the coronation procession unless Brown arrests Mackie. When Mackie is forced to flee, Polly takes over and makes the business legitimate by buying a bank, which later co-opts both Brown and Peachum. As Polly puts it, 'one can rob a bank, or one can tread the path of a respectable and law-abiding business', or – as a colleague interjects succinctly – 'use a bank to rob others'. While Mackie and the rest 'consume the poor man's bread', the poor themselves 'live in darkness and … fade from sight'.

Despite the film's greater narrative transparency and loss of songs, it works well as a 'ballad opera', retaining much distinctive non-naturalistic formal invention. Mackie is introduced and deftly characterised in the show's best-known song, 'Die Moritat von Mackie Messer' ('The Ballad of Mack the Knife'), accompanied by sketches of his criminal exploits. The chorus-like Street Singer (the wonderful Ernst Busch – he and Lotte Lenya were the only performers retained from the stage production) helps maintain the feel of a Brechtian parable, commenting on the action: speaking direct to camera shortly before Polly acquires the bank, for example, he tells us he will now reveal how 'things take a turn that even *you* wouldn't expect'.

Die Dreigroschenoper opened up new possibilities for the future of musical theatre. Weill and Brecht collaborated on several further projects in Germany and, in exile, in Paris. After settling in the US, Weill contributed significantly to the development of the Broadway musical and wrote the score for Fritz Lang's 'Brechtian' 1938 film, *You and Me**. The Nazis banned Pabst's film in 1933 and tried to destroy all copies, but the stage version of *The Threepenny Opera* has been performed many times in many different countries. Later film versions were made in West Germany in 1962 (directed by Wolfgang Staudte) and in the US in 1989 (as *Mack the Knife*, directed by Menahem Golan). It also inspired a Brazilian film adaptation, *Ópera do Malandro* (directed by Ruy Guerra, 1986). JH

Dir: G. W. Pabst; **Prod**: Seymour Nebenzal; **Scr**: Béla Balázs, Léo Lania, Ladislaus Vajda, from the stage play by Bertolt Brecht, Kurt Weill, based on *The Beggar's Opera* by John Gay; **DOP**: Fritz Arno Wagner (b&w); **Song Music/Lyrics**: Kurt Weill/Bertolt Brecht; **Art**: Andrej Andrejew; **Main Cast**: Rudolf Forster, Carola Neher, Reinhold Schünzel, Fritz Rasp, Valeska Gert, Lotte Lenya, Ernst Busch; **Prod Co**: Tobis Filmkunst/Nero-Film AG (in association with Warner Bros.).

Easter Parade
USA, 1948 – 104 mins
Charles Walters

'Drum Crazy', Fred Astaire's first main musical number in *Easter Parade*, has much in common with numbers like 'Fancy Free' in *Top Hat**, largely solo dances that the character seems to improvise, using the props and furniture of whatever space he finds himself in. Here, it is a toyshop and the number is partly a ruse to appropriate a toy rabbit from a small boy and add it to the heap of Easter presents he has been buying. But in ways that we are not aware of at the time, the spontaneous energy of 'Drum Crazy' reveals a need in Don Hewes (Astaire) for fun and free self-expression that will be answered when he partners Hannah Brown (Judy Garland).

It was only when Gene Kelly broke his ankle that Arthur Freed tempted Astaire out of retirement with the attraction of working again with Irving Berlin, around whose songs *Easter Parade* was built, and of partnering Judy Garland. Yet playing Don Hewes began a decisive redefinition of the Astaire persona. Much older than his dance partners in the post-Ginger Rogers movies, there is now a conscious play on his reputation and his age: Don is abandoned by Nadine (Ann Miller in her first MGM role), the recipient of those presents and his partner in a successful vaudeville dance act (this is the early twentieth century), and cast adrift.

The story of *Easter Parade* is Pygmalion-like – but with a twist. Don announces that he can train anyone as his new partner, picks Hannah out of a chorus line and with grim persistence attempts to turn her into a replica of Nadine. When he realises his mistake, the transformation is immediate: he plays 'I Love the Piano' on the pianola and the pedantic artifice of their previous dances gives way to Hannah's exuberant singing and spontaneous movement. They dance together and there is an immediate transition to the same number on stage, followed by a succession of comic vaudeville numbers ('Snooky Ookums', 'Fiddle

Up', 'Midnight Choo Choo') charting the rise of 'Hannah & Hewes'. It is as if in relinquishing his role as teacher, Don enables Hannah to be herself and she releases in him the qualities he displayed in 'Drum Crazy'. In their own show, Don celebrates his new identity in 'Steppin' Out with My Baby', a brilliant medley of styles, concluding with a solo tap sequence filmed in slow motion, backed by a chorus moving at normal speed. But the number that perfectly embodies the parity in partnership he and Hannah have embraced is their double act as comedy tramps in 'We're a Couple of Swells'.

The film ends with a playful gender reversal that completes the formation of Don and Hannah as a romantic couple. Hannah is distraught after Nadine pulls Don from the audience of the Follies to dance with her ('It Only Happens When I Dance with You'). Prompted by Johnny (Peter Lawford), who has been pursuing Hannah only to realise she is in love with Don, Hannah takes action. In a scene that recalls his Easter presents for Nadine, a perplexed Don receives flowers and a ribboned top hat (with a live rabbit in it, echoing the toy of the opening). Hannah arrives, beautifully dressed but acting the traditional male part ('I never saw you look quite so pretty'), chivying Don to finish dressing and put on his Easter bonnet. The final scene, on the film's impressive recreation of Fifth Avenue, is the Easter Parade itself, with the couple definitively united as equals. DP

Dir: Charles Walters; **Prod**: Arthur Freed; **Scr**: Sidney Sheldon, Frances Goodrich, Albert Hackett, from a story by Frances Goodrich and Albert Hackett; **DOP**: Harry Stradling (colour); **Song Music/Lyrics**: Irving Berlin; **Musical Dir**: Johnny Green; **Choreog**: Robert Alton, Fred Astaire (uncredited); **Art**: Cedric Gibbons and Jack Martin Smith; **Main Cast**: Judy Garland, Fred Astaire, Ann Miller, Peter Lawford, Jules Munshin, Clinton Sundberg; **Prod Co**: Metro-Goldwyn-Mayer.

(*Opposite page*) Fred Astaire, Judy Garland, 'We're a Couple of Swells'

Evergreen
UK, 1934 – 91mins
Victor Saville

Though her popularity never matched that of Gracie Fields (see *Sing as We Go**), Jessie Matthews was a major musical star of 1930s British cinema. From working-class origins, Matthews had established herself as a star stage actor and dancer – notably in the stage version of Rodgers and Hart's musical *Ever Green* (1930). Although many musicals were being made in Britain, it was feared that they could not compete with Hollywood, and Matthews was used in straight comedies until *Evergreen*, her first musical film. Unlike Fields, she combined conventional glamour (fine legs, pert breasts and bottom) with excellent dancing skills – much admired by Fred Astaire – and a good singing voice.

Fields appealed almost exclusively to domestic audiences, whereas Matthews was recognised as having potentially international appeal and *Evergreen* competed successfully in the US market with Hollywood musicals, both Warner Bros./Busby Berkeley backstage musicals like *42nd Street** and *Footlight Parade** and Astaire–Rogers musicals like *Flying Down to Rio** and *Top Hat**. With a large budget for a British film, an American cinematographer and US-born choreographer, it incorporated, as well as Rodgers and Hart songs, extravagant set designs (by Alfred Junge). The Depression theme of finding work and success is present here, though very muted by comparison with, say, *42nd Street*, but *Evergreen* also owed something to much-admired contemporary German musicals like *Der Kongress tanzt** and *Viktor und Viktoria** (of which Matthews's 1935 film *First a Girl* was a – slightly tame – remake). Like the German films, *Evergreen* explores issues of gender, sexuality and masquerade barely touched upon in Fields's films.

Like the Astaire–Rogers musicals and other 1930s comedies, *Evergreen* turns on the comic and romantic consequences of deception, mistaken identities and coincidence. In the somewhat convoluted narrative, set first in Edwardian times, the celebrated music-hall/variety artiste Harriet Green (Matthews), about to retire and marry into society, suddenly decides to disappear (to South Africa) when threatened by the exposure that she has a daughter. Thirty years later, in the film's present, daughter Harriet (also Matthews), seeking to break into theatre, agrees to impersonate her miraculously youthful mother making a comeback, with inevitable complications.

Evergreen boasts several strikingly successful musical numbers – some simple, some spectacular, some quite risqué – comparable with the Hollywood films. There are two standout production numbers. In 'When You've Got a Little Springtime in Your Heart' (one of two songs by Harry M. Woods added to the stage show), the confines of the proscenium-arch stage – already well breached by earlier numbers – are definitively exploded: encapsulating the film's play with time, an hourglass motif, with extensive montage, turns the clock back to the 1920s Jazz Age and the Charleston, then back to 1914 with striking *Metropolis*-type costumes and sets, and back again to 1904 and a formal dance. In the film's extended finale, 'Over My Shoulder', Harriet decides to reveal all by, as it were, revealing all: on the first night, dancing wildly in an impromptu frenzy of abandonment and paean to youthful sexuality and display, she rips off her semi-Edwardian costume, bonnet and wig to show her youthful body, 'free at last', as the song has it, to be herself. This sexual display, accompanied by revolving circular stages packed with chorus girls, is then incorporated into the show, in which she discards a feathery dress and reappears in a revealingly diaphanous shift. JH

Dir: Victor Saville; **Prod**: Michael Balcon (uncredited); **Scr**: Emlyn Williams, Marjorie Gaffney, from Benn W. Levy's play *Ever Green*; **DOP**: Glen MacWilliams (b&w); **Song Music/Lyrics**: Richard Rodgers/Lorenz Hart; Harry M. Woods, *et al*.; **Art**: Alfred Junge, Peter Proud (uncredited); **Main Cast**: Jessie Matthews, Sonnie Hale, Betty Balfour, Barry MacKay, Ivor McLaren, Hartley Power; **Prod Co**: Gaumont British Picture Corporation.

Flying Down to Rio
USA, 1933 – 89 mins
Thornton Freeland

Flying Down to Rio, the first teaming of Fred Astaire and Ginger Rogers as dance partners, is only a prelude to their later 1930s RKO musicals, notably *The Gay Divorcée**, *Top Hat** and *Swing Time**. Billed fourth and fifth, they dance only one number together, are neither a romantic couple nor central to the main romantic triangle and backstage story, although Rogers's somewhat sexually forward persona and Astaire's greater refinement are already in evidence. Astaire plays Fred, best friend of bandleader Roger (Gene Raymond), who can't resist pretty women, and Rogers plays Honey, the band's singer. Roger pursues Belinha (Dolores del Rio), already engaged to her compatriot Julio (Raul Roulien), from Miami to Rio, where the romantic triangle continues and Roger and Fred help to mount a show.

    Though intended as Astaire's first musical after his successful stage career, production delays meant that he appeared first (as himself) in *Dancing Lady*, singing and dancing with Joan Crawford. Rogers had already appeared in minor roles in over twenty films, notably *42nd Street** and *Gold Diggers of 1933**, and was not the initial choice for the film. Nevertheless, what with Rogers singing on her own ('Music Makes Me'), Astaire singing with both del Rio ('Orchids in the Moonlight') and solo ('Flying Down to Rio') and dancing on his own (the rehearsal dance), and the two of them dancing together only once ('The Carioca'), one cannot help feeling (in retrospect) that RKO was wilfully refusing to see what had to be. Though not the main stars, Astaire and Rogers, their characters happily drunk together, close the picture, as if announcing their partnership and the films to come. The film was also the first to bring together choreographer Hermes Pan and production designer Van Nest Polglase, and its commercial success helped RKO through a period of financial problems.

    In the early 1930s, Hollywood studios vied with each other in the extravagance of their musical production numbers. The climactic 'Flying

Down to Rio' number here represents a particular kind of excess: unable to present a show at the hotel, instead they strap showgirls on aeroplane wings, complete with Busby Berkeley-type 'dance' and leggy display as parts of their costumes are whipped away by parachute. The extended 'Carioca' number, though less outlandish, is even more extravagantly staged. Supposedly ordinary Carioca-dancing couples – all suggestive body movements – encourage Fred and Honey to take to the floor, where they perform their own version, with noticeably fewer suggestive gyrations but incorporating a tap routine and a wonderful 'banged-head' moment when they totter dizzily away from each other.

Professional, costumed Carioca dancing couples then take over, themselves followed by a black singer and black dancers in a more Afro version, followed *again* by more of Fred and Honey. Much simpler, but very striking, is Fred's rehearsal dance, in which uptempo band music propels him, as if against his will, into tap, incorporating some wonderful 'out-of-control' dance moves.

By comparison with later Astaire–Rogers films, *Flying* is noticeably pre-Code. Not only do Honey and the chorus girls wear see-through costumes and appear in various states of undress, but many of the dialogue exchanges are openly risqué. After being warned not to get familiar with hotel guests, Honey pointedly replies, 'But what if the hotel guests get familiar with us?', while another woman character asks, 'What have these South Americans got below the equator that we haven't?' JH

Dir: Thornton Freeland; **Prod**: Lou Brock, Merian C. Cooper; **Scr**: Cyril Hume, H. W. Hanemann, Erwin Gelsey, from a play by Anne Caldwell, based on a story by Lou Brock; **DOP**: J. Roy Hunt (b&w); **Song Music/Lyrics**: Vincent Youmans/Gus Kahn, Edward Eliscu; **Choreog**: Dave Gould, Hermes Pan; **Art**: Van Nest Polglase, Carroll Clark; **Main Cast**: Dolores del Rio, Gene Raymond, Raul Roulien, Ginger Rogers, Fred Astaire; **Prod Co**: Radio Pictures.

Footlight Parade
USA, 1933 – 104 mins
Lloyd Bacon

Like its immediate predecessors, *42nd Street** and *Gold Diggers of 1933**, *Footlight Parade* follows the personal and professional struggles of a New York musical theatre company to stage a show – represented by the spectacular Busby Berkeley-directed numbers for which the Warners musicals are most famous. *Footlight Parade* also maintains the close relationship established in the earlier films between the story and the off-screen social world of Depression America, although here the threat to the show, or to musical theatre as a whole, with which all three films open, is not the lack of money caused by the Crash but Hollywood's wholesale switch from silent movies to 'talkies'. This is one way in which the problems of the Depression are somewhat muted in *Footlight Parade*.

In this inflection of the backstage story, the director Chester Kent (James Cagney) achieves a role for musical theatre in the new world of talking pictures by mass-producing live 'prologues' to tour the country's cinemas in support of feature films. The film's exhilarating momentum is powered by Kent's drive to meet the constant demand for new prologue ideas – and finally by a tight deadline to win a contract with a major exhibition chain. Although the exhaustion that shadows the rehearsal process in *42nd Street* is present here, the tone of *Footlight Parade* is notably more upbeat. Central to this are Cagney's extraordinary dynamism, which makes Kent a much more positive figure than the directors in the previous two films, and his enhanced role in the plot, as lover and finally as performer. The regular pairing of Dick Powell and Ruby Keeler as the young couple falling in love (and performing together in the extravagantly staged 'Honeymoon Hotel' and 'By a Waterfall' numbers) is paralleled here by Kent's troubled relationships with women and his cheating business partners, and by his final recognition that his

(Opposite page) 'By a Waterfall'

secretary, Nan (Joan Blondell), is the partner he needs. Unlike the Warner Baxter character in *42nd Street*, who is never involved in performance, Kent constantly demonstrates dance steps in rehearsal and it is appropriate as well as very satisfying when he accidentally finds himself starring in the final number, 'Shanghai Lil', falling on stage in a struggle with his unwilling leading man. The director's greater integration in the various strands of the plot makes *Footlight Parade* the most aesthetically pleasing of the three films.

It is also the film that most overtly acknowledges Warner Bros.' support for the recently elected President Franklin Roosevelt, incorporating in the affirmative, patriotic climax of 'Shanghai Lil' images of the president and of a central emblem of his New Deal policies, the eagle of the National Recovery Administration. But, as Mark Roth (1981) was the first to argue, we should see the New Deal values of communal effort and common purpose pervading the films, embodied in the interdependence of performers in the shows and particularly in the subordination of individuality to the patterning of Berkeley's extraordinary designs. Kent, not standing apart from his company but absorbed into the show, becomes the very image of the strong but benign new leader. DP

Dir: Lloyd Bacon; **Prod**: Robert Lord; **Scr**: Manuel Seff, James Seymour; **DOP**: George Barnes (b&w); **Song Music/Lyrics**: Harry Warren/Al Dubin; Sammy Fain/Irvin Kahal; **Choreog/Co Dir**: Busby Berkeley; **Art**: Anton Grot, Jack Okey; **Main Cast**: James Cagney, Joan Blondell, Ruby Keeler, Dick Powell, Frank McHugh, Guy Kibbee; **Prod Co**: Warner Bros.

Footloose

USA, 1984 – 107 mins
Herbert Ross

Given the long-established symbiotic relationship between popular music and cinema, particularly in Hollywood, with its major studio conglomerates operating across movies, music and television, major changes in one medium inevitably have radical effects on the others. The advent of MTV in the early 1980s, aimed at the same youth demographic that most movies were targeting, quickly established 'music videos' – which rapidly became as much image- as music-centred – as essential for the promotion of popular music. Rather than recordings of performance, music videos/pop promos became, in effect, musical 'numbers' without the surrounding narrative. Although the narratives in some older musicals were sometimes little more than hooks on which to hang a string of numbers and performances (see, among others, *Anchors Aweigh**, *Stormy Weather**), the numbers in 'classical' musicals more generally arose from their narratives, whether as showbiz performances or spontaneously from the action. In a significant shift, the tendency in post-MTV musicals has been for musical numbers to be more decoupled from narrative, or even float free.

 Footloose is clearly calculated to appeal to a youth audience: Chicago boy Ren (Kevin Bacon) comes to live in ultra conservative, uptight small-town Bomont, which, led by minister Shaw Moore (John Lithgow), has banned rock music and dancing, to the chagrin of the town's restless teenagers, not least the rebellious, daredevil, sexually precocious minister's daughter Ariel (Lori Singer). The film declares its allegiances in the opening juxtaposition of dancing feet and shots of the Utah landscape and a deathly sermon about rock music being devil's work. Needless to say, Ren gets together with Ariel and after various battles (in which Ariel coaches Ren on biblical quotations about dancing), the minister has a change of heart and the young people have their prom.

Films like *Footloose* and *Flashdance* (1983) were made only a few years after *Saturday Night Fever** and *Grease** – pop music-centred films aimed at more or less the same audiences – but the relationships between narrative and numbers already feel different. The big numbers in *Footloose*, such as Ren's spectacular solo dance in the empty mill ('Never') or the sequence in which Ren teaches his friend, farm boy Willard (Chris Penn), how to dance ('Let's Hear It for the Boy'), seem designed to have an impact that outstrips any narrative function. Both also depend on rapid editing, elaborate staging and, in the case of 'Never', on dance doubles (like the similarly spectacular 'What a Feeling' audition in *Flashdance*). Elsewhere, with an eye on the soundtrack album, the film indulges in the now ubiquitous, almost gratuitous use of rock songs by various artists to drive action sequences, like Bonnie Tyler's 'Holding Out for a Hero' for the *Rebel without a Cause*-referencing 'chicken run' on tractors. In each case, the sequences feel like ready-made music promos.

The witty title sequence, perhaps the highlight of the movie, is a montage of variously dressed and shod legs and feet dancing to 'Footloose', an almost abstract evocation of the energy and pleasure of dance, and completely separate from the rest of the film (although, of course, credit sequences often are). It reminds us that Herbert Ross was a dancer and choreographer (*Carmen Jones**; Cliff Richard's musicals *The Young Ones*, 1961, and *Summer Holiday*, 1963; *Funny Girl*, 1968) before becoming a fully-fledged director (including *Funny Lady** and *Pennies from Heaven*, 1981). As a considerable box-office success with a cult following (parodied in, for example, *The Simpsons*), it was no surprise that *Footloose* was adapted into a successful stage musical (Broadway, 1998, London, 2006). JH

Dir: Herbert Ross; **Prod**: Lewis J. Rachmil, Craig Zadan; **Scr**: Dean Pitchford; **DOP**: Ric Waite (colour); **Song Music/Lyrics**: Kenny Loggins, *et al.*/Dean Pitchford; **Choreog**: Lynne Taylor-Corbett; **Art**: Ron Hobbs; **Main Cast**: Kevin Bacon, Lori Singer, John Lithgow, Dianne Wiest, Christopher Penn, Sarah Jessica Parker; **Prod Co**: IndieProd Company Productions/Paramount.

42nd Street
USA, 1933 – 89 mins
Lloyd Bacon

42nd Street was the first of the 1933 Warner Bros. films that revived the popularity of the Hollywood musical and established the 'backstage' story as one of its basic forms. Like its successors, *Gold Diggers of 1933** and *Footlight Parade**, the film is set in the world of musical theatre and follows the struggle to produce a show in the midst of the Great Depression. In all three, the need for money drives the narrative, and its pursuit or the power it confers often distorts the romantic relationships that are interwoven with the show's development. Several of the central performers appear in all three movies, establishing a continuity that is intensified by the films' most famous feature, the extravagant, elaborately patterned musical numbers created by Busby Berkeley. In this version of the musical, numbers belong exclusively to the theatre, not to the characters' ordinary lives.

42nd Street is the film that most directly dramatises the impact of the Depression. As it opens, reports of a new show galvanise prospective performers, but the director, Julian Marsh (Warner Baxter), is recovering from a breakdown after losing all his money in the Wall Street Crash; in poor health, he is desperate for a 'last shot' at success. The character of the director is a significant index of the changing tone of the three films: here, Marsh drives rehearsals mercilessly, in a state of permanent anxiety. Here too, the exhaustion of the dancers in the gruelling rehearsal process is at its most intense.

The show's finance depends on wealthy Abner Dillon (Guy Kibbee), the sugar daddy of the show's star, Dorothy Brock (Bebe Daniels), but everything is threatened by her love for Pat Denning (George Brent). The complications of these relationships, together with the growing romance between inexperienced Peggy Sawyer (Ruby Keeler) and juvenile lead Billy Lawler (Dick Powell) and desperate attempts to prevent Abner finding out about Pat, are interwoven with the increasingly frantic pace of rehearsal and the out-of-town tour. Inevitably, Abner discovers the truth and in the crisis that ensues, Peggy is plucked from the chorus to replace Dorothy in the show ('You're going out a youngster – but come back a star!').

The success of the show is embodied in the three Busby Berkeley numbers (with songs written by Harry Warren and Al Dubin in the first of many movies for Warners), 'Shuffle off to Buffalo', 'Young and Healthy' and the climactic '42nd Street'. A central paradox of the Warner musicals is that while their narratives are about theatre and the numbers are therefore performed for a live audience, theatrical space dissolves in Berkeley's hands and the numbers become celebrations of the wondrous freedom of the camera and editing to create a purely filmic space. 'Young and Healthy' also contains the profusion of female bodies, reduced at times to abstract patterns in kaleidoscopic overhead shots, for which Berkeley is notorious, and, with 'Shuffle off to Buffalo', makes explicit the sexual energy that remains more muted in the narrative.

The film ends, though, not with the show's triumph but with Marsh, who has driven the show to success but is now alone, slumped on a step outside the theatre as the audience leaves. In dramatising the rewards of communal effort in the face of the Depression, these films carry a significant political charge in the year of the New Deal, but here Marsh has no place in the unity he has inspired. In *Footlight Parade*, made several months later, the director's fate is very different

A successful show based on *42nd Street* opened on Broadway in 1980 and in London in 1984. DP

Dir: Lloyd Bacon; **Prod**: Daryl F. Zanuck; **Scr**: Rian James, James Seymour, from Bradford Ropes's novel; **DOP**: Sol Polito (b&w); **Song Music/Lyrics**: Harry Warren/Al Dubin; **Choreog/Co Dir**: Busby Berkeley; **Art**: Jack Okey; **Main Cast**: Warner Baxter, Bebe Daniels, George Brent, Ruby Keeler, Guy Kibbee, Dick Powell, Ginger Rogers; **Prod Co**: Warner Bros.

Funny Face
USA, 1957 – 103 mins
Stanley Donen

The last sequence of *Funny Face* returns to the grounds of the Chantilly church in which, much earlier, the obtuse Dick Avery (Fred Astaire) finally realised his love for Jo Stockton (Audrey Hepburn) and they sang and danced 'He Loves and She Loves'. Now, after Jo has run – distressed – from the fashion show in her final outfit, the wedding dress she was also wearing in the earlier scene, Dick intuits where she has gone and the film ends with their lovely musical reconciliation, ''S Wonderful', filmed, like the earlier number, in self-consciously dreamy soft focus.

It is a fittingly romantic conclusion but one that, unlike some other key late Astaire movies (*Easter Parade**, *The Band Wagon**), isolates the couple from the social world. In those films, as the woman falls for Astaire's character, she finds or recovers her true self and wholeheartedly embraces his world. Here, the ending is (implicitly) more equivocal: Jo is disenchanted with the lecherous Emile Flostre (Michel Auclair), the founder of 'Empathicalism', the philosophy to which she was devoted, but she does not identify herself with the fashion world Dick works in. As in *Silk Stockings**, the 'happy ending' closes off rather than resolves the couple's differences.

In satirical sequences set in gloomy and angst-ridden Parisian Left-Bank venues, the film itself is fairly unequivocal about the humourless pretensions of Empathicalism. About fashion, it is more poised. Its absurdities are wonderfully sent up in the early sequences in *Quality* magazine's New York offices, with the editor, Maggie Prescott (the splendid Kay Thompson in one of her rare screen appearances), galvanising her staff in 'Think Pink', and in the magazine's invasion of a bookshop for a photo-shoot. It is here that Dick, a fashion photographer working for the magazine, meets Jo and sets out to recruit her as the new-style '*Quality* woman' for the magazine's crucial Paris show. The film foregrounds but also embraces the artifice of photography and fashion

as Jo is transformed: the emergence of her portraits from developing fluid in the red light of the darkroom as Dick sings 'Funny Face' and they dance for the first time; Jo's stunning first appearance in her new guise after the fashion house has worked its magic; each moment in the Paris shoot completed with a spectacular fashion plate, via freeze-frame, monochrome and colour manipulation. Yet the film's evident delight in its bravura display of these and other image-manipulating techniques (such as the split-screen montage of the three principals in various Paris locations for the number 'Bonjour Paris') does not lead it to endorse the fashion world's values.

In a parallel way, for Jo, being a model can be fun but it is mere pretence. Audrey Hepburn gives Jo qualities of innocence and openness that make entirely credible and touching her inability to simulate feelings close to her heart (like the happiness of a bride in her wedding dress). Such feelings can be expressed only in private – especially in the numbers with Dick that only we witness. In backstage musicals, public performance and romance go hand in hand; in *Funny Face*, private and public realms are out of synch.

The film seems like an MGM musical in all but studio. Roger Edens developed the project, combining Leonard Gershe's libretto with Gershwin songs written for the entirely different 1927 show *Funny Face*, starring Adele and Fred Astaire. When Paramount would not loan out Hepburn, MGM sold them the package and with it went key 'Freed unit' personnel, including director Stanley Donen, producer Roger Edens, musical director Adolph Deutsch and choreographer Eugene Loring. DP

Dir: Stanley Donen; **Prod**: Roger Edens; **Scr**: Leonard Gershe; **DOP**: Ray June (colour); **Song Music/Lyrics**: George Gershwin/Ira Gershwin; Roger Edens/Leonard Gershe; **Musical Dir**: Adolph Deutsch; **Choreog**: Eugene Loring, Fred Astaire; **Art**: Hal Pereira, George W. Davis; **Main Cast**: Audrey Hepburn, Fred Astaire, Kay Thompson, Michel Auclair, Robert Flemyng; **Prod Co**: Paramount.

(*Opposite page*) Audrey Hepburn, 'How Long Has This Been Going On'

Funny Girl
USA, 1968 – 155 mins
William Wyler

After 1960, many hopes for the survival of the classic studio musical fell
upon Julie Andrews and the phenomenal success of *Mary Poppins** and
The Sound of Music*. In the late 1960s, when her films *Thoroughly
Modern Millie* (1967) and *Star!* (1968) brought diminishing returns,
Barbra Streisand's first films, *Funny Girl*, then *Hello, Dolly!* (1969) and
On a Clear Day You Can See Forever (1970), offered another moment of
optimism for the genre. *Funny Girl* was adapted from the Broadway
show based on Jewish comedienne Fanny Brice's early career in
1910s/20s New York. Producer Ray Stark (Brice's son-in-law) had first
imagined a dramatic play; as it became a stage musical, various leading
ladies were considered before Streisand – Jewish, and almost as quirky
looking as Brice – was chosen. Streisand had released successful albums,
won Grammy awards and starred on television, but had limited musical
comedy theatre experience. *Funny Girl* opened in March 1964 to great
acclaim and ran for 1,348 performances, picking up a raft of Tony
nominations (but losing out to *Hello, Dolly!*).

Despite the acclaim, Columbia first wanted Shirley MacLaine for the
film; Stark insisted on Streisand, who thus achieved the feat of
translating Broadway success to Hollywood which had eluded many
theatre stars. *Funny Girl* resembles the showbiz narratives of *A Star Is
Born** and *Love Me or Leave Me**, in which masculine self-esteem is
destroyed by a woman partner's rise to stardom. Much of Brice's success
came in Florenz Ziegfeld's *Follies* (see *Ziegfeld Follies**), where she often
sent up 'glamour': in the spectacular 'His Love Makes Me Beautiful',
Fanny brings the house down by appearing in a white wedding dress
only to turn sideways and reveal, scandalously, a large pregnant 'bump'.

William Wyler, who had never directed a musical, was supposedly
responsible for the story sequences of *Funny Girl*, while stage and movie
choreographer Herbert Ross (see *Footloose**) took care of the

choreography and directing the musical numbers. The film's dramatic narrative is too slow-moving, but Wyler is effective enough, for example in the fluid, reflective opening and closing passages which lead in and out of the film's flashback. However, the film is more remarkable for its musical numbers. Several of the best combine multi-location shots with Streisand both singing and singing in voice-over: during 'Don't Rain on My Parade', Fanny rushes through a station and takes a train, taxi and then tugboat. 'People', however, takes place in real time: though it works by its simplicity – and Streisand's wonderful performance – its effect depends on subtle camera movements. The division of directorial labour is less clear with the fine number which ends the film, 'My Man', apparently shot by Wyler, which transforms a stage performance into a dramatic private moment by judicious use of lighting, framing and costume. We know that Streisand disliked lip-synching and that 'My Man' was the only number sung 'live', and it shows: this song – the number most associated with Brice – is the film's most deeply felt, and its most Streisand moment.

Funny Girl established Streisand as a movie star – though it also gave her a reputation for being perfectionist and 'difficult'. It was 1968's top-grossing film, and Streisand shared the Best Actress Oscar with Katharine Hepburn. Herbert Ross later directed Streisand in both *The Owl and the Pussycat* (1970), which cemented her image as both sexy and a fine comic, and the Fanny Brice sequel, *Funny Lady* (1975). Streisand stuck with musicals in her 'rock' remake of *A Star Is Born* (1976) and her own directing debut, *Yentl* (1983). JH

Dir: William Wyler (musical sequences choreographed and directed by Herbert Ross); **Prod**: Ray Stark; **Scr**: Isobel Lennart, from the Broadway show, book by Lennart, music by Jule Styne, lyrics by Robert Merrill; **DOP**: Harry Stradling (colour); **Song Music/Lyrics**: Jule Styne/Robert Merrill; Maurice Yvain/A. Willemetz, Jacques Charles, Channing Pollack; James F. Hanley/Grant Clarke; Fred Fisher, Billy Rose; **Musical Dir**: Walter Scharf; **Art**: Gene Callahan, Robert Luthardt; **Main Cast**: Barbra Streisand, Omar Sharif, Kay Medford, Anne Francis, Walter Pidgeon, Lee Allen; **Prod Co**: Columbia/Rastar.

The Gay Divorcee
USA, 1934 – 107 mins
Mark Sandrich

From the perspective of RKO, *The Gay Divorcee* was very much a try-out for a new star couple following *Flying Down to Rio**, in which they had appeared in secondary roles. In the history of the musical, it is a landmark: the first film in which Fred Astaire and Ginger Rogers co-starred and the first of eight films produced between 1934 and 1939 that made them the most popular star couple of their era and the most enduring in the history of the Hollywood musical (see also *Top Hat** and *Swing Time**). Their films brought new vitality to the genre by combining aspects of the show musical with settings and stories owing a good deal to operetta, a fusion that retains some of the glamour of operetta but with characters and music that are emphatically American. Crucially, too, dance is at the heart of these films – romance finds its perfect expression in a couple dancing.

Adapted from Astaire's 1932 stage hit, *The Gay Divorce* (from which only one of Cole Porter's numbers was retained), *The Gay Divorcee* became in a number of ways a prototype for the cycle. The setting is contemporary, though geographically and economically distanced from Depression America (the action takes place in France and England and the central characters are well off). Astaire's character is a professional dancer, and spaces designed for performance (including the Big White Set, which became a recurrent feature of the films) figure extensively in the narrative. The script centres on the witty interplay of the central couple. When the Astaire and Rogers characters meet, he is immediately smitten but she is alienated, and he must gradually persuade her that they belong together. Here, Guy meets Mimi in the customs hall after he has just landed from France, later looks for her all over London, finds her again by accident, loses her once more, until they meet again in the seaside resort of Brightbourne.

In the meantime, Guy's solo number, 'Needle in a Haystack', performed as he prepares to look for Mimi in London, establishes the

Astaire character's ability to move spontaneously into song and dance, as though they were entirely natural extensions of speech and walking, and to integrate his surroundings wittily into performance: he sings as he dresses and the room's furniture and fittings effortlessly become props for his dance. The film ends with a parallel outburst of playful spontaneity, now with Guy and Mimi dancing together on and over the furniture in her hotel suite as they prepare to leave. Between these moments, Guy's task is in effect to find ways of drawing Mimi into the dance, and he first achieves this on the empty dance floor in Brightbourne, singing Cole Porter's 'Night and Day', blocking Mimi's escape and entrancing her into perfectly matching him in the dance. All these numbers also establish the fluid method of filming dance that marks Astaire's approach – shooting in extended takes, the camera framing the dancers at full length.

The plot complications turn, as in most of the later films, on issues to do with marriage. Here, uniquely in the series, the Rogers character is already married and mistakes Guy for the professional co-respondent (played by Erik Rhodes) hired to facilitate her divorce. Mistaken identity is relatively soon resolved but Mimi is still not free. She and Guy publicly mark their commitment to each other by joining in 'The Continental', the huge production number that is being staged as part of the hotel's entertainment; and when Mimi's husband is exposed as a philanderer, the way is cleared for the couple's celebration in dance. DP

Dir: Mark Sandrich; **Prod**: Pandro S. Berman; **Scr**: George Marion Jr, Dorothy Yost, Edward Kaufman, from the show *The Gay Divorce*, book by Dwight Taylor, musical adaptation by Kenneth Webb and Samuel Hoffenstein; **DOP**: David Abel (b&w); **Song Music/Lyrics**: Cole Porter; Mack Gordon/Harry Revel; Con Conrad/Herb Magidson; **Musical Dir**: Max Steiner; **Choreog**: Dave Gould, Fred Astaire (uncredited), Hermes Pan (uncredited); **Art**: Van Nest Polglase, Carroll Clark; **Main Cast**: Fred Astaire, Ginger Rogers, Alice Brady, Edward Everett Horton, Erik Rhodes, Eric Blore, Betty Grable; **Prod Co**: RKO.

Gentlemen Prefer Blondes
USA, 1953 – 91 mins
Howard Hawks

Gentlemen Prefer Blondes begins boldly and its opening sequences set out what it wants to say: the Fox logo gives way to blue curtains; showgirls Dorothy (Jane Russell) and Lorelei (Marilyn Monroe) emerge in daring sparkly red costumes and jewels and launch into the brash 'Little Girl from Little Rock', in which girls from the wrong side of the tracks are done wrong by men and discover all about love and money. The credits disposed of, we cut back to the song and then to the film's first male, Gus (Tommy Noonan), Lorelei's sugar daddy, watching in the audience and, shortly, meeting fiancée Lorelei backstage. Nervous and awkward around the simpering, pouting Lorelei, Gus almost faints when she kisses him, while tougher, wise-cracking Dorothy looks on, amused.

Though very different from each other, Dorothy and Lorelei make a formidable partnership, happy and relaxed around each other (apparently, Russell and Monroe did get along very well, and it shows, particularly in their lovely joint number 'When Loves Go Wrong'). Lorelei is (much) smarter than she looks and acts: she tells Gus's wealthy, suspicious father: 'Don't you know that a man being rich is like a girl being pretty. You might not marry a girl just because she is pretty but my goodness, doesn't it help?', a philosophy which takes spectacular form in 'Diamonds Are a Girl's Best Friend'. She aims to 'educate' Dorothy, who, as Lorelei puts it, is 'always falling in love with some man just because he's good looking'. Dorothy's approach to sex and men comes across in 'Is There Anyone Here for Love?': the two women are sailing to France, and Dorothy, in a low-cut black playsuit, finds herself surrounded by the male athletes of the US Olympic team as they work out. Dressed only in flesh-coloured shorts, the athletes are choreographed so that they become objectified and 'demasculinised', preoccupied with their physical fitness and not at all interested in her, despite her invitation to 'tennis' – 'Doubles anyone? Court's free. Doesn't anyone want to play?'

Other male characters also can't measure up to the confident, assertive women. Lorelei is ogled by both randy, aged diamond-mine-owner 'Piggy' Beekman (Charles Coburn) and gravelly voiced precocious twelve-year-old Henry Spofford III (George Winslow). The private detective Malone (Elliott Reid), spying on Lorelei and attracted to Dorothy, is a halfway presentable male but hardly dynamic hero material. The film does end with a double marriage – Dorothy with Malone, Lorelei with Gus – but neither prospect seems very promising, and the *mise en scène* suggests that the real union is between the two women.

Although the film has many 'Hawksian' qualities, musicals were not Hawks's forte, and the fine musical numbers in *Gentlemen Prefer Blondes* owe most to choreographer Jack Cole. The successful 1949 Broadway stage version (which made a star of Carol Channing and was choreographed by Agnes de Mille) remained faithful to the 1920s Jazz Age, gold-digging flapper setting of Anita Loos's original 1925 novel and 1926 stage play, but this version updates the story, and it is very much a 1950s film. As Laura Mulvey (1996) suggests, 'the theme of the woman who commodifies herself through her desire to accumulate commodities' is entirely appropriate for the 'consumer-obsessed 50s'. For a film which plays heavily on the male gaze (while also deconstructing it), Russell and Monroe were inspired choices. Both were quintessential 'glamour' icons of the period – Monroe appeared on the cover of *Playboy* just a few months later – but their performances do much to ironise their status as sex symbols. JH

Dir: Howard Hawks; **Prod**: Sol C. Siegel; **Scr**: Charles Lederer, adapted from the Broadway stage musical by Joseph Fields, Anita Loos, itself adapted from the novel and stage play by Anita Loos; **DOP**: Harry J. Wild (colour); **Song Music/Lyrics**: Jule Styne/Leo Robin; Hoagy Carmichael/Harold Adamson; **Musical Dir**: Lionel Newman; **Choreog**: Jack Cole; **Art**: Lyle R. Wheeler, Joseph C. Wright; **Main Cast**: Jane Russell, Marilyn Monroe, Charles Coburn, Elliott Reed, Tommy Noonan, George Winslow, Marcel Dalio; **Prod Co**: 20th Century-Fox.

(*Next page*) *Gentlemen Prefer Blondes*: Jane Russell, Marilyn Monroe, 'When Love Goes Wrong'

The Girl Can't Help It
USA, 1956 – 93 mins
Frank Tashlin

In 1957, when French film critics were beginning to enthuse about Frank Tashlin's comedies, Jean-Luc Godard (1972) wrote that *The Girl Can't Help It* was a 'fountain of youth from which the cinema … has drawn fresh inspiration'. It seems an unlikely claim for a film that is in part a compendium of numbers designed to showcase emerging stars of rock and roll, but *The Girl Can't Help It* was very different in look and approach from other rock and roll movies, such as *Rock around the Clock* and *Don't Knock the Rock*, that were rushed out in 1956 to meet the new demand. Embracing both the music and the opportunities of the exploitation format with evident enthusiasm, Tashlin produced one of the definitive film comedies about 1950s America.

In fact, the film flaunts the demand to cram in numbers (seventeen in 93 minutes) by making most of them essentially set pieces: Tashlin merely nods to the conventions of the integrated musical by placing them in nightclubs, on TV or in a rehearsal studio. Gene Vincent, The Platters, Fats Domino, Little Richard and others erupt into the film with performances that are almost independent of the narrative as well as, at times, incongruously displaced from their familiar contexts (Little Richard in a refined nightclub!). Across the film, shot with glamour lighting and in glossy colour – *The Girl Can't Help It* was the first rock and roll movie in colour – the numbers brilliantly show off the music but also come to function as consumer images for the film's narrative about instant celebrity and the absurdities of 1950s American life.

The story proceeds largely in juxtaposition to the numbers, evoking contrasting aspects of the 1950s. Alcoholic theatrical agent Tom Miller (Tom Ewell) is hired by ex-racketeer Marty ('Fats') Murdoch (Edmond O'Brien) to turn his girlfriend Jerri (Jayne Mansfield) into a star. Tom is haunted by his previous client and girlfriend (Julie London as herself), who appears spectrally in his drunken visions, singing 'Cry Me a River', but eventually falls for Jerri. Central characters called Tom and Jerri, and another called Mousey (Henry Jones) signal something of Tashlin's intentions, and a good deal of the film's comedy is played out around Jayne Mansfield's remarkable figure and its effect on men: ice melts, milk boils and spectacles crack as she passes. Mansfield is a delight – a talented comedian who, as John Waters puts it in the DVD extras, was in on – not the butt of – the joke in which she becomes a cartoon-like parody of 1950s sex symbols (Tashlin's early career was in cartoons). Apparently unable to sing, Jerri becomes a star with a siren-like scream at the end of Marty's song 'Rock around the Rock Pile', sung by Ray Anthony.

Among the various twists of the plot, Jerri (real name Georgiana) wants nothing more than domestic bliss; she falls for Tom; it turns out that she can sing after all; Marty inadvertently becomes a rock star, singing his own number; he gives Jerri up on their wedding day, leaving the way for Tom and Jerri. In Tashlin's ironic play with 1950s images and ideals, celebrity is both contrived and whimsical, and happily ever after neatly subverts stereotypes: the iconic Jayne Mansfield can fall in love with Tom Ewell (lovelorn and unromantic in several 50s movies); Jayne wants nothing more than to cook and have babies; and Edmond O'Brien can get to be the latest star of rock and roll. *The Girl Can't Help It* is much the best of the early rock and roll movies – and a great deal more. DP

Dir/**Prod**: Frank Tashlin; **Scr**: Frank Tashlin, Herbert Baker, from Garson Kanin's novel *Do Re Mi*; **DOP**: Leon Shamroy (colour); **Song Music**/**Lyrics**: Bobby Troop; John Marascalco/ Robert Blackwell; Arthur Hamilton; Gene Vincent; Fats Domino, *et al*.; **Music**: Lionel Newman, Leigh Harline; **Musical Dir**: Lionel Newman; **Art**: Leland Fuller, Lyle R. Wheeler; **Main Cast**: Tom Ewell, Jayne Mansfield, Edmond O'Brien, Henry Jones, Julie London, Ray Anthony, John Emery, Little Richard, Gene Vincent, The Platters, Eddie Cochrane, Fats Domino; **Prod Co**: 20th Century-Fox.

Gold Diggers of 1933
USA, 1933 – 94 mins
Mervyn LeRoy

Gold Diggers of 1933 was the second Warner Bros. backstage musical of that year and it gave birth to a whole series of *Gold Digger* movies. An immediate follow-up to *42nd Street**, using many of the same cast and with Busby Berkeley directing the numbers, the film is based on a 1919 play, *The Gold Diggers*, and the early colour movie, *Gold Diggers of Broadway* (1929). Combined with a story of musical theatre in the Depression, the play's emphasis on class and female friendship produces a different balance between personal and professional strands of the plot to that in *42nd Street*, with its tighter focus on the show.

We see much more here of the characters outside the theatre – a good deal of the action takes place in the apartment shared by Polly (Ruby Keeler), Carol (Joan Blondell) and Trixie (Aline MacMahon), the three women who dominate the film. Correspondingly, we see less of the rehearsal process than in *42nd Street* and the role of the director is significantly reduced. He is at the heart of *42nd Street* but his equivalent here, the show's producer, Barney Hopkins (Ned Sparks), is relatively marginal to the drama.

The anxieties of the Depression are also less urgently present across the film. The film begins with an apparently optimistic number, 'We're in the Money' ('Never see a headline about a breadline today'), abruptly interrupted by the sheriff arriving to seize the set and costumes – the fourth show in four months to be shut down. We are introduced to the three women, out of work and broke, but the immediacy of the Depression context then recedes until the last section of the movie and its famous final number, 'My Forgotten Man', with its lament for the destitute veterans of World War I.

Reflecting this changed dynamic, instead of building to a climactic theatrical event, here the film is divided into two parts which pivot on the show's opening, represented by the number 'Pettin' in the Park'.

In the first, we meet the central characters, including Barney, in the women's apartment. Dick Powell and Ruby Keeler again play the young couple – this time Powell is Brad, a musician living next door, who Barney hires as his composer. The central mysteries of the first part – how Brad is able to fund the show and why he refuses to perform in public – are unlocked when he saves the day by replacing the incapacitated juvenile but is recognised and exposed as a member of a Boston 'Blueblood' family.

The family insists that Brad must give Polly up or be disinherited, and the backstage story is largely displaced by Carol and Trixie's plot to help Polly and Brad by ensnaring Brad's snobbish and pompous brother, Lawrence (Warren William), and the family lawyer, Peabody (Guy Kibbee). The comic convolutions, skilfully handled by Mervyn LeRoy, begin with Trixie and Carol aiming to 'take 'em for a ride', and lead, via episodes of mistaken identity, drunkenness and humiliation, to Carol falling in love with Lawrence. Love and marriage reward the women's triumph over privilege and bigotry. When the film returns to the show for its concluding movement and the final numbers, 'In the Shadows Let Me Sing to You' and 'My Forgotten Man', three couples have been formed (Trixie has even married the corpulent Peabody) and Lawrence finally relents. The abrupt shift of tone with the final number makes returning to the Depression feel almost like an afterthought and, indeed, 'My Forgotten Man' was a late addition, but what lingers as the film ends is its extraordinary power. DP

Dir: Mervyn LeRoy; **Prod**: Robert Lord; **Scr**: Erwin Gelsey, James Seymour, based on Arthur Hopwood's play *Gold Diggers* and the film *Gold Diggers of Broadway*; **DOP**: Sol Polito (b&w); **Song Music/Lyrics**: Harry Warren/Al Dubin; **Choreog/Co Dir**: Busby Berkeley; **Art**: Anton Grot; **Main Cast**: Joan Blondell, Aline MacMahon, Ruby Keeler, Dick Powell, Warren William, Guy Kibbee; **Prod Co**: Warner Bros.

(*Next page*) *Gold Diggers of 1933*: 'My Forgotten Man'

Golden Eighties
France/Belgium/Switzerland, 1986 – 96 mins
Chantal Akerman

Chantal Akerman is among the most interesting contemporary
experimental film-makers and installation artists. Influenced by film-
makers as diverse as Jean-Luc Godard and Michael Snow, films like
Jeanne Dielman, 23 Quai du Commerce, 1080 Bruxelles (1975), *News
from Home* (1977) and *Toute une nuit* (1982) deconstruct the
conventions of narrative cinema and explore new ways of representing
the everyday. *Golden Eighties* (known in the US as *Window Shopping*), a
musical set in a shopping mall, was a long-cherished project: in 1983,
trying to raise funds for the film, Akerman put together *Les Années 80*, a
feature-length 'preview' comprising an hour of video footage of
auditions, rehearsals and recording, and 20 minutes of sample scenes on
35mm. It was always likely that *Golden Eighties* would be a reflection on
the genre's formal and thematic conventions, more a 'counter-musical'
than 'a musical'. Songs and dance routines are performed, in part,
directly to camera; Akerman foregrounds the film frame, particularly
with the choruses of male loafers and female salon assistants who
make fun of the characters, spread gossip and predict 'trouble ahead'.
The singing and dancing is some way short of perfection, but this is part
of the film's charm.

Characters play out variations on heterosexual romance: bar-owner
Sylvie (Myriam Boyer) gets letters from a lover who is trying to make his
fortune in Canada; Jeanne (Delphine Seyrig), who runs the dress shop
with her husband, Monsieur Schwartz (Charles Denner), is thrown into
confusion when her long-lost American lover Eli (John Berry) returns
looking for her; their son Robert (Nicolas Tronc) is infatuated with Lili
(Fanny Cottençon), who runs the next-door hair salon for her boss,
Monsieur Jean (Jean-François Balmer); M. Jean, married but sleeping with
Lili, cannot abide her flirting with Robert; Mado (Lio), one of the salon
workers, is in love with Robert. But, as in other musicals of the period

like *New York, New York** and *One from the Heart**, 'happy endings' are a distant prospect: as the *ronde* of love and infatuation unravels, Sylvie's interest in her long-distance lover wanes; Jeanne decides against reuniting with Eli; distracted by Lili's infidelity, M. Jean wrecks the salon but turns up at the end with his wife and children; let down by Lili, Robert proposes to Mado but abandons her when Lili turns up.

Like the desperate lovers in *Toute une nuit*, the characters cannot bear *not* being in love, but, as Jeanne says, 'love only brings misery'. Pragmatic M. Schwartz tells the devastated Mado not to worry: 'You'll see how fickle the heart is. It has to love somebody. It's like dresses. You see one you've got to have … [it] looks great on the rack, but not on you. So you have to choose another one. After all, you can't walk around naked. If people did that, we'd be out of business.' M. Schwartz's summation of life, love, clothes-buying and the movies is made as he, Jeanne and Mado emerge from the mall into daylight, but otherwise the film takes place entirely within the claustrophobic mall, a goldfish bowl of shop windows and artifice, a space for looking and being looked at, an arena for the characters' 'ritualised games of flirtation and display' (Fowler, 2000).

The interconnectedness between Akerman's characters is reminiscent of Jacques Demy's *Lola* (1961) (not a musical, but very 'musical'), *Les Parapluies de Cherbourg** and particularly *Les Demoiselles de Rochefort**, and no doubt Akerman had Demy in mind. French cinema has thrown up several other recent explorations of the musical genre, such as Alain Resnais's *Pas sur la bouche** and François Ozon's *8 femmes**. JH

Dir: Chantal Akerman; **Prod**: Martine Marignac; **Scr**: Chantal Akerman, Jean Gruault, Leora Barish, Henry Bean, Pascal Bonitzer; **DOP**: Gilberto Azevedo (colour); **Song Music/Lyrics**: Marc Hérouet/Chantal Akerman; **Art**: Serge Marzolff; **Main Cast**: Delphine Seyrig, Myriam Boyer, Fanny Cottençon, Lio, Pascale Salkin, Charles Denner, Jean-François Balmer, John Berry, Nicolas Tronc; **Prod Co**: La Cecilia/Paradise Films (Bruxelles)/Limbo Film (Zurich).

Grease
USA, 1978 – 110 mins
Randal Kleiser

Grease is a phenomenon. It began as an amateur show in Chicago, started its professional life in revised form off-Broadway early in 1972 and word-of-mouth success powered its transfer a few months later to Broadway, where it stayed for 3,388 performances, a Broadway record when the show finally closed in 1980. Released in 1978, the film grossed $150 million on its first run alone, a staggering sum for a musical. There have been successful revivals (sometimes incorporating numbers from the film) in New York and London, and professional productions in at least twenty other countries.

The film considerably toned down the 'rowdy, dangerous, over-sexed and insightful' original (Miller, 2006–7). Changes were made that diluted the rock and roll-inspired score: some songs were dropped, others reordered; new ones were introduced (including the title track by Barry Gibb) and various period numbers imported. With a shift from the city to seemingly more suburban settings, the original's urban edge was softened. The basic story remained, anchored around two groups of teenage friends, 'The Pink Ladies' and 'The T-Birds' (renamed from the show's 'Burger Palace Boys'), at Rydell High School, but the film's vision of the late 1950s became largely nostalgic. One index of this is the casting of fondly remembered faces from the past, including Joan Blondell, Eve Arden and Sid Caesar, to play adults in the school and diner. Another is that John Travolta, cast as Danny Zuko on the back of his huge success in *Saturday Night Fever**, is a much less edgy figure here. The film's opening itself – tongue-in-cheek prologue of Danny's summer beach romance with Sandy (Olivia Newton-John) ('Love Is a Many Splendored Thing' on the soundtrack) and the witty animated credits that follow – seems to promise a world that will be fundamentally benign.

The characters' dilemmas – centrally those of sexuality, polarised gender roles and peer-group pressure – are intensely felt, but in the utopian tradition of the integrated musical, they can be expressed with infectious energy and drive in song and dance. Turning up as a new girl at Rydell High, not knowing Danny is there, Sandy gives her companions a romantic account of her 'Summer Nights' ('He got friendly, holding my hand'), which is intercut with Danny feeding his friends a much raunchier version ('We made out under the dock'). It is the cynical Rizzo (Stockard Channing) who offers a commentary on 1950s feminine ideals in her great number aimed at Sandy, 'Look at Me, I'm Sandra Dee' ('lousy with virginity/Won't go to bed till I'm legally wed'). When she thinks she might be pregnant by Danny's T-Bird friend Kenickie (Jeff Conaway), Rizzo's 'There Are Worse Things I Could Do' also challenges romantic fantasy and the sexual double standard: 'There are worse things I could do/than go with a boy or two … take cold showers everyday/ And throw my life away, on a dream that won't come true.'

The final movements play self-consciously on image and wish-fulfilment. At the graduation carnival, Danny's new athletics student persona – his bid to win Sandy – is overshadowed by Sandy's apparent transformation from Sandra Dee to sexually provocative vision in skin-tight black. As everyone sings and dances 'We Go Together', the film acknowledges the cheerful fantasy of its resolution as Danny's car carries the couple into the air. A little before, as Rizzo (not in fact pregnant) is happily reconciled with Kenickie, she had added her customary note of more earth-bound realism: 'It ain't moonlight and roses'. DP

Dir: Randal Kleiser; **Prod**: Robert Stigwood, Allan Carr; **Scr**: Brontë Woodard, from the stage musical, music and lyrics by Jim Jacobs and Warren Casey; **DOP**: Bill Butler (colour); **Song Music/Lyrics**: Jim Jacobs/Warren Casey; Barry Gibb; Louis St Louis/Scott J. Simon; John Farrar, *et al*.; **Choreog**: Patricia Birch; **Art**: Phil Jefferies; **Main Cast**: John Travolta, Olivia Newton-John, Stockard Channing, Jeff Conaway, Barry Pearl, Michael Tucci, Didi Conn, Kelly Ward, Dinah Manoff, Frankie Avalon, Eve Arden, Joan Blondell, Sid Caesar; **Prod Co**: Paramount Pictures.

Guys and Dolls
USA, 1955 – 150 mins
Joseph L. Mankiewicz

Guys and Dolls, based on Damon Runyon's 1932 stories about
gamblers and hustlers in New York's mid-town, was a huge Broadway
hit, running for 1,200 performances after its 1950 opening.
Producer Samuel Goldwyn beat off competition from other studios for
the film rights and chose writer-director Joseph L. Mankiewicz to direct
his first and only musical. There was also intense competition for the
central male parts of Nathan Detroit and Sky Masterson. Gene Kelly
might well have been cast as Sky but MGM refused to loan him out;
Frank Sinatra was also a contender but Goldwyn controversially cast
Marlon Brando, a non-singer and non-dancer, for his box-office appeal,
and Sinatra became Nathan Detroit. Members of the Broadway
company – notably Vivian Blaine as Adelaide and Stubby Kaye as
Nicely-Nicely Johnson – reprised their roles in the film and Michael
Kidd was retained for the distinctive choreography that was so crucial
to the style of the show.

   The film is valuable partly for these links to the original production.
It has been criticised for being stage-bound but its stylised settings are a
vital accompaniment to Kidd's angular, athletic choreography and the
distinctive formality of Runyon's vernacular dialogue. As in the show,
stylisation is the key to dramatising Runyon's Manhattan demi-monde.
The opening is one of the movie's highlights: Kidd's pulsating dance
introduction to the social variety of Broadway street life segues into
Loesser's wonderfully ingenious 'Fugue for Tinhorns' on the theme of
picking winners at the races, with its three intermeshed vocal lines (Kaye,
Johnny Silver, Danny Dayton). There are other exhilarating ensemble
numbers: the guys in the barber shop greeting Nathan, leading into 'The
Oldest Established, Permanent, Floating, Crap Game in New York', Kidd's
'Ballet for Crapshooters' and Nicely-Nicely's show-stopper, 'Sit Down,
You're Rocking the Boat' in the mission hall.

The film is less successful in integrating dialogue and musical sequences. There is much pleasure in the working through of the plot as Nathan tries desperately to continue his crap game and bets Sky he cannot persuade missionary Sarah Brown (Jean Simmons) to go to Havana with him, but Mankiewicz's script is very wordy and between numbers the film's impetus often flags (it is much too long at 150 minutes). Much of the splendid texture of the film's world comes from the casting of the minor parts – Sheldon Leonard, B. S. Pully, Silver, Dayton, among others. Loesser was unhappy with the choice of Sinatra for Nathan Detroit, but part of the film's continuing appeal comes from the casting of Sinatra and Brando in their only movie together. It is certainly difficult to regret Sinatra's musical contributions, especially in two of Loesser's brilliant duets, 'Guys and Dolls' with Kaye and 'Sue Me' with Blaine's Adelaide (Nathan's fiancée of fourteen years), and the casting of two actors who could each be the romantic lead gives the film a dynamic clearly not anticipated by Loesser. It is still startling to see Brando in a musical, but he is very good as Sky. Even the limitations of his singing voice (neither he nor Simmons were dubbed), which constrain one of the film's main numbers, 'Luck Be a Lady Tonight', create an appropriate intimacy in Sky's songs with Sara, such as 'Your Eyes Are the Eyes of a Woman in Love'.

There have been numerous revivals of the stage show on Broadway and in London, including two very successful National Theatre productions in 1982 and 1996. DP

Dir: Joseph L. Mankiewicz; **Prod**: Samuel Goldwyn; **Scr**: Joseph L. Mankiewicz, based on the musical play, book by Jo Swerling, Abe Burrows, from stories by Damon Runyon; **DOP**: Harry Stradling (colour); **Song Music/Lyrics**: Frank Loesser; **Musical Dir**: Jay Blackton; **Choreog**: Michael Kidd; **Art**: Joseph Wright, Oliver Smith; **Main Cast**: Marlon Brando, Frank Sinatra, Jean Simmons, Vivian Blaine, Stubby Kaye, Robert Keith, B. S. Pully, Sheldon Leonard, Danny Dayton, Johnny Silver; **Prod Co**: Goldwyn/Metro-Goldwyn-Mayer.

Hallelujah!
USA, 1929 – 100 mins
King Vidor

Hallelujah! is a landmark musical that deserves to be much better known. It was one of the first Hollywood feature films with an entirely African-American cast and a personal project (as well as his first talkie) for King Vidor, who had to invest his own salary in order to persuade MGM to back the film. It is also one of the first musicals to explore the rich seam of Americana, scenes from traditional American life, initiating what Rick Altman (1987) terms the 'folk musical', a central strand of the Hollywood genre.

As the tradition developed, it focused, like most Hollywood films, almost exclusively on white American experience, with African-American characters, where they appeared at all, generally occupying demeaning and crudely stereotyped social roles (see, for example, *The Littlest Rebel**). Vidor's film certainly rests on familiar stereotypes of a simple – even primitive – people but goes well beyond these in its positive creation of a black society in the South and the characters who inhabit it. This is a make-believe Deep South (no whites and therefore no racism) but the location sequences shot in Tennessee and Alabama (without sound – synchronising the sound later was a major technical feat in 1929) ground much of the action in observed reality, with sequences of cotton picking, processing at the cotton gin, revival meetings and mass baptism creating the rhythms and rituals of a textured social world.

At the heart of the film (and of the folk musical) are family and community, the settings with which the film begins and ends and the centre of the values it endorses. Community is the focus of music and religion, the two inseparably linked through their roots in hard labour on the land. The early sequences of work and communal life are dominated by the singing of spirituals and folk tunes, as well as by dance that, like the songs, is presented as spontaneous and improvised, as though the world is suffused by music. Most of the film's music, in fact, is drawn from traditional sources in African-American culture, spirituals and folk songs giving way in later settings to the rhythms of jazz, which come to embody the unruly forces repressed by religion.

Much of the film's power derives from the way in which Vidor intertwines the religious enthusiasm of family and community with the force of sexual desire. The eldest son, Zeke (Daniel L. Haynes), falls for the attractions of saloon girl Chick (Nina Mae McKinney), loses his family's money to her crooked gambler boyfriend Hotshot (William Fountaine) and in the ensuing fracas, accidentally shoots his younger brother. Becoming a revivalist preacher, Zeke travels the South conducting meetings and baptising the faithful. In a series of increasingly intense sequences, Vidor dramatises Chick's conversion in terms of an almost hysterical confusion of religious fervour and sexual passion. Zeke struggles to resist his own desire but finally surrenders all control and carries Chick off. When, months later, she returns to Hotshot, Zeke chases them and kills Hotshot after a long pursuit through the bayou. Finally released from prison on probation, Zeke travels back to his family, his song 'I'm Going Home' running through the journey and taken up by the cotton pickers as the film ends with the family reunited.

Zeke is redeemed but it is central to Vidor's ambivalent vision that the forces underlying the utopia of family and community should shadow the lovely ending. The film enjoyed some critical success and Vidor was nominated for an Oscar, but it lost money; regrettably, *Hallelujah!* was soon largely forgotten, though it established approaches that inform later black-cast musicals (see *Cabin in the Sky**, *Stormy Weather**, *Carmen Jones**). DP

Dir: King Vidor; **Prod**: King Vidor, Irving Thalberg; **Scr**: King Vidor, Wanda Tuchock, Ransom Rideout; **DOP**: Gordon Avil (b&w); **Song Music/Lyrics**: Irving Berlin, *et al*.; **Art**: Cedric Gibbons; **Main Cast**: Daniel L. Haynes, Nina Mae McKinney, William Fountaine, Victoria Spivey, Harry Gray, Fanny Belle DeKnight, Everett McGarrity; **Prod Co**: Metro-Goldwyn-Mayer.

A Hard Day's Night
UK, 1964 – 84 mins
Richard Lester

By late 1963, the Beatles were establishing their image, defining their 'sound' and becoming the biggest ever pop music phenomenon. The movie industry, never slow to exploit the success of recording artists (see, for example, *Holiday Inn**, *Calamity Jane** and, in the rock era, *Jailhouse Rock**), inevitably wanted a Beatles movie. Cliff Richard, then Britain's most popular male 'rock' artist, had already made three musicals (*Expresso Bongo*, 1960, *The Young Ones*, 1961, *Summer Holiday*, 1963). The low-budget, quickly made *Hard Day's Night* teamed the Beatles with director Richard Lester, an expatriate American whose work in 1950s British television and advertising included helping to adapt the radio *Goon Show* for television, and writer Alun Owen, who, like the Beatles, grew up in Liverpool and had written working-class television plays set there for Armchair Theatre (*No Trams to Lime Street*, *Lena, O My Lena*, both 1959).

In effect, *Hard Day's Night* is about 'Beatlemania': under the opening credits, we see documentary-type shots of John, George and Ringo, laughing as they run away from pursuing young fans, to the strains of the film's title song. Already, the boys' sense of fun, of not taking themselves too seriously and the feeling that it's all a bit of a 'lark', comes across powerfully. The plot, such as it is, is an almost symbolic narrative, following the Beatles travelling by train from Liverpool to perform in a live television variety show in London, where they proceed to deflate the pretensions and mock the snobbery of various middle-class figures and media types. Trading heavily on the down-to-earth, 'authentic' qualities of its young working-class characters, the film can be seen as a late entry in the 'Northern' invasion of British culture spearheaded by works like *Room at the Top* (novel 1957, film 1959), *A Taste of Honey* (play 1958, film 1962) and *Saturday Night and Sunday Morning* (novel 1958, film 1960). Contradictorily, *Hard Day's Night* also presages the heavily metropolitan 'swinging 60s': the Beatles are, perhaps, as one of them remarks, 'an early clue to the new direction'.

Although no doubt the intention was to make something very different from Cliff Richard's films, the basic requirements were similar: a lot of Beatles songs and a showcase for their cheeky personae. This is what we get, despite rather lame subplots involving Paul's grandfather (Wilfrid Brambell, the irascible father from the television sitcom *Steptoe*

The Beatles, 'Can't Buy Me Love'

and Son) and the group's manager Norm (Norman Rossington) and roadie Shake (John Junkin). The film's nice contrast between the songs' uncomplicated, almost innocent lyrics and the sophisticated humour of its sight and verbal gags endeared the film to many critics, who were surprised at how attractive they found it.

Stylistically, the film borrows heavily from current documentary styles. 'I Should Have Known Better', set in a train guard's van, is all hand-held, rapidly edited shots, beginning as a card game with the song playing in the background then morphing into performance before morphing back to the card game. 'Can't Buy Me Love' is played over the four racing, running and jumping around an empty playing field to dizzying, humorous effect (directly influenced by Lester's 1960 short film *The Running, Jumping and Standing Still Film* with Goons Peter Sellers and Spike Milligan). Though most of the other songs are more or less straight performances, these two sequences surely announce the later strategies of music video.

The Beatles' later films – *Help!* (1965), the made-for-television *Magical Mystery Tour* (1967), the animated *Yellow Submarine* (1968) and the documentary *Let It Be* (1970) – charted the shifts in the group and their music. JH

Dir: Richard Lester; **Prod**: Walter Shenson; **Scr**: Alun Owen; **DOP**: Gilbert Taylor (b&w); **Song Music/Lyrics**: John Lennon, Paul McCartney; **Musical Dir**: George Martin; **Art**: Ray Simm; **Main Cast**: John Lennon, Paul McCartney, George Harrison, Ringo Starr, Wilfrid Brambell, Norman Rossington, John Junkin, Victor Spinetti; **Prod Co**: Maljack Productions/Proscenium Films/Walter Shenson Films/United Artists.

The Harder They Come
Jamaica, 1972 – 120 mins
Perry Henzell

Jamaican reggae music developed out of ska and rocksteady music in the late 1960s, producing singer-songwriter stars like Bob Marley, Desmond Dekker and Jimmy Cliff. Perry Henzell's *The Harder They Come*, featuring Jimmy Cliff, helped to popularise reggae music outside Jamaica (doing for reggae what *Saturday Night Fever** later did for disco) and effectively reflected the music's political and social dimension, exploring the struggles of Jamaica's disadvantaged and powerless. The film's 'hero', Ivan (Jimmy Cliff) – based on a real-life 1940s criminal – arrives in Kingston from the countryside hoping to find success as a singer-songwriter. However, the music industry is controlled by a fat cat who rips off artists. Refusing such exploitation but without work, Ivan turns to the (illegal) ganja business, but finds the same corruption, with powerful players getting rich at the expense of the poor who take the risks. Trying to 'get what's his', Ivan is hunted down by the police: Ivan achieves celebrity, but not as he had imagined. His gunning down is intercut with shots from an earlier scene in which an enthralled audience watches the hero of Sergio Corbucci's spaghetti western *Django* (1966) mow down his foes.

Though unique in many ways, not least as the first ever Jamaican feature film, *The Harder They Come* appears influenced by other similar films with similar ideas – *Bonnie and Clyde* (1967), for example, made only a few years earlier, also features outlaws on the run who become folk heroes but get taken down by the law. It may have been inspired by Melvin Van Peebles's independently made *Sweet Sweetback's Baadasssss Song* (1971), whose outlaw hero takes on mythic proportions and which was more radical in its exploration of the situation of poor blacks than studio blaxploitation pictures like *Shaft* (1971) and *Superfly* (1972). Certainly, *The Harder They Come*, shot on 16mm over a long time period with different camera personnel, jaggedly edited, sometimes grainy, with lots of long lens and zoom camerawork, *looks* like the low-budget *Sweet Sweetback* (though a more general influence here may be the various 1960s 'new waves'). The film's images of teeming streets and shanty-town slums have a strong documentary quality.

Music is part of the fabric of Jamaican culture, and Jimmy Cliff's songs (as well as some by other singer-songwriters) are integral to the film. The songs are mostly confined to the soundtrack (though Cliff gives a wonderful performance of the title song in an audition), where they provide a commentary on the action. 'You Can Get It If You Really Want' ('You can get it if you really want/But you must try, try and try/Try and try, you'll succeed at last') accompanies Ivan's journey from countryside to city – but also his later, fateful involvement in ganja distribution. Ivan's fruitless search for work is accompanied by the plaintive 'Many Rivers to Cross' and the pursuit of the doomed Ivan by 'The Harder They Come' ('I keep fighting for the things I want/Though I know when you're dead you can't/But I'd rather be a free man in my grave/Than living as a puppet or a slave'). There is a religious quality to songs like 'Many Rivers to Cross' and the film takes on the important role that religion plays in Jamaican culture: religion is depicted as harshly hypocritical, its gospel-type music offering worshippers a kind of ecstatic release.

The Harder They Come received limited distribution initially but became a successful 'midnight movie'. Henzell adapted the film as a stage musical, which opened at London's Theatre Royal Stratford East in 2005. JH

Dir: Perry Henzell; **Prod**: Perry Henzell, Chris Blackwell **Scr**: Perry Henzell, Trevor D. Rhone; **DOP**: Peter Jessop, David McDonald, Franklyn St Juste (colour); **Song Music/Lyrics**: Jimmy Cliff; Desmond Dekker; Brent Dowe/Trevor McNaughton, *et al*.; **Art**: Sally Henzell; **Main Cast**: Jimmy Cliff, Janet Bartley, Carl Bradshaw, Basil Keane, Ras Daniel Hartman, Bob Charlton; **Prod Co**: International Films Inc./Xenon Pictures.

High School Musical
USA, 2006 – 98 mins
Kenny Ortega

Television – poised between Broadway and Hollywood – has played an important role in preserving the American musical (see Introduction). Disney has persisted with musicals aimed at youthful audiences, with shows like *Hannah Montana* (2006–10, theatrical movie 2009) and *The Cheetah Girls* television movies (2003–8). The *High School Musical* television movies have been particularly successful. Director Kenny Ortega choreographed films like *One from the Heart** and *Dirty Dancing* (1987), and worked with Madonna and Michael Jackson, among others, as well as directing television shows like *Dirty Dancing* (1988), *Chicago Hope* (1998–9) and *Ally McBeal* (2001). Directing and choreographing several episodes of the short-lived 1990 high school musical show *Hull High* and directing a dozen episodes of *Gilmore Girls* (2002–6) provided ideal preparation for *High School Musical*.

During a resort New Year's Eve party, jock Troy (Zac Efron) and bookworm Gabriella (Vanessa Hudgens) are thrown together for a karaoke duet ('Start of Something New') only to find that they enjoy both singing and each other (they even stop having to read the lyrics). In a nod to *Grease**, Gabriella then transfers to Troy's school; she and Troy remain attracted to each other and want to audition for the school musical but are held back by Troy's basketball and Gabriella's commitment to studying. Despite scheming rivals and, more importantly, having to figure out who they really are, all ends happily.

The film is carefully crafted to respond to the anxieties and dilemmas of pre- and post-pubescent 'tweens' (roughly eight- to thirteen-year-olds, although, of course, the film's characters are older): it's OK to play basketball or be studious *and* want to sing and dance in the school musical or enjoy baking; whites, Latinos, Asians and African-Americans are really all the same and get along; attraction to the opposite sex won't go smoothly but things will quickly work out; parents won't understand immediately but will come around. The film's numbers – some integrated, some performances – reinforce and celebrate its reassuring messages: basketball and musical theatre aren't supposed to go together, but the choreographed basketball players of the first big number, 'Getcha Head in the Game', imply that they can, and everyone confesses to multiple rather than single identities in the ensemble 'Stick to the Status Quo'. After Troy leads the basketball team to victory, Gabriella helps win the Scholastic Decathlon and together they get the lead roles in the school musical, and everybody lets their hair down and comes together in the gym for the finale, 'We're All in This Together'. It's all very wholesome – more *Gilmore Girls* than *Dirty Dancing*.

What began as a simple made-for-television movie quickly became a phenomenon and franchise. *High School Musical* was Disney Channel's most-watched 2006 film (over 8 million viewers on its first broadcast), the best-selling television film on DVD ever and an enormous success worldwide. *High School Musical 2* (2007) was watched by over 17 million US viewers, the record for a television movie. *High School Musical 3: Senior Year* (2008), a theatrical feature, became the highest-grossing musical ever in its US opening weekend. *High School Musical 4: East Meets West* – with a different cast and director – will be broadcast in 2010. Spin-offs include Argentine, Brazilian and Chinese versions, a 2006–7 concert tour, a 2007 touring ice show, novelisations, video games and a television reality talent show.

Without *High School Musical*, we would probably be without the innovative television high school musical comedy series *Glee*, which uses many of the same ingredients but more boldly, more reflexively and more caustically.   JH

Dir: Kenny Ortega; **Prod**: Don Schain; **Scr**: Peter Barsocchini; **DOP**: Gordon C. Lonsdale (colour); **Song Music/Lyrics**: Matthew Gerard, Robbie Nevil; David Lawrence, Faye Greenberg; Ray Cham, Greg Cham, Andrew Seeley; Randy Petersen, Kevin Quinn; Jamie Houston, *et al*.; **Art**: Mark Hofeling; **Choreog**: Kenny Ortega, Charles Klapow, Bonnie Story; **Main Cast**: Zac Efron, Vanessa Anne Hudgens, Ashley Tisdale, Lucas Grabeel, Alyson Reed, Corbin Bleu, Monique Coleman; **Prod Co**: Disney Channel/Salty Pictures/First Street Films.

Holiday Inn
USA, 1942 – 100 mins
Mark Sandrich

Holiday Inn brought together Fred Astaire, the most popular dancer of
his generation, and Bing Crosby, among the top 1934–54 box-office
performers and one of the most popular stars in Hollywood history.
Crosby had established the laid-back, almost conversational style of jazz-
influenced 'crooning', and was a major recording artist as well making
over seventy movies. Following his RKO musicals with Ginger Rogers,
notably *The Gay Divorcée**, *Top Hat** and *Swing Time**, Astaire worked
with several other partners, including Eleanor Powell (*Broadway Melody
of 1940*, 1940) and Rita Hayworth (*You'll Never Get Rich*, 1941, *You
Were Never Lovelier*, 1942); here, he dances with two relatively
unknowns, Marjorie Reynolds and Virginia Dale.

The film's full title is *Irving Berlin's Holiday Inn*, and the concept
originated with Berlin's 'Easter Parade': he and Moss Hart had the idea
for a Broadway revue based around the major US public holidays.
The plot involves singer Jim (Crosby) and dancer Ted (Astaire) competing
for women and centres on Jim semi-retiring and turning a Connecticut
farm into an inn which opens only on national holidays. Crosby, typically,
plays the somewhat retiring, easygoing good-guy singer, while dancer
Astaire is more ambitious, wily and scheming, a 'bad guy' by comparison,
but humorous and much more engaging than Crosby's Jim. The film is
structured around nine holidays, each with a dedicated song and
production number, most of them staged as performances. Crosby
croons 'Lazy', 'White Christmas', 'Happy Holidays', 'Easter Parade' and
other Berlin songs (including the problematic 'Abraham', performed in
blackface with a verse about 'setting the darkies free' by Jim's black
housekeeper Mamie, played by Louise Beavers, and the patriotic 'Song of
Freedom' – the film was in mid-production at the time of Pearl Harbor
and the US entry into war and affords appropriately reassuring
entertainment). Astaire provides several remarkable dance numbers,

including a 4th July solo routine with firecrackers; the wonderful New Year's Eve number when, drunk, he dances with Linda (Marjorie Reynolds); and the Washington's Birthday number when Jim causes Ted and Linda to keep switching between minuet and jazz dancing.

The film has a pleasurably reflexive quality, with the initial rivalry between Jim and Ted for Lila (Virginia Dale) immediately realised in 'I'll Capture Your Heart Singing' (reprised at the end), in which Jim bets he will win the girl with his singing and Ted wagers he will win her with his dancing. Near the film's conclusion, in Hollywood, Jim wanders into replica exterior and interior studio sets of his inn – the film's actual sets – and we watch from behind the camera and crew as Linda moves through the set and is reunited with him.

Confusingly, *Holiday Inn*, rather than the sort-of 1954 sequel *White Christmas*, was the film in which Irving Berlin's 'White Christmas', the West's most celebrated Christmas song and all-time best-selling record, was first sung by Bing Crosby (though *White Christmas* reprises it). Astaire and Crosby were reunited for *Blue Skies* (1946), which has a similar plot and was also very commercially successful. It was originally intended that the pair would also play together in *White Christmas* (reusing the earlier film's set), but the role intended for Astaire was eventually played by Danny Kaye. Both *Blue Skies* and *White Christmas*, Crosby's most commercially successful picture, featured abundant popular Irving Berlin songs. The Holiday Inn hotel chain borrowed its name from the film. JH

Dir/Prod: Mark Sandrich; **Scr**: Claude Binyon, adapted by Elmer Rice from an idea by Irving Berlin; **DOP**: David Abel (b&w); **Song Music/Lyrics**: Irving Berlin; **Music**: Bob Alcivar; **Art**: Roland Anderson, Hans Dreier; **Main Cast**: Bing Crosby, Fred Astaire, Marjorie Reynolds, Virginia Dale, Walter Abel, Louise Beavers; **Prod Co**: Paramount.

8 femmes
France/Italy, 2002 – 111 mins
François Ozon

No European national cinema has done more in the last thirty years or so to keep alive and explore the possibilities of music and song (and sometimes dance too) than French cinema (see also, for example, Alain Resnais's *Pas sur la bouche**, Chantal Akerman's *Golden Eighties** and, of course, Jacques Demy's *Les Parapluies de Cherbourg** and *Les Demoiselles de Rochefort**). *Enfant terrible* and darling of recent French cinema, François Ozon originally wanted to remake MGM's 1931 film *The Women*, with its renowned female stars (Joan Crawford, Rosalind Russell, Norma Shearer *et al.*) and exploration of bitchiness, but ended up freely adapting a 1960 play by popular playwright and screenwriter Robert Thomas. *8 femmes* (*8 Women*) had already been filmed in 1960 as *La Nuit des suspectes*, in the Agatha Christie-type tradition of an isolated setting in which a murder has been committed and any one of the characters might be guilty. Cinephile as well as cineaste, Ozon turns the play into an extraordinary concoction of melodrama, musical, whodunit and farce, peopled by a clutch of the *grandes dames* of contemporary French cinema.

In a snow-bound country house in a sort of time-warped 1950s, complete with settings and costumes borrowed from Douglas Sirk and *All That Heaven Allows* (1955), where three generations of women are assembled, Marcel/Daddy (husband, father, son, lover to the women characters) is found with a knife in his back, apparently dead. Wild family tensions are on open display, in a heady mixture of suspicions, jealousies, secrets, lies, real and false flashbacks, sudden changes of character and inexplicable action centred on the women characters' relationships with each other and with Marcel. Danielle Darrieux (Mamy), supposedly confined to a wheelchair, suddenly gets up and walks, for example, and Isabelle Huppert (Augustine) acts out a hysterically repressed Bette Davis/Agnes Moorehead type of role, until she suddenly feels like 'looking pretty' and reappears glamorously transformed.

Using their own voices, each actor performs a pop song and dance number written by or associated with 1950s/60s singer-songwriters like Georges Brassens, Sheila and Françoise Hardy. The youthful Ludivine Sagnier (Catherine), for example, performs a boisterous 'Papa t'es plus dans le coup' ('Papa, You're Not with It'), while Catherine Deneuve (Gaby) sings a melancholy 'Toi jamais' ('You, Never'), Fanny Ardant (Pierrette) a breathlessly sexual 'A quoi sert de vivre libre' ('What's the Use of Living Free'), Darrieux a resigned 'Il n'y a pas d'amour heureux' ('There Is No Such Thing as Happy Love'), and so on. In reality, the songs, which focus on different versions of female sexuality, relate more to the actors' star personas – Huppert's dangerous unpredictability, for example – than to their 'characters'. The songs are very different from each other: in postmodern fashion and like a number of other recent French 'musicals' – Resnais's *On connaît la chanson* (1997) and *Pas sur la bouche*, for example – *8 femmes* makes no attempt at the integrated scores central to Jacques Demy's films, and it is part of the film's wayward charm that the numbers interrupt the action rather than unify it. It is all delicious fun: at the end, after a formal dance, the women line up and link hands across the stage/frame and 'take their bow'. JH

Dir: François Ozon; **Prod**: Stéphane Célérier, Olivier Delbosc, Marc Missonnier; **Scr**: Marina de Van, François Ozon, from the play by Robert Thomas; **DOP**: Jeanne Lapoirie (colour); **Song Music/Lyrics**: Georges Brassens/Louis Aragon; Jean-Louis d'Onofrio; Jan and Jacques Plait; Françoise Hardy/Michel Berger, *et al*.; **Art**: Arnaud de Moleron; **Main Cast**: Danielle Darrieux, Catherine Deneuve, Isabelle Huppert, Emmanuelle Béart, Fanny Ardant, Virginie Ledoyen, Ludivine Sagnier; **Prod Co**: BIM/Canal+/Centre National de la Cinématographie/France 2 Cinéma (*et al*.).

It's Always Fair Weather
USA, 1955 – 102 mins
Gene Kelly, Stanley Donen

In the middle of *It's Always Fair Weather*, Ted Riley (Gene Kelly) celebrates his discovery of love in a number ('I Like Myself') that recalls Kelly's much more famous 'Singin' in the Rain'. Ted's virtuoso dance through the streets on roller skates is as exuberant in its way as Don Lockwood's great number in *Singin' in the Rain**, but the self-loathing that Ted is breaking free from ('Always used to dislike myself … Can it be I like myself?') has no parallel in Don's buoyant self-rediscovery through love in the earlier film.

This shift in tone from earlier, more affirmative musicals has divided critics. For Michael Wood (1975), the film is symptomatic of a failure in the underlying optimism of the genre; for Bruce Babington and Peter Evans (1985), it anticipates later films that play 'the ideals of earlier musicals against more bitter experience'. Certainly, there is nothing accidental in the film's mood: Kelly's original ambition of reuniting the three stars of *On the Town** in a film that 'treat[ed] a serious subject within the context of musical comedy' (Fordin, 1975) implied from the outset a reflective dialogue with the earlier film.

Something of the energy and comradeship of the three sailors in *On the Town* is present in the *It's Always Fair Weather* scenes set in 1945, though the number in which the three army buddies (Gene Kelly, Dan Dailey and Michael Kidd) dance in the New York streets is an exhilarating but increasingly frantic outburst of drunken energy after Ted has received a 'Dear John' letter. Correspondingly, there is much in the film that is unusually downbeat, notably the montage sequence bridging the ten years from 1945 that charts in split screen the compromises and disillusion of the men's lives. When they meet in 1955 as they promised, it is a disaster: in 'Why Are We Here?', they sing their bitterness in interior monologue, trapped in separate frames.

The later plot intertwines the three men becoming unwitting guests on a TV show, the growing relationship between Ted and Miss Leighton

(Cyd Charisse), who hatches the TV plan but gradually falls for Ted, and a rigged boxing match that Ted and Miss Leighton foil. The film has a good deal of fun at the expense of sponsored TV programmes and the advertising industry (Doug [Dan Dailey]'s solo number, 'Situation-Wise', is an outburst of frustration, fuelled by drink, at his life in advertising). The TV show climaxes in the exposure on live TV of the hoods who are threatening Ted for wrecking their fight-fixing plans, and a cathartic on-camera fight in which the friends reunite and triumph. Ted and Doug begin a tentative process of remaking their lives, Doug possibly saving his marriage and Ted and Miss Leighton acknowledging the emotional hurt that has held them back in the past from romantic commitment. It is indicative of the film's mood, however, that there is no song or dance to embody the compatibility of the couple. In fact, Cyd Charisse's single major number, 'You Knock Me Out', is performed with the pugilists and trainers of a boxing gym as a celebration of her remarkable grasp of boxing history rather than of romance.

There is measured optimism in the friends' final parting, but also an implied note of caution: the crane shot with which the film ends, rising from the street to look down on the action, is identical to the one that showed us their well-intentioned leave-taking in 1945. DP

Dir: Gene Kelly, Stanley Donen; **Prod**: Arthur Freed; **Scr**: Betty Comden, Adolph Green; **DOP**: Robert Bronner (colour); **Song Music/Lyrics**: André Previn/Betty Comden, Adolph Green; **Musical Dir**: André Previn; **Choreog**: Gene Kelly, Stanley Donen; **Art**: Cedric Gibbons, Arthur Lonergan; **Main Cast**: Gene Kelly, Dan Dailey, Cyd Charisse, Michael Kidd, Dolores Gray, Jay C. Flippen; **Prod Co**: Metro-Goldwyn-Mayer.

Jailhouse Rock
USA, 1957 – 96 mins
Richard Thorpe

It would be difficult to make a case for any of Elvis Presley's thirty films as distinguished musicals but together they form a remarkable phenomenon in the genre's history. As times became increasingly uncertain for Hollywood in the 1960s, the veteran Hal Wallis, who produced nine of Presley's films, suggested that 'A Presley picture is the only sure thing in Hollywood'. *Jailhouse Rock* was Elvis's third film, just over a year after his first number one record, 'Heartbreak Hotel'. The global explosion of American popular music that became generically known as 'rock and roll' was triggered in 1955 by the use of Bill Haley and His Comets' 'Rock around the Clock' in Richard Brooks's film *Blackboard Jungle*. Although the music itself, some of its performers (notably Elvis) and the reactions of teenage fans induced massive controversy and even moral panic, Hollywood studios were keen to exploit the new craze and Elvis himself was enthusiastic to begin a film career.

Emblematically, *Jailhouse Rock* was made by MGM in the same year in which the studio saw Fred Astaire play his final romantic lead (in *Silk Stockings**) and Gene Kelly make his last film (George Cukor's *Les Girls*) under the contract with MGM that began in 1942. But if in some ways the contrasts are stark – black and white not colour, Leiber and Stoller not Cole Porter, Presley not Astaire or Kelly, plus the differences in setting and budget – *Jailhouse Rock* is firmly grounded in the genre and in Hollywood tradition. Producer Pandro S. Berman had recently produced *Blackboard Jungle* but had a history going back to Astaire and Rogers at RKO in the 1930s; the director assigned was Richard Thorpe, director of dozens of films from the 20s on. Presley was never teamed with film-makers who might have responded more adventurously to his music and his persona (though special mention should be made of Don Siegel for *Flaming Star*, 1960).

Even in a film that is, on the whole, so stylistically conservative, it is still exciting to see Elvis before he was completely tamed. He plays Vince

Everett, jailed for manslaughter after a bar-room fight he did not start, and introduced to music by his cell-mate, Hunk Houghton (Mickey Shaughnessy), an ageing country singer. Vince is unlike the basically nice guys Elvis played in most of his films, less a rebel (despite elements of that) than money-driven, self-centred and careless of others – the only time he played something like an anti-hero (even if he reforms by the end). The plot follows the familiar rise to fame trajectory of many backstage musicals, tracing a path that parallels Presley's own, as the numbers chart the emergence of the characteristic Presley vocal and performance style.

In his first recording session, a lifeless first take of 'Don't Leave Me Now' is transformed in the second take after Peggy (Judy Tyler) urges Vince to sing it with feeling. The film's most famous song and its only production number, 'Jailhouse Rock', is the highlight of the movie and an iconic moment in Presley's film career. Presented as part of a TV extravaganza, with Vince and dancers as convicts in a set backed by prison bars, it was choreographed by Alex Romero, who revised his initial plans to incorporate the trademark gyrations that had produced outrage and ecstasy in Elvis's stage and TV performances. The energy and evident enjoyment of Presley's performance, channelled by Romero's choreography, produced one of the defining early images of both Elvis and rock and roll. DP

Dir: Richard Thorpe; **Prod**: Pandro S. Berman; **Scr**: Guy Trosper; **DOP**: Robert Bronner (b&w); **Song Music/Lyrics**: Mike Stoller/Jerry Leiber; additional songs by Roy C. Bennett, Sid Tepper; Aaron Schroeder, Abner Silver, Ben Weisman; **Choreog**: Alex Romero; **Art**: William A. Horning, Randall Duell; **Main Cast**: Elvis Presley, Judy Tyler, Mickey Shaughnessy, Vaughn Taylor, Jennifer Holden, Dean Jones; **Prod Co**: Metro-Goldwyn-Mayer.

Janken musume
Japan, 1955 – 92 mins
Sugie Toshio

Western audiences associate Japanese popular cinema with monster movies and period dramas such as samurai films but, as with most national cinemas, comedies and musicals were industry mainstays. Very popular with domestic audiences, they were generally considered not to travel well. *Janken musume* (*Janken Girls*, also known as *So Young, So Bright*) is a good 1950s example.

Japanese tradition is emphasised in the opening shots of Kyoto and orderly columns of uniformed schoolchildren. But not for long: we soon find a comic dozing teacher and two girls on the bus expressing their boredom with shrines and temples. Shortly after, Ruri (Misora Hibari) and Yumi (Chiemi Eri) fall into the river, spend the night with a friend of Ruri's mother and meet *maiko* (apprentice geisha) Pyua-chan (Yukimura Izumi). Tomboy Yumi reveals that she has never worn a kimono; Ruri and Pyua-chan sing and dance a traditional number, but Pyua-chan prefers jazz and mambo, which she, in traditional costume, and Yumi, in a dress, dance together. The film explores tensions between traditional and modern attitudes, and between Japanese and foreign cultures, as they manifest themselves in these three teenage girls, amid sleepovers and great romantic and family dramas: Ruri, raised by her single-parent geisha mother, needs to resolve the problems posed by her wealthy father and his wife wanting to adopt her; Yumi has a budding romance with the same boy who Pyua-chan hopes will save her from the geisha life.

At another level, the plot serves as a vehicle for three popular singers who were brought together for the film (and its sequels). Misora Hibari was Japan's most popular 1950s singing star. In a key sequence, the girls decide to change their mood and go off to the 'Girls' Opera Grand Show'. Each girl in turn closes her eyes and imagines herself performing on stage: Pyua-chan sings and dances a cha-cha-cha in Japanese and English; Yumi performs the mambo 'Happy, Happy Africa'; Ruri sings 'La

Vie en rose'. They come across as elegant, confident, international young women, ideal versions of themselves.

Most of the film's numbers, traditional or modern, real or imagined, are performances; even when Pyua-chan sings 'Smile' (in Japanese), she has to tell herself to sing. Only in the closing roller-coaster sequence do the girls 'break into song': each sings a solo (Pyua-chan sings 'Mambo Jambo', Yumi the cha-cha-cha 'Blue Sky' and Ruri the 'Rendezvous Song') before all three together sing the 'Rock, Scissors, Paper' song that opened the film. This celebration of triumph over their various dilemmas is given only a slightly unreal feel by the intercutting between very obvious rear projection for the song close-ups and location long shots of the roller coaster itself. *Janken musume* was Toho's biggest hit of the year and spawned sequels and imitations. Though it owed much of its success to its starring popular singers, the film no doubt played out the cultural dilemmas of its youthful audiences. Certainly, it is a fascinating document as well as a charming movie.

Some Japanese musicals were closer to the Hollywood model. *Kimi mo shusse ga dekiru* (*You Too Can Succeed*, 1964) builds on the popular 'salarymen' comedies: Toho sent its personnel to the US to familiarise themselves with Broadway, and the film is clearly influenced by both *How to Succeed in Business without Really Trying*, then one of Broadway's most successful shows, and the movie version of *West Side Story**. More recently, cult auteurs Miike Takashi and Suzuki Seijun gained notice for their musicals *The Happiness of the Katakuris* (2001) and *Princess Raccoon* (2005). Both are too eccentric to be considered mainstream, but *Linda Linda Linda* (directed by Yamashita Nobuhiro, 2005) is closer in spirit to *Janken musume*. JH

Dir: Sugie Toshio; **Prod**: Sugihara Sadao; **Scr**: Nakanor Minoru; **DOP**: Kankura Taiichi (colour); **Music/Lyrics/Musical Dir**: not known; **Art**: Muraki Shinobu; **Main Cast**: Misora Hibari, Chiemi Eri, Yukimura Izumi, Yamada Shinji, Ehara Tatsuyoshi; **Prod Co**: Toho.

The Jazz Singer
USA, 1927 – 89 mins
Alan Crosland

The Jazz Singer was not the first 'all-talking' (and singing) feature film, as was claimed, but it remains a film historical landmark. Its success confirmed Warner Bros. as a major studio and forced other studios to switch to sound (though Warners' sound-on-disc Vitaphone system was soon jettisoned in favour of sound-on-film systems) and to begin to wire up theatres. Ironically, early sound films like *The Jazz Singer* were seen as silent pictures by far greater audiences than saw them as sound films.

Adding sound to moving pictures (or vice versa) had been an ambition since Edison. In the 1920s, vaudeville and theatre performances were recorded on film and some reviewers saw *The Jazz Singer* more as a record of Al Jolson performances than as a dramatic narrative. The Broadway production of Samson Raphaelson's 1925 play (based on Jolson) starred George Jessel, but Jolson himself, a more established star, with origins in vaudeville and minstrel shows, was eventually preferred for the film. The story, centred on the conflict Jakie Rabinowitz feels between remaining true to his Jewish roots and his desire to succeed as a 'jazz singer' on Broadway, had a special resonance in a movie industry dominated by Jewish producers (including the Warner brothers) making mainstream American entertainment. Naturally, the film concludes with Jakie managing both to grant his dying cantor father's wish that he should sing 'Nol Kidre' at Yom Kippur and (as Jack Robin) become a Broadway star.

African-American culture profoundly influenced American popular music in the 1920s Jazz Age, and Jolson's use of blackface poses obvious problems. Blackface, originating in minstrelsy, acknowledges the black roots of popular music yet engages in grotesque African-American stereotypes. Does blackface function in the film (and more widely) as a mask for Jakie's unresolved sense of whether he is Jewish or 'white', or does it suggest that blackface masks his Jewishness and implies

Al Jolson serenades Eugenie Besserer with 'Blue Skies'

whiteness? Jakie is first seen in blackface at a critical moment near the end of the film, a dramatic device employed to heighten his crisis of identity. Certainly, though jazz allows Jakie to adopt a modern 'American' identity, this is not dependent on blackface.

The Jazz Singer was made as a silent film and it comes across now as straddling silent cinema and sound cinema. The early club sequence in which Jakie's sync sound 'Dirty Hands, Dirty Face' and 'Toot, Toot, Tootsie', with his interjected 'Wait a minute, wait a minute, you ain't heard nothin' yet', is bracketed with all the more noticeably silent shots and title cards for his first encounter with *shiksa* Mary (May McAvoy). The sense of two sets of film conventions colliding with each other is perhaps most obvious when Jakie sings 'Blue Skies' for his mother (Eugenie Besserer), bringing out the palpable difference between Jolson's naturalistic singing and ad-libbed dialogue, and Besserer's silent film 'mugging' in intercut, masked shots (though her performance is markedly different in the sound two-shot with Jakie).

Jolson's part-talkie *The Singing Fool* (1928), with more favourite Jolson songs, was an even greater popular success. He appeared regularly in musicals in the 1930s, including the unusual *Hallelujah, I'm a Bum* (1933), and provided the singing voice for Larry Parks in the popular biopics *The Jolson Story* (1946) and *Jolson Sings Again* (1949). *The Jazz Singer*, adapted for the times, was remade in 1952, with Danny Thomas, and in 1980, with Neil Diamond (and for television in 1959, with Jerry Lewis), and has provided a kind of narrative template for other stories of showbiz rise to fame. JH

Dir: Alan Crosland; **Prod**: Darryl F. Zanuck; **Scr**: Alfred A. Cohn from the play by Samson Raphaelson; **DOP**: Hal Mohr (b&w); **Song Music/Lyrics**: James V. Monaco/Edgar Leslie, Grant Clarke, Al Jolson; Dan Russo, Ernie Erdman/Gus Kahn; Irving Berlin; Louis Silvers/Grant Clarke, *et al*.; **Musical Dir**: Louis Silvers; **Choreog**: Ernest Belcher; **Art**: not known; **Main Cast**: Al Jolson, May McAvoy, Warner Oland, Eugenie Besserer; **Prod Co**: Warner Bros./Vitaphone.

Kiss Me Kate
USA, 1953 – 110 mins
George Sidney

Kiss Me Kate is a musical within a musical, in which the off-stage conflicts and final reconciliation of divorced theatre stars Lilli Vanessi and Fred Graham are paralleled by their roles as Kate and Petruchio in a musical version of *The Taming of the Shrew*, the action switching between on and off stage on the show's first night. Cole Porter, hired to write the songs after many years without a Broadway hit, produced a remarkable range of numbers in various idioms of both music and language to reflect the dual levels of Samuel and Bella Spewack's book; the 1948 show ran for over 1,000 performances on Broadway – Porter's biggest hit.

Dorothy Kingsley's film adaptation introduced an opening scene with Fred Graham (Howard Keel) and Cole Porter (Ron Randell) persuading Lilli (Kathryn Grayson) to appear as Kate in Porter's musical of *The Taming of the Shrew*, and Fred's new girlfriend, Lois Lane (Ann Miller), auditioning for the role of Kate's sister, Bianca. The glory of this otherwise redundant addition is Ann Miller's explosive solo performance of 'Too Darned Hot', an early indication that her portrayal of Lois/Bianca will be a highlight of the film (and of her career). In fact, the dancing is consistently brilliant. The choreography of Fred Astaire's longtime collaborator, Hermes Pan, provides several more showcases for Miller, including 'Tom, Dick or Harry', with the trio of Tommy Rall, Bobby Van and Bob Fosse playing Bianca's suitors, and 'Why Can't You Behave?', with Tommy Rall in his off-stage role as Bill Calhoun, Lois's real boyfriend. Perhaps most remarkable in dance terms is 'From This Moment On', the one song added for the film, in which Miller and the three men are joined in an extended number by dancers Carol Haney and Jeanne Coyne, and it is startling to see, in the angularity, finger-clicking and business with hats of the sexually charged section danced by Haney and Bob Fosse, an early example of Fosse's distinctive choreography (see *The Pajama Game** and *Cabaret**).

Principals Howard Keel and Kathryn Grayson have great scenes, especially as Petruchio and Kate, when their voices match the histrionic demands of their roles, in songs like Petruchio's 'I've Come to Wive It Wealthily in Padua' and 'Where Is the Life That Late I Led?' and Kate's fervent anthem, 'I Hate Men!'. The dual roles make almost conflicting demands, however, and neither has the subtlety or lightness of touch to make the screwball comedy-like backstage drama sparkle. The writing and direction are not helpful here: the film struggles to animate the heavy-handed plotting involving two gangsters (Keenan Wynn and James Whitmore) who have come to collect a gambling debt (though Whitmore and Wynn – non-singers and dancers both – provide one of the film's most pleasurable numbers in 'Brush up Your Shakespeare').

Ann Miller makes of Lois a woman whose libido (for all her claims of fidelity to Bill) seems unlikely to be tamed. The difficulty of the ingenious doubling of Fred/Lilli and Petruchio/Kate is that Shakespeare's play, notoriously problematic for modern productions, requires Kate to accept her taming. When Lilli suddenly returns for the play's finale, after abandoning the production with her stolid Texan fiancée, Grayson manages Kate's acquiescence speech with grace, but as play and film end euphorically with 'Kiss Me Kate', Fred and Lilli's remade marriage has to be taken on trust.

The film had a limited release in (reputedly very effective) 3D, one of the few musicals made for 3D exhibition during that process's short 1950s vogue. The musical show was successfully revived most recently on Broadway in 1999 and London in 2001. DP

Dir: George Sidney; **Prod**: Jack Cummings; **Scr**: Dorothy Kingsley, from the musical play by Samuel and Bella Spewack; **DOP**: Charles Rosher (colour); **Song Music/Lyrics**: Cole Porter; **Musical Dir**: André Previn, Saul Chaplin; **Choreog**: Hermes Pan; **Art**: Cedric Gibbons, Urie McCleary; **Main Cast**: Howard Keel, Kathryn Grayson, Ann Miller, Tommy Rall, Keenan Wynn, James Whitmore, Bobby Van, Bob Fosse, Ron Randell; **Prod Co**: Metro-Goldwyn-Mayer.

Der Kongress tanzt
Germany, 1931 – 85 mins
Erik Charell

'Until the advent of the Third Reich, the *Operettenfilm* was UFA's most successful weapon in its fight against Hollywood's dominance of the world market' (Claus and Jäckel, 2000), and the superproduction *Der Kongress tanzt* (*Congress Dances*) was seen as a key film to compete against popular Hollywood operetta musicals like *The Love Parade**, *The Merry Widow** and *Love Me Tonight** (see also *Viktor und Viktoria**). It is not surprising that *Der Kongress tanzt*, a fairy-tale musical whose Vienna setting is as much a fantasy as the settings in Ernst Lubitsch's films, resembles its Hollywood rivals. Just as 1930s Hollywood musicals diverted audiences from the Depression, German musicals offered diversion from contemporary economic and political problems (whereas films like Slatan Dudow and Bertolt Brecht's *Kuhle Wampe*, 1932, focused sharply on them).

Like *Love Me Tonight*, the story involves a romance across social class lines: the Congress of Vienna (called in 1815 to negotiate a post-Napoleon European settlement) is about to take place, and shopgirl Christel (Lilian Harvey) becomes romantically involved with the visiting Russian Tsar, Alexander (Willi Fritsch). Wily German Chancellor Metternich (Conrad Veidt) hopes to inveigle Alexander into taking more interest in romantic dalliance than in diplomacy, but comic complications arise when (for security reasons) the equally wily Tsar, unbeknown to Metternich, brings a double with him.

The period settings and costumes of *Der Kongress tanzt* are sumptuous and there are grand dance sequences both at the theatre (the 'Polovtsian Dances' from Borodin's *Prince Igor*, staged in honour of the Tsar) and in the Congress ballroom. The film shares some of the almost innocent pre-Code 'naughtiness' of the Hollywood films, with its fetishistic preoccupation with ladies' elaborate underwear. All the stops are pulled out for two remarkable musical sequences, which showcase the technical virtuosity of the UFA studios in this early sound period, with complex, fluid camera movements and long takes worthy of Murnau's silent films like *Der letzte Mann* (1924) and *Sunrise* (1927). In the first, celebrated singer Paul Hörbiger serenades the denizens of a tavern in which Christel and Alexander are pursuing their tryst with the popular romantic song 'Das muss ein Stück von Himmel sein, Wien und der Wein' ('That Must Be a Little Bit of Heaven, Vienna and Wine') as the camera glides along and among the drinkers of different social classes. Later, Christel is transported in the Tsar's open carriage from her shop to a rendezvous with him at a country chateau. A series of complex tracking and dolly shots adds an exhilarating feeling of elation and escape as she sings 'Das gibt's nur einmal, das kommt nie wieder' ('It only happens once, and never comes again').

As part of its strategy for reaching international markets, *Der Kongress tanzt* was also made in French (*Le Congrès s'amuse*) and English (*Congress Dances*) versions. Most of the German cast was replaced in these adaptations, but trilingual British-born Lilian Harvey starred in them all. Harvey's Hollywood career never really took off and she returned to Germany in 1935, where she made many successful films; problems with the regime caused her to emigrate to France and then back to the US, only returning to Germany in 1949. Erik Charell, Erich Pommer and Robert Liebmann, all Jews, were dismissed by UFA in 1933 and left Germany to work in exile, as did Werner Richard Heymann. Regularly shown on postwar East and West German television, *Der Kongress tanzt* was remade (in colour) in Austria in 1955, a dubbed version of which was released in the US in 1957. JH

Dir: Erik Charell; **Prod**: Eberhard Klagemann, Erich Pommer; **Scr**: Norbert Falk, Robert Liebmann; **DOP**: Carl Hoffmann (b&w); **Song Music/Lyrics**: Werner R. Heymann/Robert Gilbert; **Art**: Robert Herlth, Walter Röhrig; **Main Cast**: Lilian Harvey, Willy Fritsch, Otto Walburg, Conrad Veidt, Carl-Heinz Schroth, Lil Dagover; **Prod Co**: Universum-Film (UFA).

Little Shop of Horrors
USA, 1986 – 90 mins
Frank Oz

Like *The Rocky Horror Show* (1973), *Little Shop of Horrors* (1982) was a comedy stage musical which exploited camp taste for schlock horror/science fiction; both were successful long-running shows and were adapted into very popular movies (see *The Rocky Horror Picture Show**). Both demonstrate the ways musical theatre and movies feed off each other and exemplify the period's taste for parody and pastiche.

The inspiration for *Little Shop of Horrors* was very specific – Roger Corman's B (or maybe Z) 1960 no-budget horror/science-fiction film of the same name, itself already a tongue-in-cheek spoof.

The show and film story sticks close to Corman's movie: nerdy Seymour (Rick Moranis in the film) works in a Skid Row florist shop; he harbours a secret passion for shop assistant Audrey (Ellen Greene), who is in an abusive relationship with a leather-clad, motorbike-riding sadistic dentist (Steve Martin) although secretly attracted to Seymour. Seymour acquires a flytrap-type plant; he christens it Audrey II and it attracts interest and transforms the shop's fortunes. As it grows spectacularly (and acquires a voice), Audrey II needs to be fed human flesh and blood. The stage show ends with Audrey II consuming both Seymour and Audrey and threatening the audience, and a comparable ending – Audrey II taking over New York City – was intended for the film. However, in response to test audiences, the ending was changed: Seymour rescues Audrey from Audrey II's maw, saves himself and destroys Audrey II.

The film is set in the early 1960s and the music is particularly pleasurable, teetering somewhere between doo-wop and Tamla Motown. The chorus of black singers, Crystal, Ronette and Chiffon (all named after doo-wop 1960s girl groups), sporting beehive hairdos, provide a kind of commentary, while Audrey II's voice is provided by Motown's Four Tops lead singer Levi Stubbs. The songs are good but perhaps too narratively specific to become popular standards, though 'Suddenly Seymour', in which Seymour and Audrey declare their love, comes closest, despite some odd sentiments. 'Skid Row (Downtown)', the film's first and most elaborate production number, impressively incorporates the main characters with Skid Row's zombie-like, dispossessed inhabitants. When Audrey sings about 'Somewhere That's Green', she imagines a stylised, brightly coloured suburban world straight out of consumer lifestyle magazines, and the film's happy end is undermined when this is the world Seymour and Audrey escape to (especially since the final shot is of a new flytrap plant growing in their garden). Popular culture provides a frame of reference: Audrey, lured into the shop by the voracious Audrey II, asks (in the spirit of *The Wizard of Oz**), 'Am I dreaming?', to which Audrey II replies, 'No, and you ain't in Kansas either', adding later in the rocking 'Mean Green Mother from *Outer Space*' that he 'don't come from no black lagoon'. In turn, *Little Shop of Horrors* has become a cult film, widely referenced and imitated in films and television shows like *South Park* and *Family Guy*.

Howard Ashman, who wrote the libretto and lyrics, and Alan Menken, who composed the score, later worked together on Disney's *The Little Mermaid* (1989), *Beauty and the Beast* (1991), *Aladdin* (1992) and others (until Ashman's early death in 1991). The film's director, Frank Oz, had worked as a puppeteer on the *Muppets* and *Sesame Street*, a useful background for a film in which the cheesily wonderful animatronic Audrey II takes centre stage. Several graduates of Chicago's comedy revue group Second City – John Candy, Jim Belushi, Christopher Guest and Bill Murray – make cameo appearances. JH

Dir: Frank Oz; **Prod**: David Geffen; **Scr**: Howard Ashman, adapted from the 1982 off-Broadway production, itself based on the script by Charles B. Griffith for the 1960 film; **DOP**. Robert Paynter (colour); **Song Music/Lyrics**: Alan Menken/Howard Ashman; **Choreog**: Pat Garrett; **Art**: Roy Walker, Stephen Spence; **Main Cast**: Rick Moranis, Ellen Greene, Vincent Gardenia, Steve Martin, Tichina Arnold, Michelle Weeks, Tisha Campbell, James Belushi, John Candy, Bill Murray; **Prod Co**: The Geffen Company.

The Littlest Rebel
USA, 1935 – 70 mins
David Butler

In the mid-1930s, Shirley Temple was the most popular movie star in the US. In 1935, when she was seven years old, the Academy made her the first recipient of its Juvenile Award (paving the way for later stars like Deanna Durbin – see *100 Men and a Girl**). Her studio, Fox, fully exploited her popularity, starring her in eighteen features between her debut, *Little Miss Marker* (1934), and *Just around the Corner* (1938). Temple's films combined drama, comedy and musical in resolutely upbeat narratives in which her cutely precocious charm overcomes barriers and brings people together: in *The Littlest Rebel*, she even brings together the two sides in the American Civil War. Though the *raison d'être* of Temple's films was not their quota of song and/or dance musical routines, singing and dancing were integral to her star persona. A typical Temple film might contain only three or four such sequences, many shared with established adult singers or dancers; her song repertoire would include traditional songs (here, for example, 'Those Enduring Young Charms', 'Dixie' and 'Polly Wolly Doodle') as well as contemporary standard popular songs.

In *The Littlest Rebel*, Temple plays Virgie, daughter of a Virginian plantation-owner and Confederate army captain (John Boles), celebrating her sixth birthday on the day the Civil War breaks out. The war keeps her father away and, after losing their house and wealth, her mother (Karen Morley) dies, leaving Virgie a virtual orphan (a role she often played in her films). When both her father and a sympathetic Union colonel (Jack Holt) are arrested and sentenced to death by the Unionists, Virgie goes to Washington and persuades a kindly, wise President Lincoln, no less, to pardon them. As has often been noted, the overall optimism of the Temple films needs to be seen as a response to the Depression. Roosevelt remarked on how splendid it was that for just 15 cents Americans could raise their spirits watching a Shirley Temple movie.

Shirley Temple, Bill Robinson

The several films Temple made with African-American dancer Bill Robinson are among her most interesting, not least for their representation of race. *The Littlest Rebel* shows the black workers on her family's plantation as happy, willing participants in a benevolent slave system (though very different from the idealised all-black community of *Hallelujah!**). Significantly, the main black characters, 'Uncle' Billy (Bill Robinson), head manservant and Virgie's mentor and constant companion (before being sidelined at the very end), and James Henry (Willie Best), are seen as natural companions for white children. Billy is essentially an 'Uncle Tom' character, loyal and devoted and without any real narrative of his own, while James Henry, as one would expect from Best's other roles, plays out the worst black stereotypes – slow-moving, eyes popping, apparently stupid, though the film may not be quite as unconscious of its stereotypes as critics claim.

Bill 'Bojangles' Robinson was probably the best tap dancer of his generation, denied mainstream stardom by racial prejudice. Nevertheless, one of the major purposes of *The Littlest Rebel* (and Temple's other films with Robinson, who was one of her idols) was to showcase Robinson's skills, particularly in the complex tap routines at Virgie's party ('Cotton-Eyed Joe') and when he and Virgie dance to raise the rail fare to Washington. Fred Astaire plays tribute to Robinson in the 'Bojangles' sequence in *Swing Time** and a heavily fictionalised version of Robinson's life story forms the basis of *Stormy Weather**. JH

Dir: David Butler; **Prod**: Darryl F. Zanuck, Buddy G. DeSylva; **Scr**: Edwin J. Burke, Harry Tugend from the play by Edward Peple; **DOP**: John F. Seitz (b&w); **Song Music/Lyrics**: Sidney Clare/Buddy G. DeSylva, *et al.*; **Music**: Cyril Mockridge; **Art**: William S. Darling; **Main Cast**: Shirley Temple, John Boles, Karen Morley, Bill Robinson, Guinn Williams, Willie Best, Frank McGlynn Sr; **Prod Co**: 20th Century-Fox.

Love Me or Leave Me
USA, 1955 – 122 mins
Charles Vidor

Love Me or Leave Me, a biopic of the 1920s/30s singer Ruth Etting, was Doris Day's first film after her seven-year contract with Warner Bros., during which she became a best-selling recording artist and one of Hollywood's most popular musical stars (see *Calamity Jane**, *The Pajama Game**). James Cagney had already been cast as the Chicago racketeer Marty Snyder, who discovered Etting and became her manager and husband, when he suggested Day for a role that caused controversy among her fans and marked a major shift in her film career.

Love Me or Leave Me is Doris Day's *A Star Is Born**, another backstage musical charting a singer's rise to fame and a tormented marriage in which the husband is increasingly overshadowed by his wife, though even darker in mood than George Cukor's film. Marty is a much more oppressive figure than Norman Maine in *A Star Is Born*, an ageing version of Cagney's gangster persona, enforcing his club-land laundry franchise with threats of violence. Ruth resists Marty's advances after she is fired as a dime-a-dance hostess and he offers to kickstart her performing career, but she is still able to manipulate him into launching her as a singer. Part of the strength of Day's performance is that she conveys both Ruth's probity and a steely ambition that suggests she is in her own way as unscrupulous as Marty. Ruth stays with him even though she is attracted to her pianist, Johnny Alderman (Cameron Mitchell), and it is in New York, with her opening in Florenz Ziegfeld's *Follies* and Marty increasingly angry at his exclusion from decisions about the show, that Ruth fully realises the trap she has created for herself. She marries Marty after he threatens to pull her out of the *Follies* and, enraged, tries to force himself on her.

Musical numbers throughout the film (almost all associated with Etting) are confined to Ruth's performances and rehearsals. After the marriage, as Ruth becomes successful but increasingly unhappy and

Doris Day, James Cagney

withdrawn, the songs act as intense monologues, giving voice to feelings she cannot express in other ways. After the montage of her burgeoning career, the dramatic '10 Cents a Dance' both evokes where she started and eloquently implies how she sees her continuing situation (she says to Marty after they marry, 'You don't have to sell me, I'm sold'). When she meets Johnny again, working for her Hollywood studio, 'I'll Never Stop Loving You' – delivered by Day into the middle distance as they rehearse after she has confronted Marty – is as much self-assertion as love song. 'Never Look Back' ('we've reached a parting of the ways'), sung in a recording studio with Marty looking on from outside, is even more pointed.

The film's last movement is extraordinary. Paranoid and vengeful, Marty shoots Johnny, although he does not kill him. Released on bail, he finds that Ruth, though now committed to Johnny, has not only completed to Marty's own designs the nightclub he had bought to demonstrate what he could achieve on his own but is singing on its opening night. As Ruth performs 'Love Me or Leave Me' to the packed audience, Marty – initially furious and resentful – has to accept that, even as they divorce, this is her way of thanking him. It is a satisfyingly ironic resolution.

Perhaps the only other musical to contain a performance of insecure, possessive masculinity as disturbing as Cagney's is *New York, New York**. And Cagney was certainly right about Doris Day: in a mode that could hardly be more different from her previous roles, she is very impressive. DP

Dir: Charles Vidor; **Prod**: Joe Pasternak; **Scr**: Daniel Fuchs, Isobel Lennart; **DOP**: Arthur E. Arling (colour); **Song Music/Lyrics**: new songs: Nicholas Brodszky/Sammy Cahn; Chilton Price; Ruth Etting's songs: Irving Berlin; Richard Rodgers/Lorenz Hart; Buddy DeSylva; Ray Henderson/Lew Brown; Arthur Freed, *et al*.; **Musical Dir**: George Stoll; **Choreog**: Alex Romero; **Art**: Cedric Gibbons, Urie McCleary; **Main Cast**: Doris Day, James Cagney, Cameron Mitchell, Robert Keith, Tom Tully, Harry Bellaver; **Prod Co**: Metro-Goldwyn-Mayer.

Love Me Tonight
USA, 1932 – 104 mins
Rouben Mamoulian

Love Me Tonight appeared amid three early 1930s Maurice
Chevalier/Jeanette MacDonald Ernst Lubitsch musicals, *The Love Parade**,
One Hour with You* (co-directed by George Cukor) and *The Merry
Widow**. (Lubitsch also directed MacDonald in *Monte Carlo* [1930] and
Chevalier in *The Smiling Lieutenant* [1931]). *Love Me Tonight* shares its
social setting and risqué, witty, pre-Code sexual banter ('Can you go for
a doctor?'; 'Certainly, bring him right in') with Lubitsch's films; some
critics argue that Mamoulian's film is even more sparkling.
Certainly, Rodgers and Hart's score is outstanding. Like the Lubitsch
musicals, *Love Me Tonight*'s story is slight and tongue-in-cheek, perhaps
a pastiche of Lubitsch: a fairy tale in which, due to various
misunderstandings and mistaken identities, Maurice (Chevalier), a
common Parisian tailor, awakens the fainting-prone Princess Jeanette
(MacDonald) and love overcomes class barriers; as the aged aunts put it,
Maurice is 'a prince charming who was not a prince, but who was
charming, and they lived happily ever after'.

   Unlike many contemporary musicals, the numbers are wholly
integrated with the narrative action. Mamoulian, more assured than on
his debut film *Applause** and never one to adopt the 'invisible' classical
style of Hollywood film-making, is endlessly inventive in overcoming early
sound cinema's constraints on sound and camera. Lyricist Lorenz Hart
aimed for 'conversational rhythm … rhythmic dialogue', and Mamoulian
'decided to make it lyrical, thoroughly stylised: a film in which the whole
action of actors, as well as the movement of camera and cutting was
rhythmic' (quoted in Kemp, 2004). Right from the start, the film is
marked by its fluidity. Following some lovely shots of early morning Paris
streets, accompanied only by a clock striking six o'clock, Mamoulian
experiments with sound (as he had in his 1927 Broadway production of
Porgy): the thud of a pickaxe on (studio) cobbles is joined in rhythm by a

Maurice Chevalier takes the measure of Jeanette MacDonald

sleeping figure's snores, sweeping, a baby crying, knives being
sharpened, a rug being beaten, and so on – a veritable city 'sound
symphony' which would have delighted René Clair (see *Le Million**).
From a dolly into Chevalier's trademark straw hat on a wall and his head
emerging from a sweater comes his first song, 'The Song of Paree' ('You
would sell your wife and daughter/For just one Latin Quarter'), which
segues again into the half-song, half-recitative 'How Are You?' as
Maurice walks to his tailor's shop. One of the film's pleasures is the way
that songs emerge imperceptibly from rhyming couplet dialogue, so
much so that it is not entirely clear whether the racy 'A Woman Needs
Something Like That' is a dialogue exchange or a song. 'Isn't It
Romantic?' begins with Maurice, is taken into the street by a customer,
and is picked up by a taxi driver and his songwriting passenger; singing
the song on a train, he is joined by a group of soldiers, who carry it on as
they march through the countryside, where it is picked up by a violinist,

who takes it to his gypsy encampment; from there it is picked up by Princess Jeanette on her chateau balcony, so that even at this early stage Maurice and Jeanette's destiny is mapped out. Later, Maurice's suggestive rendition of 'Mimi' to Jeanette is picked up playfully the next day by the otherwise unbending Duke (C. Aubrey Smith) and others, as if tickled out of their crustily antiquated ways by the energetic Maurice. As Tom Milne (1969) put it, 'in a very real sense, *Love Me Tonight* is one long, unbroken production number'.

After *Love Me Tonight*, Mamoulian continued to be a major force in musical theatre and was responsible for some of the more remarkable movie musicals of the next thirty years, notably *High, Wide and Handsome* (1937), *Summer Holiday** and (his last film) *Silk Stockings**. JH

Dir/**Prod**: Rouben Mamoulian; **Scr**: Waldemar Young, Samuel Hoffenstein, George Marion Jr, from the play *Tailor in the Chateau* by Léopold Marchand, Paul Armont; **DOP**: Victor Milner (b&w); **Song Music/Lyrics**: Lorenz Hart/Richard Rodgers; **Art**: Hans Dreier; **Main Cast**: Maurice Chevalier, Jeanette MacDonald, Charlie Ruggles, Charles Butterworth, Myrna Loy, C. Aubrey Smith; **Prod Co**: Paramount.

The Love Parade
USA, 1929 – 109 mins
Ernst Lubitsch

In the history of the film musical, *The Love Parade* is a landmark in several respects. It was Ernst Lubitsch's first talkie, Jeanette MacDonald's first film, the first of the four films that made Maurice Chevalier and MacDonald the musical's original star couple (see *One Hour with You**, *Love Me Tonight**, *The Merry Widow**); and with songs that flow directly from the action, it has claims to be the first fully 'integrated' musical. The film was based on a 1919 play but as a musical it descends from European operetta, with its sexual and romantic intrigues of upper-class characters in grand European settings, a tradition that initiates the subspecies of the American film musical that Rick Altman (1987) calls 'the fairy-tale musical'.

As in *The Merry Widow*, Chevalier plays a minor aristocrat (Count Alfred Renard) whose amorous exploits are notorious but whose charm keeps him universally popular with the ladies. In the film's opening, Renard is ordered to leave Paris in disgrace as a result of his scandalous affairs. He sings his fond farewell from a window ('Paris, Please Stay the Same'), his manservant (played by British music-hall star Lupino Lane) taking up the song from another window, a paralleling of the love lives of master and servant that runs through the film. In the mythical kingdom of Sylvania, meanwhile, the Queen (MacDonald) sings of her 'Dream Lover' but is under huge pressure to marry. When Renard returns, the Queen is fascinated and amused rather than appalled by his colourful past, and their rapidly developing romance is marked by the first two numbers ('Anything to Please the Queen' and 'My Love Parade') that bring together MacDonald's operatic soprano and Chevalier's rougher and more conversational *chansonnier* style. Much of the pleasure of their interaction comes from the wit with which Lubitsch handles the sexual innuendo of dialogue and action, and the characteristic inventiveness with which the developing relationship is followed by servants and courtiers watching through windows and peering through keyholes. This intercutting is one example of Lubitsch finding ingenious ways to maintain editing freedom despite the restrictions of the new sound technology.

The difference in status between Renard and the Queen, however, produces a reversal of gender roles: in Sylvania, the Queen's husband can only be Prince Consort, not King; as they marry, Renard must promise to be 'an obedient and docile husband' and the priest pronounces them 'wife and man'. Renard finds himself in the wife's traditional position – a decorative partner for the working spouse, his sphere of action confined to the bedroom. Lubitsch makes eloquent use of the impersonal spaces and rituals of the palace in which the Queen has the central role while Renard has none. A good deal of humour is developed out of the gender reversal but when Renard rebels ('I'm a man'), threatening to return to Paris and seek a divorce, the Queen's position becomes increasingly painful, notably in the opera scene where Renard's price for remaining is to require the Queen to beg him to stay. In their final scenes, the Queen in tears and Renard feigning indifference, their conflict is resolved via a reprise of their first dialogue, with Renard now asking, 'How am I going to punish you?' The Queen's answer is to cede all her power to him, both in public and private ('My King!'). Chevalier smiles conspiratorially at the camera and draws the bedroom curtains. Lubitsch's three films with Chevalier and MacDonald are all quizzical explorations of the couple; here, gender roles revert (playfully but not without pain) to type. DP

Dir/Prod: Ernst Lubitsch; **Scr**: Ernest Vajda, Guy Bolton, from Leon Xanrof and Jules Chancel's play *The Prince Consort*; **DOP**: Victor Milner (b&w); **Song Music/Lyrics**: Victor Schertzinger/Clifford Grey; **Art**: Hans Dreier; **Main Cast**: Jeanette MacDonald, Maurice Chevalier, Lupino Lane, Lillian Roth; **Prod Co**: Paramount.

Mary Poppins
USA, 1964 – 139 mins
Robert Stevenson

With *Mary Poppins* and *The Sound of Music**, Julie Andrews appeared in the mid-1960s to be the saviour of the Hollywood studio musical. Andrews had no movie credentials but had starred on stage in *My Fair Lady* (Broadway, 1956, London, 1958) and *Camelot* (Broadway, 1960) and on television. Her lack of movie celebrity no doubt explains why Audrey Hepburn was preferred for the *My Fair Lady* movie (1964), but the lead role in Disney's *Mary Poppins* more than compensated: *My Fair Lady* cost significantly more than *Mary Poppins* and was considerably less successful at the box office.

Walt Disney had tried to secure movie rights to P. L. Travers's *Mary Poppins* novels since 1938 and finally succeeded in 1961. The film significantly softens the character of Travis's nanny Mary Poppins, who magically descends on a middle-class English family to sort out their parenting problems before magically disappearing. Among other significant changes, the story's period is switched from the 1930s (when the first *Poppins* novels were published) to 1910, that supposedly more untroubled pre-1914 period also favoured by other family-centred musicals like *Meet Me in St. Louis** and *Summer Holiday**.

Mr Banks (David Tomlinson) and his wife (Glynis Johns) are clueless about proper parenting for their children, Jane (Karen Dotrice) and Michael (Matthew Garber). Mr Banks loves his life: he works in a bank and thinks 'it's grand to be an Englishman in 1910' ('I Love the Life I Lead'). For him, the future of the empire lies in the hands of a good, stern nanny. Neither he nor Mrs Banks, who combines Suffragette activism with utter deference to her husband, has any time for their children's needs. Cue Mary Poppins, who drifts down from the clouds with her carpet-bag and brolly to provide the children with a balanced diet of stern rules, affection and, courtesy of her magic powers, enchantment. Bert (Dick Van Dyke), pavement artist, chimney sweep and hawker (non-magical, but enjoying a special relationship with the audience), accompanies Mary and the children on their adventures; he too has a store of sound parenting knowledge (he is attracted to Mary but she knows that he would 'never think of pressing his advantage').

This is rather odd, because neither Mary nor Bert has a home or a family, nor any prospect of one. 'Family', however dysfunctional, may be the preserve of the upper middle classes, but family values are not. Mary's elocution is impeccable – this is, after all, Julie Andrews – but she is clearly lower in class than the Banks family. Bert's appearance, 'mockney' speech and occupations mark him as working class: as he puts it in 'Chim-Chim-Cheree', he's on society's 'bottom-most rung' but 'there's no happier bloke' (despite the song's somewhat melancholic melody). In 'Step in Time', the spectral chimney sweeps who dance with Bert and Mary on the dingy rooftops (as if the working class was invisible, or only came out at night) display an energy and humour entirely lacking in the affluent, leafy Banks world. The celebrated combined live action/animated 'Jolly Holiday' family fantasy which Mary and Bert play out with the children is an essentially middle-class one, but 'Supercalifragilisticexpialidocious', which follows, features them dancing energetically to a pearly band.

At $6 million dollars, *Mary Poppins* was Disney's then most expensive film, but it grossed over $100 million on US release alone (and was re-released in 1973 and 1980). Disney put together a musical stage version of *Mary Poppins* in London (2004) and on Broadway (2006). The spirit of *Mary Poppins* lives on in the television reality shows in which 'Supernanny' is 'parachuted' into families with parenting problems.   JH

Dir: Robert Stevenson; **Prod**: Walt Disney, Bill Walsh; **Scr**: Bill Walsh, Don DaGradi, from the *Mary Poppins* novels by P. L. Travers; **DOP**: Edward Colman (colour); **Song Music/Lyrics**: Richard M. Sherman, Robert B. Sherman; **Musical Dir**: Irwin Kostal; **Art**: Carroll Clark, William H. Tuntke; **Choreog**: Marc Breaux, Dee Dee Wood; **Main Cast**: Julie Andrews, Dick Van Dyke, David Tomlinson, Glynis Johns, Hermione Baddeley, Reta Shaw, Karen Dotrice, Matthew Garber; **Prod Co**: Walt Disney.

Meet Me in St. Louis
USA, 1944 – 104 mins
Vincente Minnelli

Released in 1944, when many families remained fractured by war, and based on Sally Benson's stories of her turn-of-the-century childhood, *Meet Me in St. Louis* speaks directly to nostalgia for the ideals of American family life. The film's gorgeous Technicolor recreation of 1903 St Louis evokes a period before the great traumas of the twentieth century, when traditional values could seemingly coexist with the exciting but unthreatening promise of modernity (the World's Fair which the characters eagerly anticipate and with which the film ends).

Producer Arthur Freed saw the possibility of creating 'a simple story … that basically says "there's no place like home"' (Fordin, 1975). The wonderfully textured scenes of family life (like the title number that introduces members of the household and the much later 'You and I' sung by Mr and Mrs Smith [Leon Ames and Mary Astor]) place the appeal of that sentiment at the heart of the film, but as with *The Wizard of Oz**, it is shadowed in various ways. Minnelli and his collaborators emphasise the artifice of the film's world and suggest the pivotal roles that fantasy and performance play in sustaining the ideology of family life. The four seasons that structure the film are introduced by sepia photographs embedded in pages from a decorative album; the camera tracks in, colour bleeds into the photograph and the scene comes to life, our distance from the past aesthetically underlined. Motifs of performance are central to the roles adopted by the eldest daughters, Rose (Lucille Bremer) and Esther (Judy Garland), in their pursuit of boys but are also repeatedly present in Minnelli's use of doorways, windows and archways to frame action and numbers. When Esther, for example, sings longingly of 'The Boy Next Door' even before she has met him, we watch her through a window frame, across which she finally lets down a lace curtain.

Such decisions develop perspectives on a dream of harmonious family life that is qualified in other ways. Andrew Britton (1977), in fact,

Judy Garland, 'The Boy Next Door'

argues that the film is 'systematically ambivalent' about the Smiths. It is striking, for instance, that although in principle the father possesses the power in the family, he and the other men are largely ineffectual figures. The drama centres on Mr Smith's promotion to New York but it is the women who prevail when he abandons his ambition. His change of heart is decisively triggered, however, by the actions of his youngest daughter, Tootie (Margaret O'Brien), the most remarkable and disturbing figure in the film. It is on Tootie that the surprisingly dark aspects of the film centre. She is obsessed with death (she buries all her dolls); with her sister Agnes (Joan Carroll), she attempts to derail a trolley bus and then accuses Esther's beau, John Truitt (Tom Drake), of hitting her. In a Halloween sequence that evokes the horror movie, Tootie takes on the terrifying task of symbolically 'killing' the ogre-like Mr Braukoff. In an even more radical disruption of tone that feels, as Robin Wood (1972) suggests, like an attack on the image of the family itself, she later rushes out into the night and hysterically attacks the group of snow people the children have made earlier. It is after watching this in utter dismay that Mr Smith relents. The film ends with apparent harmony restored as the family visits the fair and Esther celebrates the wonder of living in St Louis. In its way, it is a lovely ending, though what Minnelli shows us of the fair is yet another image – just lights across the water.   DP

Dir: Vincente Minnelli; **Prod**: Arthur Freed; **Scr**: Irving Brecher, Fred F. Finklehoffe, from Sally Benson's stories; **DOP**: George Folsey (colour); **Song Music/Lyrics**: Hugh Martin/Ralph Blane; Nacio Herb Brown/Arthur Freed; **Musical Dir**: Roger Edens; **Choreog**: Charles Walters; **Art**: Cedric Gibbons; **Main Cast**: Judy Garland, Margaret O'Brien, Mary Astor, Lucille Bremer, Leon Ames, Tom Drake, Marjorie Main, Henry Davenport, Joan Carroll; **Prod Co**: Metro-Goldwyn-Mayer.

The Merry Widow
USA, 1934 – 98 mins
Ernst Lubitsch

The Merry Widow, a version of Franz Lehár's extremely successful 1905 operetta, reunited Ernst Lubitsch, Maurice Chevalier and Jeanette MacDonald for the last time in what also proved to be Lubitsch's final musical as well as one of Chevalier's last Hollywood films before his return to France in 1935. In many respects, the film continues the pattern of elegant and risqué musicals established in a group of Paramount productions that included the trio's previous collaborations, *The Love Parade** and *One Hour with You**, but *The Merry Widow* was made in even more lavish style at MGM.

    The film retains but transforms the operetta's central plot of a rich widow who must be prevented from marrying a foreigner in order to keep her fortune in the country. Initially set in the tiny and obscure kingdom of Marshovia, the opening number, 'Girls, Girls, Girls!', shows Count Danilo (Chevalier), marching at the head of an army parade, ecstatically greeted by the female population, his sexual exuberance only punctured by the black-clad, unsmiling figure of the widow Sonia (MacDonald) in her carriage. The sequence introduces a world joyously pervaded by guilt-free sex but also the stark contrast between the count and the widow that the film will wittily explore and work to resolve. The couple must undergo a process of mutual re-education, Sonia back to life and love, and Danilo from his life of uncommitted indulgence.

    Unlike their previous films together, the two leads sing only separately: 'Girls, Girls, Girls!' is followed by Sonia's solitary and yearning 'Vilia' and 'Tonight Will Teach Me to Forget'. It is through dance that they become a couple, a feature of *The Merry Widow* that extends the musical structure of the previous Lubitsch films and anticipates the role of dance in the Astaire/Rogers musicals (see *The Gay Divorcee**, *Swing Time**, *Top Hat**). In Paris, where Danilo has been sent by the King to marry Sonia at all costs, two settings

dominate: Maxim's, where uninhibited sexuality is joyfully celebrated, and the Embassy, where elegant formality and inhibition rule.

At Maxim's, Sonia pretends to be a good-time girl, Fifi; she and Danilo dance for the first time as Sonia sings 'The Merry Widow Waltz', but she is repelled by Danilo's insincerity. When they meet at the Embassy, the waltz once more sweeps them away but they become lost in the whirling couples of a huge, Busby Berkeley-like, production number, the public world overwhelming their growing intimacy. Just as Sonia decides to trust Danilo, a premature announcement of their engagement reveals the marriage plot. Danilo denounces the engagement and is arrested for treason.

At his trial in Marshovia, when Sonia refuses to believe his love, Danilo declares, to applause from all the men present: 'Any man who can dance through life with hundreds of women and is willing to walk through life with one should be hanged!' The film's conclusion aligns public interest and private commitment in surprising and unsettling ways. Sonia visits Danilo in prison. With the King and cabinet listening outside, and to the strains of a gypsy band playing 'The Merry Widow Waltz', Sonia reminds Danilo of his earlier declaration and he now replaces 'should be hanged' with, '… should be married!' Locked in the cell, with a priest ready at the peephole to perform the ceremony, they kiss. Does marriage equal imprisonment? The film's smile remains quizzical and its attitudes poised.

Made just as the enhanced Production Code of self-censorship was taking effect in Hollywood, several cuts apparently remained in US prints of the film until the 1960s. In 1952, MGM produced another version of Lehár's operetta. DP

Dir: Ernst Lubitsch; **Prod**: Irving Thalberg; **Scr**: Ernest Vajda, Samuel Raphaelson, based on the operetta with music by Franz Lehár, book and lyrics by Victor Léon, Leo Stein; **DOP**: Oliver T. Marsh (b&w); **Song Music/Lyrics**: Franz Lehár/Lorenz Hart, Gus Kahn; additional music by Richard Rodgers; **Musical Adapt**: Herbert Stothart; **Art**: Cedric Gibbons; **Main Cast**: Maurice Chevalier, Jeanette MacDonald, Edward Everett Horton, Una Merkel, George Barbier; **Prod Co**: Metro-Goldwyn-Mayer.

Le Million
France, 1931 – 83 mins
René Clair

Overwhelmingly, particularly in Hollywood, the coming of sound meant the advent of sound recording of people talking (or singing) – the 'talkies'. The talkies also dominated in European studios, but the greater extent of experimentation with film form in Europe in the 1920s encouraged several important film-makers, including Sergei M. Eisenstein in the Soviet Union and René Clair in France, to argue strongly for a less naturalistic approach to sound – the 'sound film' rather than the 'talkie'. Not that there was an absence of experimentation with sound in Hollywood; in fact, musicals played an important role in enhancing the possibilities of sound technology and aesthetics. Clair (1929) himself admired the use of sound in *Broadway Melody* (1929), for example – 'neither theatre nor cinema but something altogether new' (although, in truth, films like *Applause** and *The Love Parade** would have served his argument even better) – and played with sound-film conventions in his own films *Sous les toits de Paris* (1930), *Le Million* and *A nous la liberté* (1931).

As *Le Million* begins, the camera traverses a sleeping midnight Paris towards the sound of party celebrations, which the chorus of dancing figures offers to explain to onlookers. This ushers in a flashback to the start of that same day when a poor, dreamy artist (René Lefèvre, destined for later greatness as Lange/Arizona Jim in Jean Renoir's *Le Crime de M. Lange*, 1936) discovers that the jacket containing his winning lottery ticket has gone astray. The day is then taken up with the crazy goings-on involved in the search for the jacket, via a gang of thieves, the police, a night at the opera and various on–off flirtations and romances. Comically, both thieves and police introduce themselves and their missions with choruses from the same melody, and elsewhere, singing voices are used, variously, as interior voice-over, the voice of celestial moral conscience, and so on. Among the film's 'making strange' strategies are dialogue scenes played, apparently arbitrarily, with or without spoken dialogue and a sound 'slap' and noises-off within otherwise silent scenes. Famously, Clair introduces football crowd noises (complete with referee's whistle) over an extended tussle for possession of the jacket. Engagingly, the love duet between two disagreeable, overweight opera singers is played out over the romantic young couple hiding behind them amid stage scenery. As we know from the start, and as in most musical comedies (which is how *Le Million* describes itself), all ends happily, with the lottery ticket found and the young couple reunited.

The film is suffused with the whimsical spirit of Clair's earlier films, not least the Dadaist 1924 *Entr'acte*, but Alan Williams (1992) is surely right to suggest the strong possibility of some influence from Bertolt Brecht, in both the film's form, with its distanced, self-conscious narration devices, and its content ('the foot soldiers of inequality' thieves, committed to 'redistributing wealth', against 'the foot soldiers of legality' police, upholding 'public virtue and private property'). Certainly, Clair would have been acquainted with film and theatre developments in Germany: Brecht and Kurt Weill's *The Threepenny Opera* was premiered in 1928 and G. W. Pabst's film adaptation*, made in a French as well as a German version and by the same company that produced Clair's films, was released in early 1931, some months before *Le Million*. JH

Dir/Scr: René Clair, from a play by Georges Berr, Marcel Guillemaud; **Prod**: not credited; **DOP**: Georges Périnal (b&w); **Music**: Armand Bernard, Philippe Parès, Georges Van Parys; **Art**: Lazare Meerson; **Main Cast**: Annabella, René Lefèvre, Jean-Louis Allibert, Paul Ollivier, Constantin Siroesco; **Prod Co**: Films Sonores Tobis.

Moulin Rouge!
Australia/USA, 2001 – 126 mins
Baz Luhrmann

At a time when the Hollywood musical once again seemed moribund, in successive years *Moulin Rouge!* and *Chicago** became worldwide hits. In their intense theatricality, montage-based styles and use of non-musical stars, the films have much in common, but among all his contemporaries Baz Luhrmann's was the most determined attempt to make an original film musical on traditional themes for audiences immersed in the methods and images of music video but unfamiliar with the genre's traditions.

Moulin Rouge! was the third of what Luhrmann termed his 'Red Curtain' films (a reference to their informing theatricality) following *Strictly Ballroom* (1992) and *Romeo + Juliet* (1996). The stereotypical red velvet curtains of proscenium-arch theatre are the film's initial cue to an elaborately reflexive and referential approach that informs every level of decision-making. Two central motifs of the traditional musical – a showbiz setting and the heterosexual couple of romantic comedy – are cross-referenced with the mythic narrative of Orpheus and Eurydice and operatic tragedies of the Parisian demi-monde like Verdi's *La Traviata* and Puccini's *La Bohème* to create a narrative that could sustain the shifts of mode and tone that excited Luhrmann in Bollywood movies (see, for example, *Dil se ...**). An aspiring young writer, Christian (Ewan McGregor), new to the underworld of Montmartre, falls in love with the glamorous courtesan Satine (Nicole Kidman), star of the Moulin Rouge, who is also being pursued by a wealthy Duke (Richard Roxburgh). The love plot is intertwined with the production of the opening show, 'Spectacular Spectacular', in the redeveloped Moulin Rouge.

Songs are drawn eclectically from well-known popular singers and groups – making awareness of the music's varied origins central to the film and emphasising the characters' status as functions of a world created by performance. Songs by The Police, Madonna, Elton John and Queen, among many others, come and go, orchestrated in various styles and versions from opera to rock and pop. From earlier periods, Christian improvises 'The Sound of Music' as his first contribution to the theatre troupe's show, and in her first appearance, lowered from the ceiling of the Moulin Rouge on a swing, Satine sings 'Diamonds Are a Girl's Best Friend'. Dialogue is at times similarly knowing, Christian coming up, for instance, with 'Love is a many splendoured thing' and 'All you need is love'.

Intensifying levels of artifice, the film's designers, combined with Luhrmann's rapidly moving camera and often frenetically paced cutting, create a dreamlike vision of 1899 Montmartre that condenses the rich accumulated images and associations of the Moulin Rouge and its milieu. In their look and choreography, production numbers evoke styles from the can-can, through Busby Berkeley and MGM musicals of the 1940s/50s, to the overt homage to Bollywood in 'Hindi Sad Diamonds', the opening number of the climactic show. Scenes range in tone from broad physical comedy to the emotional extremes of melodrama – in both its romantic and theatrical modes. Performances, frequently filmed in big close-up, are correspondingly heightened and histrionic.

All this makes the film's attitude to its material deeply equivocal. In part a homage to various traditions of the musical, *Moulin Rouge!* is, among other things, a love story. Yet romantic love and the lovers, like everything else, are subject to the film's sensory bombardment, its deployment of pastiche, overt theatricality, clashes of tone and constant allusiveness. In an aesthetic, as Pam Cook (2010) puts it, that is 'both ironic and nostalgic', perhaps nothing is authentic, love and death merely performance, subject to the pervasive play of irony. These may be the terms on which a film musical about romantic love could be made in 2001. DP

Dir: Baz Luhrmann; **Prod**: Baz Luhrmann, Martin Brown, Fred Baron; **Scr**: Baz Luhrmann, Craig Pearce; **DOP**: Donald M. McAlpine (colour); **Song Music/Lyrics**: Eden Ahbez; Marc

Bolan; Richard Rodgers/Oscar Hammerstein; Elton John/Bernie Taupin; David Bowie; Marius DeVries/Amiel Daemion; Andrew Scott; Trevor Griffin, *et al*.; **Music**: Craig Armstrong; **Musical Dir**: Marius DeVries; **Choreog**: John O'Connell; **Art**: Catherine Martin; **Main Cast**: Nicole Kidman, Ewan McGregor, Jim Broadbent, Richard Roxburgh, John Leguizamo, Jacek Koman, Kylie Minogue; **Prod Co**: Bazmark/20th Century-Fox.

The Music Man
USA, 1962 – 151 mins
Morton DaCosta

Meredith Willson's *The Music Man* opened on Broadway in 1957 and ran for over 1,300 performances, ousting *West Side Story* in popularity and critical acclaim, and it has remained one of the most frequently toured and amateur shows. The show's popularity no doubt encouraged Warners to keep its producer-director, male lead (Robert Preston) and choreographer (Onna White) for the 1962 film; the main change was Janis Paige's replacement by Shirley Jones, the star of *Oklahoma!** and *Carousel**. Though many films reduced shows' duration by cutting songs, subplots and characters, *The Music Man* preserves almost the entire song catalogue and runs at Broadway show length.

The film/show's popularity doubtless owes something to its evocation – like *Meet Me in St. Louis** and *Summer Holiday** – of early twentieth-century small-town America. However, there is a self-reflexively 'corny' edge to *The Music Man*, not least in Preston's slyly knowing incarnation of 'Professor' Harold Hill. Flimflam man Hill plans to fleece the rubes of River City, Iowa, by organising a boys' marching band, complete with 'seventy-six trombones' and smart uniforms, but making off with the townsfolk's money. First, however, he must persuade them that they need to combat the degenerate tendencies of the young, and focuses on the town's new pool table (in the wonderful 'Ya Got Trouble': 'Are certain words creeping into his conversation? Words like "swell" … and "so's your old man"?'). Cleverly evading efforts to expose him, he falls for the town's spinsterish librarian and piano teacher, Marian (Jones), causing him, finally, to confess all. He is saved from tarring and feathering when the boys turn up with their instruments, in their uniforms: they sound terrible, but the parents are nevertheless tremendously proud, and in a fantasy finale they morph into a professional, splendidly uniformed, 76-trombone-size band marching energetically through town.

Shirley Jones, Robert Preston, Susan Luckey: 'Shipoopi'

As all this – and the title itself – suggests (and this is much of its charm), *The Music Man* is really *about* 'musical comedy'. The comically small-minded, repressed River City community desperately needs release through music, song and dance, not least in the libido and community fellow-feeling departments. In 'Marian the Librarian', Marian is slowly drawn in with the young people dancing around her habitually staid, silent library. On the basis that 'singing is just sustained talking', Hill transforms the quarrelling school board into an entirely harmonious barbershop quartet, and his 'think system' for playing music (it's like whistling) is proved entirely feasible, at least in the imagination. Appropriately, Willson's songs are wonderfully inventive: the opening 'Rock Island' employs an auctioneer/recitative style, while 'Ya Got Trouble' uses revivalist preacher call and response. Several juxtaposed songs ('76 Trombones' and 'Goodnight, My Someone', for example) use the same melody at different tempos, and 'Shipoopi' and 'Gary, Indiana' toy joyously with sheer absurdity.

Many critics thought *The Music Man*, like *The Pajama Game**, was stage-bound, more a record of the stage production than a movie in its own right, but right from 'Rock Island', staged in an open-sided train carriage set, the film purposefully foregrounds its theatricality. Many numbers are performed frontally in long takes, as if to a theatre audience, and the film adopts such highly theatrical conventions as ending scenes with characters spotlighted against a black ground. No real effort is made to persuade us that River City is anything other than a set; and in the end credits, the actors 'take their bows' to camera. The long-lasting popularity of *The Music Man* and the affection it inspires have made it a popular reference point, and cult television shows *Family Guy* and *The Simpsons* have both parodied aspects of the show/film. JH

Dir/Prod: Morton DaCosta; **Scr**: Marion Hargrove, adapted from the Broadway stage musical by Meredith Willson, Franklyn Lacey; **DOP**: Robert Burks (colour); **Song Music/Lyrics**: Meredith Willson; **Musical Dir**: Ray Heindorf; **Choreog**: Onna White, Tom Panko; **Art**: Paul Groesse; **Main Cast**: Robert Preston, Shirley Jones, Buddy Hackett, Hermione Gingold, Paul Ford, Pert Kelton, The Buffalo Bills; **Prod Co**: Warner Bros.

Nashville
USA, 1975 – 159 mins
Robert Altman

Nashville is the most ambitious of the remarkable series of revisionist genre films (M.A.S.H., 1970, *McCabe and Mrs Miller*, 1971, and *The Long Goodbye*, 1973, preceded *Nashville*) that Robert Altman directed in the 1970s. Set shortly after the end of the Vietnam War and the resignation of President Nixon, and the year before the USA's bicentennial celebrations, it is self-consciously a state-of-the-nation movie that takes Nashville, country music's capital, as its microcosm. As Rick Altman (1987) argues, it is also a 'point by point deconstruction of the folk musical', with its unifying mythology of the American past, family and community (see, for instance, *Meet Me in St. Louis**, *Summer Holiday**, *Oklahoma!**). In *Nashville*, all is fragmentation, the residual sentiments of traditional values in the lyrics of the country singers radically disconnected from the industry and society that exploits them.

In folk musicals, characters frequently express themselves directly in song and dance. In its use of music, *Nashville* is more like a dystopian backstage or showbiz musical (like *Cabaret**): its many songs – composed by the cast and musical director Richard Baskin – are all performances (mainly on stage but sometimes on tape in the background of scenes); the utopian impulses of the integrated musical have no place here. Altman actually begins with a credit sequence that presents his film itself as a rather tawdry but star-laden confection, its gaudy attractions bawled out over a montage of framed actors' faces. What follows is a multi-stranded narrative, constantly intercutting over twenty main characters in events that take place over just a few days against the background of a presidential bid by a third-party candidate, whose eccentric populist messages are interwoven through the film. The main action runs from the acclaimed return of Nashville star Barbara Jean (Ronee Blakley) from convalescence, to a concert in support of the 'Replacement Party' candidate at which singers have been cajoled, bribed and variously persuaded to appear and at which Barbara Jean is shot by the most enigmatic of the characters whose intersecting trajectories the film has followed.

Altman's use of multi-camera shooting and a mobile camera style with extensive use of the zoom lens make much of the film feel as though action is being captured rather than staged, in the manner of a fly-on-the-wall documentary – an impression heightened by his characteristic use of overlapping dialogue and a soundtrack in which ambient noise frequently competes with what would conventionally be considered the key dialogue. Songs by the major singers in the film's world – Barbara Jean, Haven Hamilton (Henry Gibson), Connie White (Karen Black), Tom Frank (Keith Carradine) – are shown at length, but even these are repeatedly intercut with other characters, action and sound, undermining the privileged status musicals traditionally accord star performances.

On the whole, the film's view of a world it presents in such extraordinary detail is bleak; it is little wonder that the Country music establishment was so enraged. Few characters invite compassion – perhaps most obviously, the emotionally frail Barbara Jean, Linnea Reese (Lily Tomlin), the leader of a gospel choir, who has two deaf sons, and Sueleen Gray (Gwen Welles), whose striptease is the film's most painful moment. There is no romance; all the sexual encounters are casual and fleeting; there are no positively presented relationships, within or outside marriage. After the shooting, the wounded Haven calls on everyone to sing ('This isn't Dallas, it's Nashville'), and Albuquerque (Barbara Harris), a marginal figure to this point, takes the microphone and begins to sing 'It Don't Bother Me', the audience gradually joining in its mechanical repetitions. It feels very much like the end of a tradition. DP

Dir/Prod: Robert Altman; **Scr**: Joan Tewkesbury; **DOP**: Paul Lohmann (colour); **Song Music/Lyrics**: Keith Carradine, Ronee Blakley, Richard Baskin, Karen Black, *et al*.; **Musical Dir**: Richard Baskin; **Main Cast**: Ronee Blakley, Karen Black, Henry Gibson, Ned Beatty, Keith Carradine, Geraldine Chaplin, Shelley Duvall, Michael Murphy, Lily Tomlin; **Prod Co**: American Broadcasting Company/Paramount.

Naughty Marietta
USA, 1935 – 106 mins
Robert Z. Leonard, W. S. Van Dyke

The establishment in 1934 of the Production Code Administration to enforce regulation of movie content made it much more difficult for Hollywood films to tackle morally controversial material. It meant the end, for instance, of the light-heartedly racy treatment of sexual themes in some of Jeanette MacDonald's earlier films (including *The Love Parade**, *One Hour with You**, *Love Me Tonight** and *The Merry Widow**). There is something emblematic, therefore, about the knowingly sexual Gallic charm of Maurice Chevalier, MacDonald's partner in those earlier films, giving way to the much more wholesome – and American – appeal of the stolid Nelson Eddy. Unfashionable now and musically conservative even then, the success of their films paved the way for MGM's large-scale commitment to the musical in the 1940s. In fact, it took MGM some time to work out how to use Eddy after he was contracted on the basis of a successful operatic and concert career, but he was eventually cast experimentally to partner MacDonald in an adaptation of Victor Herbert's 1910 operetta. The film's great success led to six more films at MGM and to MacDonald and Eddy becoming two of the most popular singing stars of the 1930s.

One theme of the film – developed from the original operetta – is the challenge of American freedoms to the class hierarchies and arranged marriages of aristocratic Europe. But in the film, unlike the operetta, America has to wait. The action opens in Paris and it is MacDonald's role as Princess Marie that drives the narrative. She is established (this is the eighteenth century) as an unconventional princess, popular and musical (she joins a large chorus of Parisians in the first number, 'Chansonette'), but also determined to resist the King's demand that she should marry Don Carlos (Walter Kingsford), an ageing Spanish aristocrat. To escape, she assumes the identity of her maid, who is about to join the *casquette* girls, virtuous young women who are being sponsored to marry French colonists in Louisiana, taking with her an unfinished song which later becomes the operetta's most famous number, 'Ah, Sweet Mystery of Life'.

Captured by pirates, the women are rescued in Louisiana by a band of American scouts (the singing of their anthem, 'Tramp, Tramp, Tramp' signals their arrival in the forest) led by Richard Warrington (Nelson Eddy). He pursues Marie/Marietta; she is put off by his arrogant self-regard but, as the complications of the plot unfold, he gradually wins her over.

Jeanette MacDonald, 'Chansonette'

Along the way, in order to avoid enforced marriage to a colonist, she pretends to be a fallen woman (a more discreet version of the Widow's masquerade as Fifi in *The Merry Widow*), is recognised as the Princess and confronted by her uncle (Douglas Dumbrille) and Don Carlos, who have followed her from France. In the great ball scene, the distraught Marie sings 'Ah, Sweet Mystery of Life', only to hear Richard's voice joining hers, and they complete the song as a duet. Richard's men contrive the couple's escape, and we last see them reprising their duet as they journey into the American wilderness.

America and freedom triumph but the musical form of the film looks back rather than forward, rooted in the operetta tradition that retained huge appeal in Middle America. Eddy's clean-cut hero fits the mode perfectly but Marie is the heart of *Naughty Marietta*, and it is MacDonald's charm and comedic skill that lift the film.   DP

Dir: W. S. Van Dyke; **Prod**: Hunt Stromberg; **Scr**: John Lee Mahin, Frances Goodrich, Albert Hackett, from the operetta, book and lyrics by Rida Johnson Young, music by Victor Herbert; **DOP**: William Daniels (b&w); **Song Music/Lyrics**: Victor Herbert/Rida Johnson Young; additional lyrics by Gus Kahn; **Musical Dir**: Herbert Stothart; **Choreog**: Chester Hale; **Art**: Cedric Gibbons, Arnold Gillespie, Edwin B. Willis; **Main Cast**: Jeanette MacDonald, Nelson Eddy, Frank Morgan, Elsa Lanchester, Douglas Dumbrille, Joseph Cawthorne, Cecilia Parker, Walter Kingsford, Greta Meyer, Akim Tamiroff; **Prod Co**: Metro-Goldwyn-Mayer.

New York, New York
USA, 1977 – 163 mins
Martin Scorsese

During the long V-J Day sequence that opens *New York, New York*, Jimmy Doyle (Robert De Niro) breaks off his persistent attempts to pick up Francine Evans (Liza Minnelli) to make a phone call; from the top of a staircase, he looks down at a sailor in white uniform silently dancing with a young woman in a white dress. It could be an image from a 1940s MGM musical: romantic love perfectly embodied in a couple dancing.

Of the 1970s dystopian musicals (*Cabaret**, *Nashville**, *All That Jazz*, 1979), *New York, New York* engages most self-consciously with tradition – its narrative, 1945 setting and stylised sets all evoking the musical's past. At its heart too is Jimmy's own utopian image, the 'major chord' – when, as he says, you have 'the woman you want … the music you want … enough money to live comfortably'. In this show musical, however, the couple (she a singer, he a jazz saxophonist) can achieve success only separately, Francine as a Hollywood singing star and Jimmy in his jazz club, The Major Chord – the name an acknowledgment of an unrealised dream. With a story of a singer's rise to fame and a husband unable to cope with his wife's stardom and independence, Scorsese also invokes *A Star Is Born** and *Love Me or Leave Me** but pushes the material even further, using the improvisatory naturalism of his central performances to root the film in (often acutely painful) psychological realism, and characteristically intensifying the focus on paranoid, insecure masculinity.

Obsessively pursuing Francine, when Jimmy catches up with her on tour he is overbearing ('You don't say goodbye to me, I say goodbye to you') and pathologically possessive – after reading her poems about him, he drags her to the Justice of the Peace in the middle of a snowy night to marry him. Francine's songs chart the development of her feelings, from 'You Brought a New Kind of Love to Me' when she saves Jimmy's early audition from disaster, to 'You Are My Lucky Star' and 'The Man I Love' with the band, while Jimmy has no comparable musical outlet.

Liza Minnelli, Robert De Niro, 'You Brought a New Kind of Love to Me'

When she returns, pregnant, to New York, Jimmy's career founders. In the city, their musical paths completely diverge – Francine achieving mainstream success while Jimmy plays bebop with a black band. In the film's most distressing scenes, Jimmy blows an increasingly aggressive solo as the heavily pregnant Francine struggles towards him across the crowded Harlem club; they quarrel hysterically and violently in Jimmy's car; when Francine has the baby, Jimmy refuses to see him.

The film's final section begins with Francine's hugely dramatic recording-studio performance of 'The World Goes Round', filmed in a single take, the light fading around the spotlit Francine. What follows, representing Francine's Hollywood stardom, is 'Happy Endings', a long and heavy-handed parody of MGM ballet sequences; and then Francine, with Liza Minnelli strongly evoking her mother's performance style, singing the title number, 'New York, New York', with tremendous intensity on her acclaimed return to the city. It is the tune Jimmy has been gradually composing through the movie, for which Francine supplied the lyrics. With Jimmy in the audience, it is, as Richard Lippe (1986) writes, 'the film's true climax, drawing together a whole complex of emotional threads …' acknowledging 'the past relationship, the unfulfilled possibilities it suggested … Francine's independence'.

The film's box-office failure led United Artists to make extensive cuts, including most of 'Happy Endings', for the film's main release. DP

Dir: Martin Scorsese; **Prod**: Robert Chartoff, Irwin Winkler; **Scr**: Mardik Martin, Earl Mac Rauch, from a story by Rauch; **DOP**: Laszlo Kovacs (colour); **Song Music/Lyrics**: John Kander/Fred Ebb; Sammy Fain/Irving Kahal; George Gershwin/Ira Gershwin; Michael Edwards/Bud Green, *et al.*; **Musical Dir**: Ralph Burns; **Choreog**: Ron Field; **Art**: Boris Leven, Harry Kemm; **Main Cast**: Robert De Niro, Liza Minnelli, Lionel Stander, Mary Kay Place, George Memmoli, Murray Moston, Barry Primus, Georgie Auld (also dubbed saxophone for Robert De Niro); **Prod Co**: United Artists.

Oklahoma!
USA, 1955 – 145 mins
Fred Zinnemann

Rouben Mamoulian's 1943 production of *Oklahoma!* was one of the great landmarks of the Broadway musical. The first collaboration between Richard Rodgers and Oscar Hammerstein II, it ran for an unprecedented 2,212 performances and toured the US continuously until 1954. Set in 1907, just before statehood was achieved, *Oklahoma!* crystallised for the musical preoccupations with the American West that had emerged in the innovative music and dance of works such as Aaron Copland's *Billy the Kid* (1938) and *Rodeo* (1942). The show coupled a nostalgic vision of the West with a form that set new standards for the integration of story, character, song and dance in the musical. Agnes de Mille's choreography, in particular – rooted in character and everyday action and drawing on folk as well as modern dance forms – proved enormously influential.

By 1955, when the film appeared, the innovations of *Oklahoma!* had been thoroughly absorbed by the movie musical, not least in Gene Kelly's choreography and MGM's widespread use of the dream ballet that *Oklahoma!* is generally credited with introducing. Fred Zinnemann introduced appropriately expansive Western landscapes – Curly (Gordon MacRea) approaches on horseback as the film opens before launching into 'Oh, What a Beautiful Morning' – but beyond that, the film remained as faithful as it could to the original show. Particularly significant in this respect is that Agnes de Mille recreated her groundbreaking choreography for the film – her only major Broadway work adapted in its entirety for the screen. The film's value in the history of the musical lies largely in this respectful adaptation of what had become, twelve years after its opening, an American classic.

De Mille's ensemble dances – numbers such as 'Kansas City', 'The Farmer and the Rancher Can Be Friends' and 'Oklahoma!' – embody the utopian vision of community that is at the heart of what Rick Altman (1987) calls the 'folk musical'. In *Oklahoma!*, the tensions between ranchers and farmers that lead to violence in many Westerns can be resolved after mild fisticuffs through a song and a communal dance, and the marriage of the cowboy Curly and his settler sweetheart, Laurey (Shirley Jones), symbolises and confirms that unity. But, as Altman also suggests, dark forces invariably shadow romance and community values in folk musicals. In *Oklahoma!*, the sexuality that is sublimated in Laurey and Curly's wholesome relationship ('People Will Think We're in Love') is the mainspring of the spirited comic subplot centring on Ado Annie (the wonderful Gloria Grahame), her suitor, Will (Gene Nelson), and the pedlar, Ali Hakim (Eddie Albert). Annie's 'I'm Just a Girl Who Can't Say No' in a way says it all, but shotgun marriages await the unwary.

Darker and more threatening is the repressed and murderous hired hand Jud Fry (Rod Steiger), Curly's rival for Laurey. The visual paralleling of Jud and Curly in the staging of 'Poor Jud Is Dead' (in which, remarkably, the hero urges the villain to suicide) is one way in which the film implies that Jud is Curly's dark double. Even more explicit is the evocation of Laurey's turbulent feelings and fears in de Mille's dream ballet, in which dancers Bambi Lynn and James Mitchell represent Laurey and Curly, but it is Steiger as Jud who suddenly materialises as her groom, surrounds her with overtly sexual saloon girls and kills 'Curly'. Jud is conveniently dispatched, as he must be, to clear the way for the optimistic ending, but Steiger's creation lingers in the memory.

In the years that followed *Oklahoma!*, Hollywood increasingly invested in adaptations of Broadway shows and the number of original film musicals gradually declined. DP

Dir: Fred Zinnemann; **Prod**: Arthur Hornblow Jr; **Scr**: Sonya Levien, William Ludwig, adapted from the musical play, music by Richard Rodgers, book and lyrics by Oscar Hammerstein II, based on Lynn Riggs's play, *Green Grow the Lilacs*; **DOP**: Robert Surtees (colour); **Song Music/Lyrics**: Richard Rodgers/Oscar Hammerstein II; **Musical Dir**: Jay Blackton; **Choreog**: Agnes de Mille; **Art**: Joseph Wright; **Main Cast**: Gordon MacRae, Shirley Jones, Gloria Grahame, Gene Nelson, Charlotte Greenwood, Eddie Albert, Rod Steiger; **Prod Co**: 20th Century-Fox.

Oliver!
UK, 1968 – 153 mins
Carol Reed

For a few years from the late 1950s, it looked as if British musical theatre might offer something both different and popular. Leslie Bricusse and Anthony Newley made a splash with *Stop the World – I Want to Get Off* (1961, New York 1963, filmed 1966) and *The Roar of the Greasepaint – The Smell of the Crowd* (1964, Broadway 1965), but Lionel Bart looked even more exciting. From a background of music hall and pop songs for singers like Tommy Steele and Cliff Richard, Bart wrote the book, music and lyrics for a series of distinctively British musicals: *Lock up Your Daughters* (Unity Theatre, 1959), *Fings Ain't Wot They Used to Be* (Theatre Workshop, 1959), *Oliver!* (1960, Broadway, 1963), *Blitz!* (1962) and *Maggie May* (1964). *Oliver!* was by far the biggest hit, in both Britain and the US (2,618 performances in London's West End, 774 on Broadway), and the large-budget film adaptation hoped to emulate Hollywood production values. It was a good investment: the film did well at the box office and won a raft of Academy Awards, including Best Picture, Best Director, Best Art Direction and an honorary award for choreographer Onna White.

Oliver! is one of only a handful of film musicals discussed in this book in which heterosexual romance is not the dominant narrative theme. Its appeal seems to derive from the familiarity of Charles Dickens's original novel, frequently adapted for film (notably by David Lean, 1948; Roman Polanski, 2005), its elaborate recreation of nineteenth-century London (which took over most of the sound stages at Shepperton Studios), its songs, several of which had become popular standards, and some extravagantly choreographed production numbers. The musical, perhaps inevitably, significantly softens the social critique in Dickens's original – the notably more sympathetic Fagin (Ron Moody, one of very few actors retained from the stage original), for example, exits with the Artful Dodger (Jack Wild) to continue a life of crime rather than getting hanged – and as a kind of 'heritage film', it romanticises the often brutal living conditions of nineteenth-century London.

Oliver! is a full-blown musical, complete with 'Overture', 'Entr'acte' and 'Exit Music', stuffed full of songs and numbers. Several of the songs arise from the narrative in an integrated way – Oliver (Mark Lester) sings 'Where Is Love?' after being locked away in the funeral parlour cellar, for example – but they can also be 'integrated' in singularly inappropriate ways: Nancy (Shani Wallis)'s 'As Long as He Needs Me', which has become a standard love song, follows an abusive beating by Bill Sikes (Oliver Reed), who, in one of the film's more disturbing moments, later batters Nancy to death. Elsewhere, the degree of integration is more debatable: the biggest numbers, 'Food, Glorious Food', 'Consider Yourself' and 'Who Will Buy?', are grand, brilliantly contrived, energetic routines, but their relationship to the narrative seems tenuous. What does 'Consider Yourself', in which Oliver and the Artful Dodger are joined by priests, policemen, butchers, street menders, fishwives and the like, celebrate – a sense of community? The film does little elsewhere to support such an idea. The function of the equally elaborate 'Who Will Buy?', which brings together tradespersons, gentlemen, a military band and much else, is equally unclear. Despite the razzle-dazzle, they contribute to an overall rather academic feel to the film, despite its popularity. JH

Dir: Carol Reed; **Prod**: John Woolf; **Scr**: Vernon Harris, adapted from the stage musical, book, music and lyrics by Lionel Bart, itself adapted from Charles Dickens's *Oliver Twist*; **DOP**: Oswald Morris (colour); **Song Music/Lyrics**: Lionel Bart; **Musical Dir**: Johnny Green; **Art**: John Box, Terence Marsh; **Choreog**: Onna White; **Main Cast**: Ron Moody, Shani Wallis, Oliver Reed, Harry Secombe, Mark Lester, Jack Wild; **Prod Co**: Romulus Films/Warwick Film Productions.

On the Town
USA, 1949 – 98 mins
Gene Kelly, Stanley Donen

When Arthur Freed suddenly revived the idea of adapting the 1944 stage show *On the Town* (which had been heartily disliked at the time by Louis B. Mayer and other MGM executives) and offered Gene Kelly and Stanley Donen their first chance to direct, the project drew back together key personnel from *Take Me Out to the Ball Game* (1949), which was opening just as *On the Town* started shooting. Kelly, Frank Sinatra and Jules Munshin became the three sailors, with Betty Garrett cast again as Sinatra's girlfriend. Betty Comden and Adolph Green, who had written the songs for *Take Me Out to the Ball Game* with Roger Edens, were now persuaded to make the radical changes Freed required to the stage version of *On the Town* they had written with Leonard Bernstein, dropping many of the numbers and working with Edens to write new ones. Much of Bernstein's music also went in the process; what emerged was a wholesale reimagining for the screen of the show's story of three sailors on one day's shore leave in New York City.

The film announces itself with one of the most striking opening sequences in any musical. On the Brooklyn dockside, a solitary worker sings 'I Feel Like I'm Not out of Bed Yet' as he ambles to his crane past a US navy destroyer. It is 6.00 a.m. – the ship's whistle blows and sailors race down the gangplank. Three of them, Gabey (Kelly), Chip (Sinatra) and Ozzie (Munshin), burst into 'New York, New York (It's a Wonderful Town)' and the number continues in an upbeat montage of the sailors serenading the city in multiple New York settings (very unusually for a musical of its time, the whole sequence was shot on location). Release from work produces an explosion of pent-up energy that then powers the film's action: three innocents abroad in New York encountering three young women; the episodic narrative and frequent musical numbers played out across the city; everything intensified by the 24-hour time span.

Jules Munshin, Frank Sinatra, Gene Kelly, Ann Miller, Betty Garrett, 'Prehistoric Man'

The film celebrates the modern city in a way no Hollywood musical had previously done, though this is a singularly benign vision of the metropolis. On the one hand, it can accommodate the comforting familiarity of small-town American values: vivaciously wholesome but anodyne Ivy Smith (Vera-Ellen), whom Gabey pursues as his dream of New York glamour, turns out to be from his own hometown, and when they dance together for the first time, it is to share their nostalgic memories of 'Main Street'. A much more unusual – and much more vibrant – view of female sexuality is joyously embodied by New Yorkers Hildy (Betty Garrett) and Claire (Ann Miller). Hildy throws herself at Chip (Frank Sinatra) when they first meet, and one of the film's great numbers is their battling duet in her taxi cab ('Come up to My Place') as Chip tries to focus on sightseeing while Hildy has other things on her mind. Exhilarating in a different way is Ann Miller's extraordinary number

('Prehistoric Man') in the Anthropology Museum, when Claire, whose guardian hoped her studies of anthropology would distract her from men, is enraptured by Ozzie's resemblance to 'pithecanthropus erectus'.

   The film ends as it began, with the crane driver reprising his lament. But now Gabey, Chip and Ozzie are back on board, the three women on the dockside waving them off. As the 6.00 a.m. whistle blows, a new batch of sailors rush down the gangplank and three of them burst into 'New York, New York'. DP

Dir: Gene Kelly, Stanley Donen; **Prod**: Arthur Freed; **Scr**: Adolph Green, Betty Comden, from the musical play, book by Adolph Green and Betty Comden, from an idea by Jerome Robbins, music by Leonard Bernstein, lyrics by Adolph Green, Betty Comden, Leonard Bernstein; **DOP**: Harold Rosson (colour); **Song Music/Lyrics**: Leonard Bernstein, Roger Edens; Adolph Green, Betty Comden; **Musical Dir**: Lennie Hayton; **Choreog**: Gene Kelly, Stanley Donen; **Art**: Cedric Gibbons, Jack Martin Smith; **Main Cast**: Gene Kelly, Frank Sinatra, Jules Munshin, Vera-Ellen, Betty Garrett, Ann Miller, Florence Bates, Alice Pearce; **Prod Co**: Metro-Goldwyn-Mayer.

One from the Heart
USA, 1982 – 107 mins
Francis Ford Coppola

Like his fellow 'movie brats', Francis Ford Coppola has aspired to rework classical Hollywood's major genres. One of Coppola's first mainstream movies was a musical comedy (*Finian's Rainbow*, 1968, starring Fred Astaire, no less). Like Martin Scorsese's *New York, New York**, *One from the Heart* is both a musical and a critique of the genre. In outline, *One from the Heart* is familiar romantic musical comedy material: a Las Vegas couple, Frannie (Teri Garr) and Hank (Frederic Forrest), after five years together, doubt their feelings for each other and reflect on what they want from life; both seek solace and excitement with new partners, before reuniting. Coppola makes some less familiar choices in dealing with such material. Although the film is full of music and songs, neither of the main characters sings and, apart from a big 4th of July street number which ends very abruptly, there is virtually no dancing. The film's gritty, bluesy songs, written by Tom Waits and sung by Waits and Crystal Gayle, provide a kind of internal commentary, almost a chorus, for the action. Early on, for example, Frannie and Hank appear on screen to engage with each other while the accompanying song ('Picking up after You') emphasises boredom and dissatisfaction.

Frannie, a travel agency worker, and Hank, a mechanic, are sympathetic enough, though 'ordinary' and not specially self-aware – although, reversing convention, he is wedded to (somewhat makeshift) house and home while she wants to wander. The combination of Waits's and Gayle's voices – Waits gravelly and growly, Gayle dreamy, romantic and bitter-sweet – already suggests a certain incompatibility between the characters. Their status as characters in a musical is perhaps encapsulated by Hank's protestation that if he could sing, he would sing to get Frannie back, but he can't (though, in desperation, he tries).

One from the Heart was made entirely on Zoetrope's sound stages. The film begins theatrically with curtains opening and ends with them closing. Many scenes achieve a 'studio' reality look, but in the central sections of the film, as the characters live out their almost fantastical trysts – Frannie with her Latin waiter-cum-pianist (Raul Julia), Hank with hopelessly exotic circus girl Leila (Nastassia Kinski) – the film's look changes. Using theatrical scrims which allow disparate spaces to merge, highly stylised lighting and other devices, Coppola emphasises through his *mise en scène* the flimsy artifice of his sets, his story and of Las Vegas itself. *One from the Heart* ends with Frannie abandoning her escape and the couple reunited, but if this is a 'happy end', as the songs suggest, then it is so only in the unromantic sense that the characters become

Teri Garr and the Las Vegas set

reconciled to the tensions, dissatisfactions and frustrations which were so evident at the start and which remain unresolved.

The film's reputation owes less to its relationship to the genre than to the contexts of its production. After the excesses of *Apocalypse Now* (1979), *One from the Heart* was intended as a small movie with a $2 million budget. It ended up costing $28 million, and grossed less than $600,000, pushing Zoetrope Studios – Coppola's grandiose attempt to recreate something like the conditions of the old studio system – into bankruptcy. Coppola has suggested that most of his 1980s/90s films were undertaken to pay off debts. One reason for the film's escalating costs was its pioneering of new video technology, in which scenes were filmed simultaneously on celluloid and video, making possible immediate decision-making and editing. JH

Dir: Francis Ford Coppola; **Prod**: Gray Frederickson, Fred Roos; **Scr**: Armyan Bernstein, Francis Ford Coppola, from a story by Bernstein; **DOP**: Vittorio Storaro, Ronald V. Garcia (colour); **Song Music/Lyrics**: Tom Waits (sung by Tom Waits, Crystal Gale); **Musical Dir**: Bob Alcivar; **Art**: Dean Tavoularis, Angelo Graham; **Main Cast**: Frederic Forrest, Teri Garr, Raul Julia, Nastassia Kinski, Lainie Kazan, Harry Dean Stanton; **Prod Co**: Zoetrope Studios.

One Hour with You
USA, 1932 – 80 mins
Ernst Lubitsch, George Cukor

One Hour with You was Ernst Lubitsch's final musical at Paramount (though production began with George Cukor directing). Reuniting Maurice Chevalier and Jeanette MacDonald three years after their success in *The Love Parade**, it is a musical remake of Lubitsch's 1924 film, *The Marriage Circle*, the title of which points to the sophisticated comedy about marriage that is the heart of the movie. Like other musicals that draw on the operetta tradition, *One Hour with You* is set among European high society, although here the social setting is the prosperous Parisian bourgeoisie rather than the aristocracy of a fictitious state.

What Paris stands for here is made clear in the film's opening scene, a police briefing (the first of several rhyming talk-songs) about the influx of springtime visitors, and the officer leaves us in no doubt what they come for: at night, he declares, the cafés are empty but the parks are full. Policemen are dispatched to clear amorous couples from the shrubbery and we meet André Bertier (Chevalier) and Colette (MacDonald) locked in an embrace – though they claim, to the policeman's disbelief, to be a married couple. In an elegant apartment, it is clear from their playfully suggestive interaction that they are heading for the bedroom, when Chevalier turns to the camera and challenges *our* suspicious minds: 'Believe me, we are married'. He will address us repeatedly during the course of the film, increasingly with direct appeals to men in the audience ('What would you do? That's what I did too').

Where *The Love Parade* moves through courtship into marriage and its vicissitudes, *One Hour with You* follows a married couple through dramas of temptation, infidelity and doubt. André and Colette celebrate their passion in the song 'What a Little Thing Like a Wedding Ring Can Do', but when Colette's old friend Mitzi (Genevieve Tobin) makes a determined play for André, he struggles to avoid entanglement ('Oh,

That Mitzi!') and is finally unable to resist. Colette, meanwhile, suspects that André is involved with a different woman and is herself being pursued by the devoted but hopelessly unsexy Adolph (Charles Ruggles). Lubitsch stages many of the comic complications around the Berthiers' dinner party, including the central characters changing partners on the dance floor, each couple taking up lines from the title number, 'One Hour with You'.

The paralleling of husband and wife in marital indiscretion has its limits, though. Adolph is largely a figure of fun and we see how little Colette is attracted to him. She never responds to Adolph's kisses, while André certainly responds to Mitzi. We do not see André and Mitzi in her apartment after the party but are left in little doubt about what has taken place. Yet at the end of the film, Colette claims parity, as though she was equally culpable ('An Adolph for a Mitzi'), and for the first time joins André in a direct appeal to the spectator ('What would you do?'), before their final kiss. The fine plea for tolerance enshrines the double standard.

Much of the pleasure of these films comes from Lubitsch's skilful control of tone – playfulness about the pleasures and temptations of sex coupled with knowing appeals to the spectator's complicity and worldliness. Such relative openness about sexuality was no longer possible after 1934 and the introduction of a more rigorous version of the industry's code of self-regulation. As was common practice in early sound days, the film was simultaneously made in a French-language version, with Lili Damita replacing Genevieve Tobin as Mitzi. DP

Dir: Ernst Lubitsch, George Cukor (uncredited); **Prod**: Ernst Lubitsch; **Scr**: Samson Raphaelson, from Lothar Schmidt's play *Only a Dream*; **DOP**: Victor Milner (b&w); **Song Music/Lyrics**: Oscar Strauss/Leo Robin; Richard A. Whiting/Leo Robin; **Musical Dir**: Nathaniel W. Finston; **Art**: Hans Dreier; **Main Cast**: Maurice Chevalier, Jeanette MacDonald, Genevieve Tobin, Charles Ruggles, Roland Young; **Prod Co**: Paramount.

100 Men and a Girl
USA, 1937 – 84 mins
Henry Koster

It's always a salutary reminder of the nature of the movie business and its audiences that the most successful films at the box office are so often not those which come to be valued and seen as characteristic in retrospect. In the mid-1930s, Shirley Temple (see *The Littlest Rebel**), Deanna Durbin and Jeanette MacDonald and Nelson Eddy (see *Naughty Marietta**) were bigger box-office draws than Astaire and Rogers (see *Flying Down to Rio**, *The Gay Divorcee**, *Top Hat**, *Swing Time**) and the Warner Bros. musicals choreographed by Busby Berkeley (see *42nd Street**, *Gold Diggers of 1933**, *Footlight Parade**). Of course, the Astaire–Rogers and Berkeley movies now look innovative, modern, 'smart', more self-aware, while the Temple, Durbin, Jeanette MacDonald–Nelson Eddy films look old-fashioned and sentimental (though, strikingly, they all still command loyal fan bases).

Canadian-born Deanna Durbin was fourteen at the time of her debut feature, *Three Smart Girls* (1936), whose box-office success supposedly saved Universal Studios from bankruptcy. The film established the persona Durbin worked with during the 1930s: a bubbly, gushing, selfless adolescent in ankle socks, her hair often tied with a bow on top, hovering between childhood and womanhood. In 1938, Durbin shared the Academy's special Juvenile Award with Mickey Rooney, for 'their significant contribution in bringing to the screen the spirit and personification of youth, and as juvenile players setting a high standard of ability and achievement'. Durbin's later attempts to establish a properly grown-up career in the 1940s never really took off, and she retired in 1948.

Durbin's characters, like Temple's, often bring people together and bridge social divisions. In *100 Men and a Girl*, Durbin plays Patsy, teenage daughter of an unemployed musician (Adolphe Menjou) who, along with many others like him, is desperate for work. Patsy persuades upper-class socialites to back the musicians and doggedly pursues Leopold Stokowski until he agrees to conduct them. This typical Depression-era tale lacks the bite of, say, *My Man Godfrey* (1936); despite their infantile antics, it is never quite clear what the film wants us to think of the wealthy upper class. Durbin herself is winningly charming; her sweet soprano voice defines the character and Durbin's success with audiences. Her repertoire extends from standards to classical arias, and *100 Men and a Girl* comes across in many ways as an 'improving' entertainment for its audience: early on, Durbin sings two popular songs ('It's Raining Sunbeams' and 'A Heart That's Free'), but as the film progresses, her vocal contributions become exclusively classical. Her rendition of Mozart's 'Alleluja' proves a turning point in the narrative, and the film climaxes with her singing the Drinking Song from Verdi's *La Traviata*.

Durbin was an ideal vehicle for 1930s attempts to popularise classical music. Producer Joe Pasternak (who later produced *Anchors Aweigh** and several operetta musical films at MGM) made this a special feature of his productions, and conductor Leopold Stokowski was well known for his commitment to widening the appeal of classical music (most notably in his collaboration with Disney on *Fantasia*, 1940). Stokowski's carefully constructed (though somewhat pompous) self-image as the slightly eccentric, almost other-worldly European musical genius is given full rein here.   JH

Dir: Henry Koster; **Prod**: Joe Pasternak, Charles R. Rogers; **Scr**: Bruce Manning, Charles Kenyon, James Mulhauser, from an idea by Hans Kraly; **DOP**: Joseph Valentine (b&w); **Song Music/Lyrics**: Frederick Hollander/Sam Coslow; Alfred G. Robyn/Thomas Railey, *et al*.; **Music**: Tchaikovsky, Berlioz, Wagner, Mozart, Liszt, Verdi; **Art**: John Harkrider; **Main Cast**: Deanna Durbin, Adolphe Menjou, Alice Brady, Eugene Pallette, Mischa Auer, Leopold Stokowski; **Prod Co**: Universal.

Opera Jawa
Indonesia/Austria/Netherlands/Sweden/UK, 2006 – 120 mins
Garin Nugroho

Opera Jawa (*Requiem from Java*), as it announces at its conclusion, is 'a requiem for the victims of violence and natural disasters throughout the world', and especially in Java. The film was commissioned for Vienna's 2006 'New Crowned Hope' festival celebrating the 250th birthday of W. A. Mozart, for which film-makers and other contemporary artists were commissioned to respond to the spirit of innovation of the composer's last works, *The Magic Flute* (magic and transformation), *La Clemenza di Tito* (truth and reconciliation) and *Requiem* (ceremonies for the dead).

    Opera Jawa is an adaptation, in a modern setting, of a story from the Sanskrit *Ramayana* in which King Rama's wife Sita is abducted by his rival Ravana. Here, Rama and Sita become the poor potter Setio (Martinus Miroto) and his wife Siti (Artika Sari Devi), who formerly portrayed Rama and Sita in dance theatre, while Ravana becomes rich butcher and local tyrant Ludiro (Eko Supriyanto), who tries to seduce Siti. While Setio is away selling pottery, Siti is sexually aroused and almost succumbs to Ludiro's blandishments. Setio, meanwhile, suspects his wife's fidelity and is driven to distraction by jealousy, finally killing her while subjecting her to the test of fire. A parallel narrative strand shows the exploited local peasants taking arms against and killing Ludiro.

    Garin Nugroho's film combines traditional and contemporary narratives and dance and musical forms, along with installation art (including Antony Gormley-like figures). Both executive producers, Simon Field and Keith Griffiths, have long associations with avant-garde film. As all this suggests, *Opera Jawa* is a very challenging work for western audiences. This is particularly true of the film's mixing of modes. Co-existing with the film's extensive naturalism are its equally extensive stylisation and symbolism. In the film's vision, everyday, natural actions merge seamlessly with events and actions taking place in the imagination. Thus, Setio's rejection of Siti in the marital bed becomes a dramatically stylised dance expressive of sexual frustration and desire; Siti no longer dances professionally but her sense of her self and her sexuality are inevitably expressed via striking dance moves; Setio, racked with jealousy, 'dances' in, and then with, a woman's mask; Ludiro's tortured relationship with his mother is expressed in an extraordinary, stylised dance in which he seems to endeavour to return to her womb. Nugroho's invention is not confined to dance, and other visual ideas – like Setio's attempt to mould Siti on his potter's wheel, or the scarlet silk 'carpet' leading Siti to Ludiro's house – are equally striking.

'No film has looked or sounded like this before', claims Tony Rayns (2007), who offers a cogent exposition, particularly in relation to the film's paralleling of Ludiro's tyranny over the village and his desire for 'ownership' of Siti. But one wonders just how 'available' his reading is. Film reviewers tended to be awed by the film's startling imagery and intrigued by its exoticism, but at a loss to make much sense of it. Perhaps the personal and the political story are insufficiently connected or out of balance, or perhaps the film's particular mixes of traditional and modern, naturalism and stylisation, are too eclectic or idiosyncratic. Certainly, the film poses questions about who it is aimed at: popular Indonesian audiences familiar with Sanskrit mythology and traditional Javanese art forms might struggle with the film's more experimental elements; western art cinema audiences might find the experimental elements more accessible but be flummoxed by the film's more local and traditional elements. JH

Dir/Prod: Garin Nugroho; **Scr**: Garin Nugroho, Aramantono; **DOP**: Gay Hian Teoh (colour); **Music**: Rahayu Supanggah; **Art**: Nanang Rakhmat Hidayat; **Main Cast**: Artika Sari Devi, Martinus Miroto, Eko Supriyanto, Retno Maruti; **Prod Co**: New Crowned Hope/SET Film Workshop/Visions Sud Est.

Original Cast Album: Company
USA, 1970 – 58 mins
D. A. Pennebaker

Since the 1940s, record companies have regularly produced audio 'original cast recordings' of Broadway and London shows. Decca's pioneering 1943 original cast recording of *Oklahoma!* sold over a million 78 rpm disc sets. Though invariably recorded in specialist studios rather than during theatrical performances, original cast recordings put on permanent record the necessarily ephemeral live performance of a show's songs, a 'souvenir' of the show and a welcome additional income stream. D. A. Pennebaker's film *Original Cast Album: Company* documents the original cast recordings for Stephen Sondheim's 1970 show *Company*. Though a documentary film, not a 'musical', it is of enormous interest to anyone interested in musical theatre.

Pennebaker and Richard Leacock helped lead the North American 'direct cinema' revolution in the early 1960s. New camera and sound-recording technology seemed to allow documentary film-makers to be (in Leacock's phrase) 'simply observers' of events, without the pre-planning typical of earlier documentaries. Celebrated early direct cinema films, like *Primary* (1960), explored political and social subjects, but Pennebaker soon found it easier to finance musical events, like the Bob Dylan film *Dont Look Back* (1966) and the festival film *Monterey Pop* (1968). *Original Cast Album: Company* was a commission, the intended pilot for a television series.

Company opened on Broadway in February 1970. Its distinctive 'concept' rather than conventionally narrative structure – character vignettes focused around the character Bobby's thirty-fifth birthday – helped win a clutch of Tony awards, and it ran for 705 performances. Original cast recordings aim to be as technically perfect as possible: as one of the actors puts it, unlike a live performance, 'this is the definitive, the end-all and the be-all of this song'. To this pressure were added inevitable time and finance constraints: the costs of hiring a recording studio and technicians and assembling the cast were high, so the album was recorded (with one exception) over a marathon continuous session. In addition, original cast recordings were invariably made at the start of a show's run: *Company* was recorded on the first Sunday – usually a day off – after opening night.

Pennebaker–Leacock direct cinema thrived on such conditions: its subjects were focused on working and therefore less aware of intrusive cameras and tape recorders, and the film-makers' central interest is observing a group of professionals working under pressure. The film foregrounds the technical and creative work of both the actors and those whose work is 'invisible' or taken for granted during live performance (including the musicians). The actors themselves are partly in role but much more preoccupied than they would be on stage with the intricate mechanics of lyrics and music, so the complexity of Sondheim's songs comes across here more than in the 'flow' of stage performance. It is fascinating to observe Sondheim, a notorious perfectionist, working with the actors to correct pronunciation or tweak musical notes, and watch errors and repeat takes on technically difficult songs like 'Getting Married Today' (Beth Howland) and 'Another Hundred People' (Pamela Myers).

The 'crisis structure' that Stephen Mamber (1974) argued generated narrative tension in direct cinema films informs the close observation of Dean Jones making it through 'Being Alive', a song about married life, to applause from the other actors: under pressure from an ongoing messy divorce, Jones had wanted to leave the show but had agreed to open it and then contribute to the cast recording. Similarly, at 4.30 a.m. after fifteen hours in the studio, Elaine Stritch struggles to get 'Ladies Who Lunch' right; finally, everyone gives up, but in a coda she returns the next day, alone, and nails it. JH

Dir: D. A. Pennebaker; **Prod**: Chris Dalrymple, Delia Doherty, Peter Hansen, Daniel Melnick; **Cinematography**: Jim Desmond, Richard Leacock, D. A. Pennebaker (colour); **Song Music/Lyrics**: Stephen Sondheim; **Musical Dir**: Harold Hastings; **Main Cast**: Barbara Barrie, Charles Braswell, Beth Howland, Dean Jones, Charles Kimbrough, Pamela Myers, Harold Prince, Thomas Z. Shepherd, Stephen Sondheim, Elaine Stritch; **Prod Co**: Pennebaker Associates Inc.

The Pajama Game
USA, 1957 – 102 mins
George Abbott, Stanley Donen

In his seminal essay 'Entertainment and Utopia', Richard Dyer (1977) argued that entertainment – particularly the musical – provided qualities of energy, abundance, intensity, transparency and community which responded to issues such as poverty, alienated labour, monotony and social fragmentation. Thus, what many have seen as the 'escapism' of the musical genre figures instead as a kind of utopianism, both in narrative outcomes (heterosexual romance, happy endings) and in non-representational elements like colour, texture, movement, melody and camerawork.

The Pajama Game, unusually for a musical, is set in a factory. Its workers spend their days cutting and sewing pyjamas under pressure ('Racing with the Clock'), with a demanding manager and an exploitative boss, and are demanding a wage increase ('$7\frac{1}{2}$ *Cents*'). Playing out the dynamic suggested by Dyer, when the workers go on their union-organised annual picnic, the extended production number 'Once-A-Year-Day', staged and shot in exteriors, generates a palpable sense of release. Even the 'Independence Day' number in *Summer Holiday** looks gently sedate beside the explosion of energy here. Bob Fosse's choreography and Stanley Donen's *mise en scène* combine some degree of order in the polka-based ensemble dancing with a frenzy of crazy movements and gestures which only make sense as the shaking off of constraint. Something of the same effect is achieved in the film's most quintessentially Fosse sequence, 'Steam Heat' (very like 'Who's Got the Pain?' in *Damn Yankees*, George Abbott and Donen's 1958 follow-up musical), all staccato, angular movements, floorwork and hats.

Broadway shows were (and remain) a major source of Hollywood musicals, the more so as the golden period of the 1930s–50s neared its end. Though Broadway success would, it was hoped, guarantee movie success, it was common practice nevertheless to replace a show's leading

Bob Fosse's 'Steam Heat' number, with Carol Haney (centre)

players and other personnel and to modify story and music. *The Pajama Game* was something of an exception: though Broadway lead Janis Paige as Babe, the union grievance convener, was replaced by Doris Day – by then a major recording artist and star of both musical (for example, *Calamity Jane**) and non-musical films (as well as combining musical and straight roles in the biopic *Love Me or Leave Me**) – baritone John Raitt, primarily a television and Broadway star (*Carousel*, 1945, for example), was retained as aggressively ambitious new manager Sid, along with most of the main cast. There were prior discussions about Frank Sinatra (who had starred with Day in *Young at Heart*, 1954) for the male lead; no doubt the movie would feel very different with Sinatra instead of the rather stiff Raitt.

Musical shows and films, perhaps even more than straight dramas, are highly collaborative. Much of the popularity of *The Pajama Game* was down to its plentiful Richard Adler/Jerry Ross hit songs ('I'm Not at All in Love', 'Hey There', 'Small Talk', 'There Once Was a Man'). Co-director/producer George Abbott had produced and directed the show on Broadway and supposedly ensured some fidelity to the original. Stanley Donen, by then a respected film director and choreographer both with Gene Kelly (see *Cover Girl**, *On the Town**, *Singin' in the Rain**, *It's Always Fair Weather**) and on his own (*Royal Wedding*, 1951, *Seven Brides for Seven Brothers**, *Funny Face**), took primary responsibility for directing the movie, though some critics felt the film (not withstanding the opened-out 'Once-A-Year-Day') was *too* close to, or too static a reproduction of, the stage show. In addition, *The Pajama Game* was Bob Fosse's first major Broadway choreography, though his distinctive dance style had already registered in films like *Kiss Me Kate** and *My Sister Eileen* (1955). JH

Dir/Prod: George Abbott, Stanley Donen; **Scr**: George Abbott, Richard Bissell, adapted from their Broadway show, directed by Abbott and Jerome Robbins, based on Bissell's novel, *7$^{1}/_{2}$ Cents*; **DOP**: Harry Stradling (colour); **Song Music/Lyrics**: Richard Adler, Jerry Ross; **Musical Dir**: Nelson Riddle, Buddy Bregman; **Choreog**: Bob Fosse; **Art Dir**: Malcolm Bert; **Main Cast**: Doris Day, John Raitt, Carol Haney, Eddie Foy Jr, Reta Shaw, Barbara Nichols, Thelma Pelish; **Prod Co**: Warner Bros.

Pakeezah
India, 1972 – 175 mins
Kamal Amrohi

As *Pakeezah* (*Pure Heart* or *Pure One*) opens, the courtesan Nargis (Meena Kumari), just married to high-born Shahabuddin (Ashok Kumar), is rejected by his family and flees to self-imposed exile, dying nine months later, after giving birth to a daughter, Sahibjaan. Seventeen years later, Sahibjaan (also played by Kumari) has been schooled in the courtesan arts of poetry, dance and seduction (very different from the common prostitute in *Pyaasa**). In a chance encounter on the train journey from Lucknow to Delhi, a stranger admires the sleeping Sahibjaan's feet, and the anonymous poetic note he leaves becomes an obsession. Again by chance, Sahibjaan later discovers the stranger, who is Salim (Raaj Kumar), Shahabuddin's nephew. Salim courts Sahibjaan but, fearing the shame she would bring on him, she flees back to the *kotha* (salon/brothel). When Salim asks Sahibjaan to dance at his arranged wedding, the truth about Nargis and Sahibjaan comes out and their honour is redeemed when Sahibjaan is carried from the *kotha* in a bride's palanquin.

Kamal Amrohi's bold approach has all the characteristics of outright melodrama in its excessive *mise en scène*, its use of chance to propel the narrative, its expressive music and poetic lyrics and its employment of motifs like the passing train and the caged bird. There is little subtle or buried about Amrohi's wonderful images: in a celebrated scene after Sahibjaan returns to the *kotha* a broken woman ('every courtesan is a corpse'), for example, she compares herself to the broken kite stranded in the branches of a tree – a self-conscious and explicit effect, but very powerful nevertheless.

The courtesan narrative has several attractions for film-makers: it looks back at a now vanished but vital part of Mughal Indian culture; it makes possible a discourse about women's roles in society – courtesans have a certain status and independence but are nevertheless 'fallen' women, trapped in their profession, with men their only possible saviours; like the backstage musical, it offers ample opportunities for the song and dance performances, both traditional *kathak* and *mujra* and modern *filmi*, central to both courtesan culture and popular Indian cinema. Most of the film's song and dance sequences are performances by Sahibjaan/Kumari (though, as always, they feature playback singers – here Lata Mangeshkar – and, at times, also a dance double), notably 'Inhi logon ne' ('These People … Have Snatched My Veil, My Pride'), 'Thade rahiyo'('Wait for Me'), 'Aaj hum apni' ('Tonight I Wait for My Prayers to

Meena Kumari

Be Answered') and 'Chalte, Chalte' ('In the Journey of Life').
These 'numbers' explore some of the contradictions of the courtesan's
position: Sahibjaan performs, seductively, for a paying audience (both in
the *kotha* and in the cinema); she is objectified, on display, but her
coquettish, knowing delivery implies also a measure of control.
These performances are played out as if in real time and space, whereas
'Mausam hai aashiqana' ('Love Is in the Air'), following her encounter
with Salim, takes on a dreamlike quality, floating free of the constraints
of time and space, a characteristic feature of popular cinema songs
designed to encapsulate a subjective ecstatic moment.

    The film's legendary status owes something to its production and
reception. Planned by Amrohi and Kumari while still married in the late
1950s, the marriage was breaking up when shooting began in 1964 and
the partly shot film was abandoned, and only restarted in the late 1960s,
when they were persuaded to reconcile sufficiently to continue, though
Kumari was already very ill. Though the film was not an immediate hit, it
became so when Kumari died three weeks after its premiere.   JH

Dir/Prod/Scr: Kamal Amrohi; **DOP**: Josef Wirsching (colour); **Music**: Ghulam Mohammed,
Naushad; **Lyrics**: Kaifi Azmi, Kaif Bhopali, Majrooh Sultanpuri; **Playback**: Lata Mangeshkar,
Mohammed Rafi; **Choreog**: Lachchu Maharaj, Gauri Shanker; **Art**: N. B. Kulkarni; **Main
Cast**: Ashok Kumar, Meena Kumari, Raaj Kumar, Veena, D. K. Sapru, Kamal Kapoor; **Prod
Co**: Mahal Pictures/Sangeeta Enterprises.

Les Parapluies de Cherbourg
France/West Germany, 1964 – 91 mins
Jacques Demy

Musicals were not a major genre in French postwar cinema (though there were exotic vehicles designed to showcase popular singers like Luis Mariano) and Jacques Demy's *Les Parapluies de Cherbourg* offered a completely new kind of film musical, just as the *nouvelle vague* in general was reinventing other film conventions. The film's poster promised a film '*en musique, en couleurs, en chanté*', and delivered handsomely on each promise. Most notably it was '*en chanté*' – literally 'in sung', but also '*enchanté*' as in magical – in many ways more like opera or operetta than classical musicals: all the dialogue is sung (the actors all mime), from declarations of love to enquiries about the required grade of petrol. *Les Parapluies* was both a critical and commercial success, but for many purists, the lack of break between spoken dialogue and song disqualifies it from being classed as a 'musical', and it is in many ways *sui generis*. Operetta, though, was one of the major influences on film musical conventions and the overall effect here is akin to operatic recitative, with the occasional more song-like melody (notably 'Mon amour, je t'attendrai toute ma vie', the international hit 'I Will Wait for You') emerging from the continuous, thematically structured music.

As so often with melodrama, the three-part story (Departure, Absence, Return), covering a five-year period, is suitably banal: young lovers Geneviève (Catherine Deneuve) and Guy (Nino Castelnuovo) are separated when Guy is called up for military service and sent to war in Algeria; Geneviève promises to wait for him but discovers she is pregnant; with no news from Guy, and under maternal pressure, she agrees to marry rich diamond merchant Roland Cassard (Marc Michel, playing the same character from Demy's 1961 *Lola*); Guy returns and, after a period of painful adjustment, settles down with his secret admirer Madeleine (Ellen Farner); together, Guy and Madeleine have a child and

Nino Castelnuovo, Catherine Deneuve

run an Esso service station, to which, one snowy Christmas Eve, the now wealthy Geneviève pulls up with her daughter …

It's a brief, chance encounter, at once low-key and high melodrama. Paths cross, diverge, recross and life continues, which is not really how 'musicals' are supposed to end. Both characters feel the pull of the past but Guy's petit-bourgeois lifestyle and compromise happiness suggest a kind of closure, while Geneviève, comfortably bourgeois in her smart coiffure, fur coat and black Mercedes, seems regretful. As they part, Demy's camera cranes up into the falling snow and Michel Legrand's score soars to its highest pitch, before subsiding as the film ends. Rarely has '*melos*' propelled 'drama' so powerfully.

As the poster announced, *Les Parapluies* is also '*en couleurs*', one of the first *nouvelle vague* colour films, making stylised use of bold, saturated primary and pastel colours for both location and interior scenes: Demy and designer Bernard Evein were not averse to repainting bits of Cherbourg to achieve their effects. But, paradoxically, stylisation co-exists here with a rootedness in a 'realism' of story and place, and Demy was right to regret the reverse track in which Guy and Geneviève start moving, as it were, without moving (prompting the question: what on earth are they standing on?).

Demy's film offers no hostages to fortune: one of Guy's workmates reveals that he doesn't like opera ('all that singing') and prefers cinema, while Geneviève's mother tells her that people only die of love in the movies. Demy's next film, *Les Demoiselles de Rochefort**, was much more like a classical musical comedy, but he returned to a more strictly operatic form in *Une Chambre en ville* (1982), centred round a workers' strike.

Dir/Scr: Jacques Demy; **Prod**: Mag Bodard; **DOP**: Jean Rabier (colour); **Song Music/Lyrics**: Michel Legrand/Jacques Demy; **Art**: Bernard Evein; **Main Cast**: Catherine Deneuve, Nino Castelnuovo, Anne Vernon, Mireille Perrey, Marc Michel, Ellen Farner; **Prod Co**: Parc Film/Madeleine Films/Beta Films.

Pas sur la bouche
France/Switzerland, 2003 – 117 mins
Alain Resnais

The recent career of Alain Resnais – once, with *Hiroshima mon amour* (1959), *L'Année dernière à Marienbad* (1961) and *Muriel* (1963), the epitome of the high-art film director – has puzzled many commentators. The intensely cinematic-cum-literary qualities of those early features have been replaced, in his seventies and eighties, by an attraction to popular theatre and the musical – an attraction shared by Chantal Akerman (*Golden Eighties**) and François Ozon (*8 femmes**). *Smoking/No Smoking* (1993) and *Private Fears in Public Places* (2006) were both adaptations of Alan Ayckbourn plays; *On connaît la chanson* (*The Same Old Song*, 1997), in homage to Dennis Potter television plays like *Pennies from Heaven* (1981) and *The Singing Detective* (1986), featured actors lip-synching to French popular songs.

Pas sur la bouche (*Not on the Lips*) is a largely faithful adaptation of a 1925 French light operetta-cum-bedroom farce. Its ensemble cast is stereotypical for such material: the trailer announces 'the love-struck one, the frivolous wife, the schemer, the suitor, the husband, the ex' – respectively, Huguette (Audrey Tautou), Gilberte (Sabine Azéma), Gilberte's unmarried sister Arlette (Isabelle Nanty), Charley (Jalil Lespert), Gilberte's husband Georges (Pierre Arditi), Eric Thomson (Lambert Wilson). As is the way with farce, young Huguette is pursuing pretentious artist Charley, who is pursuing the flirtatious but faithful Gilberte, who needs to stop Georges (who believes that 'a woman belongs to the man who visited her first') discovering she was formerly married to American businessman Eric, who arrives to conclude a business deal (and abhors being kissed on the lips); Arlette, harbouring a secret passion for Eric, encourages romance between Huguette and Charley; and the ineffectual Faradel (Daniel Prévost) lends his bachelor pad for a series of final-act assignations. Needless to say, threatened transgressions fail to materialise: Gilberte remains with Georges, whose deluded faith is restored; Huguette lands Charley; and Arlette, pretending that *she* was Eric's wife, opens Eric to the pleasure of kissing on the lips.

As Ginette Vincendeau (2004) suggests, the film 'delivers the unadulterated pleasures of operetta in its post-World War I "light Parisian" musical comedy incarnation' and yet manages to be 'modern under its archaic veneer'. Certainly, Resnais accentuates theatricality, shooting entirely in studio sets, often in long takes, strictly preserving the play's three-act structure, emphasising the play-within-a-play and eliciting stylised performances (with actors lip-synching to playback recordings of their own singing voices). In the finale, the characters peep through the final curtain to express the hope, in song, that we enjoyed the show. Yet much here, like the opening sequence's overhead crane shot, is also very cinematic; while preserving the theatrical 'exit', Resnais does so very cinematically, via lap dissolves in which characters 'disappear'; and character asides to camera are both theatrical and cinematic (as in *One Hour with You**). Part of the film's feeling of modernity, despite its origins, comes from Resnais's adroitness in staging the musical sequences as natural extensions of dialogue. Numbers like 'Quatuor', in which Gilberte, Arlette, Georges and Eric explore the concept of first and second sexual partners in an appropriately confusing space of masking pillars and reflecting mirrors, or the title song, 'Pas sur la bouche', in which four young women try to kiss Eric, work as well as the best Hollywood musical sequences. But the film's feeling of antique modernity arises also from its sexual politics: its largely deluded male characters are led merry dances by the sympathetically knowing women. Sabine Azéma's performance, in particular, wonderfully hits just the right note for the film's 'knowingness and sophistication'. JH

Dir: Alain Resnais; **Prod**: Bruno Pésery; **Scr**: André Barde; **DOP**: Renato Berta (colour); **Song Music/Lyrics**: Maurice Yvain/André Barde; **Musical Dir**: Bruno Fontaine; **Art**: Jacques Saulnier; **Main Cast**: Sabine Azéma, Isabelle Nanty, Audrey Tautou, Pierre Arditi, Darry Cowl, Jalil Lespert, Daniel Prévost, Lambert Wilson; **Prod Co**: Arena Films/France 2 Cinéma/France 3 Cinéma/Arcade/Vega Film (with the participation of Canal+/CinéCinéma/Télévision Suisse-Romande).

The Pirate
USA, 1948 – 102 mins
Vincente Minnelli

The Pirate, set in a fantastical version of a nineteenth-century Caribbean island, begins with Manuela (Judy Garland) leafing through a picture book of pirates and yearning to be carried off by the infamous Macoco. It ends on a stage with Manuela partnering Serafin (Gene Kelly) – both dressed as clowns – in a wonderfully skilful slapstick performance of Cole Porter's 'Be a Clown' that concludes with them collapsing in uncontrollable laughter. Manuela's paradoxical journey, from dreaming of the pirate to embracing life as a performer, becomes the basis of one of MGM's most remarkable musicals.

The film was based on the 1942 Broadway comedy by S. N. Behrman, and Minnelli's team seized the possibilities for high artifice and stylisation inherent in a send-up of swashbuckling movies. The heightened style of both design and performance (its 'over-the-top-ness', as it is sometimes seen) perfectly suits the exhibitionist side of Gene Kelly's persona, though it may have contributed to the film's poor box-office performance (it lost over $2 million) and continues to divide viewers today. But it is integral to *The Pirate*'s unusual exploration of romantic comedy's central theme, the nature of the heterosexual couple, and to the film's finally rather rueful reflection on how to imagine equality between a man and woman.

The couple's mutual re-education begins in *The Pirate* with extremes: Manuela is absorbed in her dream of submission to Macoco, while Serafin's first number pushes the confidence and energy of Kelly's star persona into a spectacularly athletic display of sexual arrogance and narcissism – every girl he meets becomes 'Niña'. Garland's answering number, 'Mac the Black', erupts when Serafin hypnotises the unsuspecting Manuela as part of his show and instead of pouring out her love for him as he had intended, she completely rejects him in a riotous celebration of Macoco. Performing in her unconscious state,

Judy Garland, Gene Kelly, 'Mac the Black'

Manuela commands the space and the men in the audience with a tremendous display of sexual energy, as if her real fantasy is not to be carried off by the pirate but to become one. The power of dream that Thomas Elsaesser (1969/70; 1981) identifies as one of Minnelli's recurrent motifs here unleashes the transforming energy of Manuela's number. Now her dream must be redirected: if the couple's potential compatibility as performers is to be realised, Manuela must consciously accept her repressed talents and Serafin's narcissism must be demolished.

The ironic complication is that Don Pedro Vargas (Walter Slezak), the corpulent mayor to whom Manuela's aunt (Gladys Cooper) has betrothed her, turns out to be Macoco, retired from the sea with his ill-gotten gains. Serafin recognises Don Pedro, threatens to expose him and takes on the role of Macoco himself in order to win Manuela. In the pirate ballet, one of the most outrageously phallic sequences in Hollywood cinema, Serafin becomes Manuela's terrifyingly perfect fantasy image of the rampaging pirate.

Several twists later, with Serafin about to be hanged as Macoco but Manuela finally in the know, she embraces her identity as a performer and (now only pretending to be hypnotised) sings the intensely romantic 'Love of My Life', goading Don Pedro, consumed with jealousy, to blow his cover. The film could end there, with villain exposed and the couple united in an embrace after the woman has poured out her love. But it has a final twist. In a wonderfully bold coda, semi-detached from the narrative, the film rejects romantic love and its conventional gender disparities for a celebration of the asexual equality of the couple as clowns. DP

Dir: Vincente Minnelli; **Prod**: Arthur Freed; **Scr**: Albert Hackett, Frances Goodrich, *et al*., from S. N. Behrman's play, as produced by the Playwrights Company and the Theatre Guild; **DOP**: Harry Stradling (colour); **Song Music/Lyrics**: Cole Porter; **Musical Dir**: Lennie Hayton; **Choreog**: Robert Alton, Gene Kelly; **Art**: Cedric Gibbons, Jack Martin Smith; **Main Cast**: Judy Garland, Gene Kelly, Walter Slezak, Gladys Cooper; **Prod Co**: Metro-Goldwyn-Mayer.

Pyaasa
India, 1957 – 139 mins
Guru Dutt

In western cinema and theatre, 'musical' is usually shorthand for 'musical comedy'. In India, by contrast, music, song and dance, so integral to Indian culture, pervade films of various types which are not 'comedies' in the western sense (though most films incorporate comic characters). *Pyaasa* (variously translated as *Thirst*, *Eternal Thirst* or *The Thirsty One*), for example, is a high melodrama (which also features 'low' comedy song sequences with the ubiquitous Johnny Walker). However, the film's uses of *melos* are very different from those of Hollywood melodramas, where non-diegetic music is a crucial shaping force. Like Raj Kapoor, Guru Dutt often directed as well as starred in his films; both told love stories in which song and dance play vital roles, but both also wished to address the condition of India in their films. However, Dutt's favoured persona – the artist suffering for his art, disillusioned, down-and-out poet in *Pyaasa*, film director in *Kagaaz ke phool* (*Paper Flowers*, 1959) – is very different from Kapoor's (see *Shree 420**).

Dutt's currently high reputation rests partly on his skilled and innovative song 'picturisation'. Although the most common popular cinema song strategy is the straightforward lip-synching by stars to songs sung by star 'playback singers', in practice the playback system is very versatile. Although most of Vijay's (Dutt) songs/poems are lip-synched, in the opening sequence he is accompanied instead by a half-singing, half-reciting voice-over, with minimal musical accompaniment, suggesting a poem being composed or remembered, picturised on alternating close-ups of Vijay and images of nature. Not that 'standard' lip-synching detracts from the expressive potential of song sequences: in a justly celebrated sequence, using the dolly as well as lighting and framing to extraordinary effect, Dutt's camera follows the drunken yet clear-eyed Vijay through a street filled with brothels and fallen women ('these auction houses of pleasure') as he lip-synchs the bitter,

Guru Dutt: 'Jinhen naaz hai Hind par woh kahaan hain'

disillusioned 'Jinhen naaz hai Hind par woh kahaan hain' ('Those Who
Are Proud of This Land, Where Are They Now?') (playback by
Mohammed Rafi).

Similarly, as the prostitute Gulab (Waheeda Rehman) tries to lure
Vijay after their first encounter, lip-synching 'Jaane kya tu ne kahi, Jaane
kya maine suni' ('Who Knows What You Said, Who Knows What I
Heard?') (playback by Geeta Dutt), our response is complicated by the
realisation that Vijay is following her because she is singing one of his
lost poems/songs.

In the film's most accomplished song sequence, in which Gulab follows the melancholic Vijay home, a very different strategy is employed: Gulab's feelings are the focus of the picturisation, but neither character 'sings' or lip-synchs; music and song accompaniment are provided by an on-screen group of street musicians, led by singer Geeta Dutt (also the film's lead female playback singer). The devotional song 'Aaj sajan mohe ang lagaa lo' ('Today, Beloved, Hold Me in Your Embrace'), about the gods Radha and Krishna (whose relationship was finely poised between the sacred and the profane), is performed both on and off screen. Dutt organises the sequence so that Gulab appropriates and internalises the song's sentiments as she ascends the stairs to the roof terrace, with cutaways to the street singer, crane shots and subjective dolly shots for her actual and imagined movements towards Vijay, who is lost in reverie, unaware of her presence, before she hurries away in distress. The song's tension between physical and spiritual longing becomes the very centre of the scene and, indeed, the film as a whole. As Olivier Assayas (2004) put it, *Pyaasa* offers 'one of the most remarkable transpositions of poetry on screen'. JH

Dir/Prod: Guru Dutt; **Scr**: Abrar Alvi (dialogues), from Saratchandra's novel *Srikanta*; **DOP**: V. K. Murthy (b&w); **Music**: S. D. Burman; **Lyrics**: Sahir Ludhianvi; **Playback**: Geeta Dutt, Mohammed Rafi, Hemant Kumar; **Art**: Biren Naag; **Choreog**: Surya Kumar; **Main Cast**: Guru Dutt, Waheeda Rehman, Mala Sinha, Rehman, Johnny Walker; **Prod Co**: Guru Dutt Films.

The Rocky Horror Picture Show
UK, 1975 – 100 mins
Jim Sharman

The Rocky Horror Picture Show is a film adaptation, written by the author and directed by the director of the British stage musical *The Rocky Horror Show*. Opening in 1973, the show ran for 3,000 performances until 1986 (often in non-standard theatrical venues) and was also produced and toured in the US, Australia and elsewhere. The relatively low-budget film, in continuous release for thirty-five years, has grossed $135 million; it became a 'cult classic' as Friday and Saturday late-night audiences turned it into *the* classic 'midnight movie'. It is not altogether clear whether audience participation sprang from spontaneous response or was a marketing ploy, but the 'midnight movie' experience of the film lies somewhere between moviegoing and participatory theatre: audience members dress up as characters, sing and dance to numbers, respond to dialogue and perform ritualised actions such as throwing rice (during the wedding sequence), firing water pistols (during the storm) and igniting cigarette lighters (for 'There's a Light'). In much the same spirit as the later *Little Shop of Horrors**, and typically for their time, both show and film draw heavily on the camp appeal of low-budget, mostly Hollywood 1930s–60s science-fiction and horror films, from *Bride of Frankenstein*, *Doctor X*, *King Kong* and *The Wizard of Oz** to *It Came from Outer Space*, *Forbidden Planet* and *The Curse of Frankenstein*, which are the subject of the opening song, 'Science Fiction, Double Feature'.

The film's criminologist-narrator introduces us to straight Brad (Barry Bostwick) and Janet (Susan Sarandon), and the film creates a creepy (though always tongue-in-cheek) horror film ambience as the engaged couple burst a tyre on a stormy night and seek help at a nearby mansion. There, they chance upon Nosferatu lookalike Riff-Raff (Richard O'Brien) and Magenta (Patricia Quinn) and the Annual Transylvanian Convention; shortly, the film's best-known dance number, 'The Time Warp', is performed, and transvestite scientist Dr Frank-N-Furter (Tim Curry) sings

'Sweet Transvestite'. When Frank brings to life his sexy creation Rocky Horror, all kinds of perverse mayhem ensues: Frank seduces both Janet and Brad (neither of whom put up much resistance), and Janet wants more ('Touch-a, Touch-a, Touch-a, Touch Me'). Finally, before Riff-Raff and Magenta stage a coup and take off for the planet Transsexual, the characters are subjected to what the narrator calls the 'indignities' of Frank's decadent floor show ('Don't Dream It, Be It'). Brad and Janet, somewhat changed (but clearly, in the film's terms, for the better), survive; a sequel, *Shock Treatment* (1981), was built around their characters.

What *The Rocky Horror Picture Show* lacks in narrative coherence it makes up for in energy and inventiveness. Curry's splendid Frank, part Mick Jagger, part Tom Jones, with a high-class British accent, sexy make-up, heels, stockings and suspenders, is completely absorbed in the pleasure of his polymorphous perversity. It's camp fun (from the parodied 20th Century-Fox fanfare onwards), of course, but both show and film embrace the permissive attitude of 'glam rock' (and figures like David Bowie) to different kinds of sexuality and gender roles. Since the actors playing Grant Wood's iconic 'American Gothic' couple and the preacher at the start later become Frank, Riff-Raff and Magenta, it is as if the rest is a (bad?) dream or a return of the repressed for the 'good', small-town characters.

Initially, the stage show did not enjoy as much popularity in the US as in Britain, but the film's 'midnight movie' success prompted a successful Broadway revival in 2000.   JH

Dir: Jim Sharman; **Prod**: Lou Adler, John Goldstone, Michael White; **Scr**: Richard O'Brien, Jim Sharman, from O'Brien's musical stage play *The Rocky Horror Show*; **DOP**: Peter Suschitzky (colour); **Song Music/Lyrics**: Richard O'Brien; **Music**: Richard Hartley; **Art**: Terry Ackland-Snow; **Main Cast**: Tim Curry, Susan Sarandon, Barry Bostwick, Richard O'Brien, Patricia Quinn, Nell Campbell, Jonathan Adams, Peter Hinwood, Meat Loaf; **Prod Co**: 20th Century-Fox.

Saturday Night Fever
USA, 1977 – 118 mins
John Badham

Since the advent of sound, the music and movie industries have been closely connected (think of Bing Crosby, 'White Christmas' and *Holiday Inn**, or Elvis Presley films like *Jailhouse Rock**). So it is no surprise, in an increasingly multimedia environment and youthful audience demographic, that movies exploited trends in popular music and vice versa. *Saturday Night Fever* was the most critically and commercially successful movie to feature 1970s disco music (others included *Thank God It's Friday*, 1978, with Donna Summer, and *Can't Stop the Music*, 1980, with the Village People). In terms of synergy, music and movie were cross-promoted: the Bee Gees' single, released in advance, promoted the film, and the film's release triggered the best-selling soundtrack album ever, reviving the Bee Gees' career (thanks, in part, to a new emphasis on Barry Gibb's idiosyncratic falsetto).

Saturday Night Fever remains the quintessential disco movie, partly for the Bee Gees' music, partly for John Travolta's dance routines (referenced in, for example, *Pulp Fiction*, 1994), but also partly for its 'time-capsule' qualities, notably the period's fashions, exemplified in Travolta's blow-dried hair, tight-fitting flared trousers, Cuban heels, tight, gaudy shirts, wide open at the neck, and gold chains. Emphasising his ethnic Brooklyn Italian roots, Travolta's room sports images of *Rocky* and Al Pacino (alongside iconic Bruce Lee and Farrah Fawcett posters).

The film (based on rock writer Nik Cohn's 1976 report, 'Tribal Rites of the New Saturday Night', later revealed as largely invented) is a familiar coming-of-age/identity crisis narrative: Tony Manero, in a dead-end job, living at home, hanging out with mates, casually misogynistic and racist, gains a sense of achievement only on the dance floor, affording him (strictly local) celebrity and a kind of (short-lived) escape. Initially narcissistically swaggering, living for the moment ('Fuck the future!'), Tony begins to question his choices when he takes a new dance partner, the aspirational Stephanie (Karen Lynn Gorney), who calls Tony 'a cliché … goin' no place'. She herself has moved from Brooklyn to Manhattan, and the Brooklyn and Verrazzano-Narrows bridges provide a potent metaphor. The ending, when Tony breaks free, is not intentionally bleak but seems unable to imagine what future the 'new' Tony might have, so that we are almost nostalgic for the opening sequence – Tony strutting down the street to the strains of 'Staying Alive' – or his masterful solo disco performance to 'You Should Be Dancing'. Nobody breaks into dance here except on the dance floor, although, like Fred Astaire, Travolta's walking style takes on a kind of pre-dance rhythm. Like Astaire, Travolta insisted that his disco dance routines be done (mostly) in long shots and long takes, rather than depend on close-ups and editing.

The 1983 sequel, *Staying Alive* (directed by Sylvester Stallone), also featuring Travolta and the Bee Gees music, was critically panned but did good box-office business. *Saturday Night Fever*, considerably sanitised, was later adapted into a successful stage musical (London, 1998, Broadway, 1999). By far the oddest 'spin-off' is the Chilean film *Tony Manero* (directed by Pablo Larraín, 2008), in which a forty-something psychotic obsessively styles himself on Travolta's character, against the sinister backdrop of Pinochet's repressive regime. But perhaps the most important follow-up to *Saturday Night Fever* was *Grease**, also made by the Robert Stigwood Organization (with Paramount and Allan Carr), starring Travolta and featuring a Barry Gibb title song.   JH

Dir: John Badham; **Prod**: Robert Stigwood; **Scr**: Norman Wexler, based on an article by Nik Cohn; **DOP**: Ralph D. Bode (colour); **Song Music/Lyrics**: the Bee Gees (Barry Gibb, Maurice Gibb, Robin Gibb); **Choreog**: Lester Wilson; **Art**: Charles Bailey; **Main Cast**: John Travolta, Karen Lynn Gorney, Barry Miller, Joseph Cali, Paul Pape, Donna Pescow; **Prod Co**: Robert Stigwood Organization/Paramount.

Seven Brides for Seven Brothers
USA, 1954 – 102 mins
Stanley Donen

Producer Jack Cummings, who originated the project, and director
Stanley Donen gathered a strong team for *Seven Brides*, including writers
Frances Goodrich and Albert Hackett (*The Pirate**, *Easter Parade**),
songwriters Johnny Mercer and Gene de Paul, and choreographer
Michael Kidd. Yet MGM expected little from the film. It invested in
making two separate versions (standard ratio and CinemaScope) in case
theatres were slow to invest in the new widescreen process, but budget
constraints remained too tight to allow the location shooting Donen
considered essential, and a film set in the scenic splendour of Oregon
had to be made almost exclusively on sound stages, using process shots
for the great outdoors. At the box office, though, the film Donen has
said MGM treated like a B-movie was a major hit, outshining its
contemporary *Brigadoon*, on which the studio had lavished a good deal
more care. The film was nominated for several Academy Awards,
including Best Picture, and Adolph Deutsch and Saul Chaplin won for
their musical direction.

In this musical comedy version of Oregon 1850, there are no outlaws
or Indians. The film asserts the vitality of the frontier male but shows
untutored masculinity being civilised – if not socialised – by women from
the town. Along the way, as in a number of other musicals (*The Pirate**
and *Singin' in the Rain**, for instance), we see the discomfiture of the
self-regarding male until he becomes a fit partner for the woman. So in
both halves of the film, Milly (Jane Powell) banishes Adam (Howard Keel)
from her bed: first after her romantic dreams of a home for two
('Wonderful, Wonderful Day!') are dashed when she discovers that
Adam married her largely to keep house for the seven brothers
('A serving girl deserves a sleeping place of her own'); and later when,
appalled by the brothers' abduction of six young women, she bans all
the men from the house.

Michael Kidd could see no opportunities for dance when he heard the score, but, with the casting of four professional dancers and a skilled tumbler, found ways of developing dances rooted in the actions of the characters, such as Milly teaching the six brothers how to talk to girls ('Goin' Courtin'') and the choreographed work movements that lead to 'I'm a Lonesome Polecat'. Most remarkable is the barn-raising sequence, which moves through a barn dance in which the brothers and townsmen compete to partner the young women, to rival feats of tumbling and

Barn-raising dance

athleticism, the barn raising itself, a free-for-all fight and the barn's collapse – all brilliantly choreographed, staged and edited in 8 minutes that constitute one of the landmark dance sequences in the film musical.

What complicates contemporary responses, but certainly doesn't trouble the film, is that the second half is a benign fantasy based on the Rape of the Sabine Women. Potential Production Code sensitivities are carefully negotiated via Milly's vehement disapproval, her punishment of Adam and her policing of the men and women's segregation. But the film's energies are elsewhere: first in the extraordinary 'Sobbin' Women', the film's nearest equivalent to a 'show-stopper', yet which is also Adam's encouragement to abduction ('They acted angry and annoyed/But really they were overjoyed'); and then in the kidnapping itself, the hectic chase and the avalanche that follow. When spring ends the women's confinement to the snow-bound house, the fantasy is complete – they have all fallen for the brothers ('Spring, Spring, Spring!'), refuse to be returned and, when the townspeople arrive, contrive to be married by all claiming to be the mother of Milly's baby.   DP

Dir: Stanley Donen **Prod**: Jack Cummings; **Scr**: Albert Hackett, Frances Goodrich, Dorothy Kingsley, from the story by Stephen Vincent Benet; **DOP**: George Folsey (colour); **Song Music/Lyrics**: Gene de Paul/Johnny Mercer; **Musical Dir**: Adolph Deutsch, Saul Chaplin; **Choreog**: Michael Kidd; **Art**: Cedric Gibbons, Urie McCleary; **Main Cast**: Howard Keel, Jane Powell, Jeff Richards, Russ Tamblyn, Tommy Rall, Marc Platt, Matt Mattox, Jacques d'Amboise, Julie Newmeyer, Nancy Kilgas, Betty Carr, Virginia Gibson, Ruta Kilmonis, Norma Doggett; **Prod Co**: Metro-Goldwyn-Mayer.

Sholay
India, 1975 – 188/199 mins
Ramesh Sippy

Sholay (translated variously as *Embers*, *Flames* or *Flames of the Sun*), one of the most popular 'Bollywood' films ever, is a quintessential 'masala' film, combining song and dance with melodrama, romance, comedy and spectacular action (like the bandits' attack on a moving train). At the same time, this 'curry Western' borrows heavily from 1960s Westerns: its parched landscapes resemble those of Italian Westerns and it combines plot elements from well-known Westerns like *The Magnificent Seven* (John Sturges, 1960) and *Butch Cassidy and the Sundance Kid* (George Roy Hill, 1969): two good-hearted petty criminal buddies, Veeru (Dharmendra) and Jai (Amitabh Bachchan), are hired to protect the village of their former captor, the Thakur (Sanjeev Kumar), from the predatory bandit Gabbar Singh (Ahmad Khan), who has rendered the Thakur defenceless by cutting off his arms; there are also significant borrowings from *Once upon a Time in the West* (Sergio Leone, 1968), most obviously when the Thakur's family is callously wiped out.

At the centre of *Sholay* is the Indian concept of 'dostana', brotherly love. Although heterosexual romance often brings tensions to close male friendships in western films, *Sholay* gives this a typically Indian twist in the famously boisterous 'Yeh dosti' ('We Will Not Break This Friendship') sequence (playback singers: Kishore Kumar, Manna Dey). Here, dressed in denim and caps – the Indian version of the 1970s counter-culture look – and riding a stolen motorcycle and sidecar, the two men celebrate a brotherly love that nothing can break – certainly not the passing distraction of an attractive village girl. The knockabout number mixes comic stunt action and speeded-up camerawork, but is none the less deeply felt for that. Tellingly, a sombre version of the same music plays over the late scene in which Jai sacrifices himself and dies in his 'brother' Veeru's arms. In a wandering/settlement theme familiar from the American Western, there are fundamental conflicts between the two men's love for each other and their happy-go-lucky, unattached lifestyle of the road and the love they come to feel for women in the village and the settled life marriage would entail. However, these are conflicts that the film never has to reconcile: Jai's death releases Veeru from their bond so that the film can end with the burgeoning heterosexual couple of Veeru and the village girl Basanti (Hema Malini), who leave the community for a future which is not spelled out.

As is often the case, most musical sequences do not feature characters breaking into song and dance (as in 'Yeh dosti') but are motivated by narrative events which involve song and dance, such as the exuberant *holi* (festival of colours) sequence here ('Holi ke din'/'Day of *Holi*') (playback: Kishore Kumar, Lata Mangeshkar), a vibrant celebration of community (shattered by Gabbar Singh's marauding bandits). Several of the other popular R. D. Burman/Anand Bakshi songs are also integrated diegetically, such as the two sequences – marked by significant differences in erotic display and narrative context – in which women dance for the villains: a gypsy woman (Helen) entertains the bandits round a night-time campfire with an erotic dance display ('Mehbooba'/'Beloved') (playback: R. D. Burman), while Basanti is forced to dance on broken glass under a scorching midday sun to save Veeru's life ('Jab tak hai jaan'/'As Long as I Have Life') (playback: Lata Mangeshkar). JH

Dir: Ramesh Sippy; **Prod**: G. P. Sippy; **Scr**: Salim–Javed (Salim Khan, Javed Akhtar); **DOP**: Dwarka Divecha (colour); **Music**: R. D. Burman; **Lyrics**: Anand Bakshi; **Playback**: R. D. Burman, Manna Dey, Kishore Kumar, Lata Mangeshkar; **Choreog**: P. L. Raj; **Art**: Ram Yedekar; **Main Cast**: Dharmendra, Amitabh Bachchan, Sanjeev Kumar, Hema Malini, Jaya Bhaduri, Amjad Khan; **Prod Co**: United Producers/Sippy Films.

Show Boat
USA, 1936 – 116 mins
James Whale

Jerome Kern's and Oscar Hammerstein II's *Show Boat*, first staged by
Florenz Ziegfeld in 1927, was the first stage musical show to fully
integrate libretto, song and lyrics with the narrative, establishing the
classic Broadway musical formula. Running for over three hours, the
show's action follows the fortunes of characters on the Mississippi River
show boat the *Cotton Blossom* from the 1880s to the 1920s.
Characters include Magnolia (Irene Dunne in the film), her
owner/impresario father Captain Andy (Charles Winninger), his harridan
wife Parthy (Helen Westley) and Gaylord Ravenal (Allan Jones),
a gentleman gambler who courts and marries Magnolia; these
characters are richly complemented by mulatto singer Julie (Helen
Morgan) and her husband Steve (Donald Cook), and black workers Joe
(Paul Robeson) and Queenie (Hattie McDaniel). The film retains most of
the show's celebrated songs (including 'Make Believe' and 'Bill');
at under two hours, it lacks the show's narrative complexity, but the
story remains dense and intricate.

 Show Boat's inclusion of mixed-race marriage and major African-
American characters proved controversial. Critics objected to the black
characters' lowly roles and to stereotyped black vernacular language.
Such objections – similar to those raised about the Gershwins' *Porgy and
Bess* (show 1935, film 1959) and Hammerstein's Bizet adaptation *Carmen
Jones* (show 1943, film 1954*) – remain difficult to unpick. *Show Boat*
tries to respect the story's period while accommodating contemporary
attitudes. (Hammerstein's original use of 'nigger' was much adapted over
the years: the film opts for 'darkies'). The film is certainly progressive in
tracing the tragic results of the social exclusion and moral condemnation
of the mixed-race couple (Julie is exiled for the 'crime' of miscegenation
and later sacrifices her career for Magnolia) and makes Joe and Queenie
important, sympathetic characters.

Paul Robeson, 'Ol' Man River'

Production numbers are integral to these representations.
Julie's mixed blood is suggested when she sings 'Can't Help Lovin' Dat
Man': Joe and Queenie join in and Magnolia makes noticeably 'black'
dance movements, while black workers dance in the background.
Most telling is 'Ol' Man River': the Mississippi is central to the film and
Robeson's rendition of the show's most famous song is the film's first big
number. A dolly round Joe, sitting on the dock as he sings, intercut with
stylised images of him working, racked with pain, getting a little drunk
and landing in jail (as the song says), is remarkably eloquent on ordinary

black men's lot: 'darkies all work while the white folks play'.
A comparison with, say, Bill Robinson's role in *The Littlest Rebel** gives
some idea of *Show Boat*'s different ambitions. Nevertheless, the black
characters do fade from the film's narrative, whose final third deals
exclusively with the white story of Magnolia's family and rise to fame,
despite the reprise of Robeson's voice-over for the finale.

James Whale, best known for Universal's horror films, seemed like an
odd choice for *Show Boat*, but he displays a deft hand with this material,
not least in the lovely, comic melodrama performance, complete with
interruptions, audience participation and Cap'n Andy acting out and
narrating key scenes whose actors are temporarily indisposed.

Carl Laemmle acquired the rights to Edna Ferber's 1926 novel before
the stage show; a film version (now considered lost) was made in 1927,
released as a silent and then as a part-talkie with songs from the show.
George Sidney's MGM 1951 remake (with Kathryn Grayson, Howard
Keel, Ava Gardner and William Warfield), the best-known version, made
significant changes to the story and weakened its racial element.
Sadly, the 1951 version made the fine 1936 version hard to access. JH

Dir: James Whale; **Prod**: Carl Laemmle Jr; **Scr**: Oscar Hammerstein II, from the stage-show
book, lyrics by Hammerstein, music by Jerome Kern, from the novel by Edna Ferber; **DOP**:
John J. Mescall (b&w); **Song Music/Lyrics**: Jerome Kern/Oscar Hammerstein II; **Choreog**:
LeRoy Prinz; **Art**: Charles D. Hall; **Main Cast**: Irene Dunne, Allan Jones, Charles Winninger,
Paul Robeson, Helen Morgan, Helen Westley, Hattie McDaniel; **Prod Co**: Universal.

Shree 420
India, 1955 – 168 mins
Raj Kapoor

Shree 420 (translated variously as *Mr 420*, or *The Gentleman Cheat* – article 420 of the Indian penal code deals with cheats and thieves) is a sentimental comedy and love story, with popular cinema's characteristic quota of songs and dances; but it is also a morality play and populist critique of the social and economic inequalities of post-Independence India – in Indian cinema generic terms, a 'social'. Raj Kapoor admired Chaplin, and the film frequently adopts a Chaplin-like silent-film comedy style; Kapoor's own much-loved happy-go-lucky tramp persona Raju/Raj (introduced in *Awaara* [*The Vagabond*], 1951) is central to *Shree 420*. The film was scripted by K. A. Abbas, who, like lyricist Shailendra, was active in the Indian People's Theatre Association, a leftist movement formed in 1943 to propagate progressive ideas via popular theatre and cinema.

Arriving in Bombay to make his fortune, Raj quickly discovers that hard work and honesty won't bring success and joins a lively community of pavement dwellers who, by chance, live outside the mansion of crooked businessman Seth (Nemo). Seth lures Raj into ever greater business scams, culminating in offering cheap homes to poor people while stealing their money. Finally seeing the error of his ways, Raj rescues the people's money and exhorts them to unite and use their courage and hard work to achieve progress and national unity. Inevitably, the worlds of poverty and community and the flashy world of crooked business are personified by two women: the devious, vampish Maya (a name associated with illusion) (Nadira) is countered by the noble schoolteacher Vidya (associated with wisdom) (Nargis), who loves Raj but rejects his crooked pursuit of money. Vidya finally saves Raj from returning to a life on the road, leading him back to a dreamlike vision of a new Bombay with homes for the poor.

Director, producer and popular star, Raj Kapoor was the dominant figure in Indian cinema's 1940s–60s 'golden age'. The enormous

Raj Kapoor: the 'Dil ka haal sune dilwala' dance number

popularity of Kapoor's films – in Russia and the Middle East as well as India – came from their combination of sentimentality, comedy and social critique, as well as their incorporation of song and dance. Music was crucial to their success (as with all Indian popular cinema: see also *Pyaasa**, *Pakeezah**, *Sholay**, *Dil se …**): the celebrated musical direction team Shankar–Jaikishan, with lyricist Shailendra and Indian cinema's greatest playback singers, was responsible for many hit songs in Kapoor films.

The film's two worlds are characterised by song and dance: the newly arrived Raj leads a number among the pavement dwellers, 'Dil ka haal sune dilwala' ('Listen to the State of My Heart'), while the evening-suited Raj, following a mirror confrontation with his earlier persona, returns and joins in a second communal number, 'Ramaiya vastavaiya' ('Lord Rama Is Coming') (playback: Mohammed Rafi, Lata Mangeshkar, Mukesh). Both numbers incorporate Indian rhythms and instrumentation, and both are presented as spontaneous celebrations. The crooked business world, by contrast, is represented by more sexualised, western-style nightclub numbers, including 'Mud mud ken a dekh' ('Don't Look Back') featuring Maya and staged as a spectacle for the wealthy. But the film's two most enduringly popular Shankar–Jaikishan/Shailendra songs are the tender duet in which Raj and Vidya declare their love in a rainswept street, 'Pyar hua ikrar hua' ('Love Arises, a Promise Is Made') (playback: Lata Mangeshkar, Manna Dey), and Raj's jaunty opening (and closing) number, 'Mera jota hai japani' (playback: Mukesh), whose refrain ('My shoes are from Japan/My pants are English style/On my head's a red Russian cap/But still my heart is Hindustani/Indian') describes both Raj's ill-assorted clothes and, metaphorically, independent India's mixed heritage and place in the world. JH

Dir/**Prod**: Raj Kapoor; **Scr**: K. A. Abbas, V. P. Sathe; **DOP**: Radhu Karmakar (b&w); **Music**: Shankar–Jaikishan [Jaikishan Dayabhai Pankal, Shankarsingh Raghuwanshi]; **Lyrics**: Hasrat Jaipuri, Shailendra; **Playback**: Asha Bhosle, Manna Dey, Lata Mangeshkar, Mukesh, Mohammed Rafi; **Choreog**: Satyanaravan; **Art**: M. R. Acharekar; **Main Cast**: Raj Kapoor, Nargis, Nadira, Nemo, Lalita Pawar; **Prod Co**: R. K. Films.

Silk Stockings
USA, 1957 – 117 mins
Rouben Mamoulian

By 1957, the great period of the Hollywood musical was coming to an end. Emblematically, *Funny Face** and *Silk Stockings* were the last musicals in which Fred Astaire played romantic leads. *Silk Stockings* also turned out to be the final film directed by Rouben Mamoulian (see *Love Me Tonight** and *Summer Holiday**). Eloquent of changing times in a different way is that Astaire's number in top hat, white tie and tails towards the end of the film is 'The Ritz Roll and Rock', Cole Porter's ironic foray into rock and roll rhythms.

Silk Stockings is a musical version of Ernst Lubitsch's 1939 film *Ninotchka*, adapted from Cole Porter's final Broadway show, and some reviewers compared it unfavourably with the earlier film. But if Cyd Charisse is no Greta Garbo, what she can do more than makes up for anything she lacks: the heart of *Silk Stockings* is what Robin Wood (1981) calls 'dance-as-liberation'. Astaire is Steve Canfield, a Hollywood producer determined to keep the Russian composer Boroff (Wim Sonneveld) in Paris to work on his new film. Cyd Charisse is Comrade Yoshenko (Ninotchka), a Communist Party stalwart sent to bring Boroff back after the first emissaries (Peter Lorre, Jules Munshin, Joseph Buloff) have been converted by Steve to the delights of capitalism. Their bulky exuberance in 'We Can't Go Back to Moscow' – the first and final number in the film – frames the main action; in rather more elevated style, it is also the movement into seemingly spontaneous dance that expresses the gradual erosion of Ninotchka's ideological resistance to Steve and to Paris. She asserts that 'Dancing is a waste of time' yet takes her first tentative steps when she allows Steve to pull her into his dance as he sings 'All of You'. Later, alone in her suite, Ninotchka dances her own physical transformation, touchingly absorbed in the sensuous wonder of 'Silk Stockings'; later still, she and Steve share a lovely extended dance ('We Were Fated to Be Mated') through empty film studio sets.

This pattern of private moments in dance, associated with the charms of Paris and with love, is quite distinct (as it is in *Funny Face*) from the brasher public world of the Astaire character's profession. Hollywood entertainment is almost as much a focus of satire here as Communism (though it is certainly more fun). Janis Paige is terrific as swimming star Peggy Dainton in numbers that variously send up Hollywood values: 'Stereophonic Sound', 'Satin and Silk' and 'Josephine'. But Hollywood is Steve's world. When Ninotchka discovers that Boroff's music is being jazzed up in a musical about Napoleon and Josephine (Paige splendidly raunchy in 'Josephine' – 'commonly called Jo'), she rebels against the 'Insulting travesty of Russian culture'. It is a startling tonal shift: in response to Steve's defence ('We do this in America all the time'), Ninotchka, who had earlier drunkenly embraced the traditional inequality of romantic love ('Without Love, What Is a Woman?'), reclaims her independent identity ('You leave me nothing of my own'); she and Boroff return directly to Russia.

The film's final movement juxtaposes frustration in Russia with 'happy ending' in France. In Moscow, Boroff's 'most decadent composition', 'Red Blues', spurs almost all the comrades in the multiple-occupation apartment, including Ninotchka, into explosive dance. In Paris, after Steve has contrived to bring her back and declared, 'We're going to get married', Ninotchka tears up her return ticket. But there is no romantic musical resolution; the couple is reunited but the rousing celebration of 'We Can't Go Back to Moscow' leaves their differences in place. DP

Dir: Rouben Mamoulian; **Prod**: Arthur Freed; **Scr**: Leonard Gershe, Leonard Spigelgass, from the musical play by George S. Kaufman, Leueen MacGrath, Abe Burrows, itself based on the screenplay for *Ninotchka*, by Billy Wilder, Charles Brackett, Walter Reisch, itself based on a story by Melchior Lengyel; **DOP**: Robert Bronner (colour); **Song Music/Lyrics**: Cole Porter; **Choreog**: Hermes Pan, Eugene Loring, Fred Astaire (uncredited); **Art**: William A. Horning, Randall Duell; **Main Cast**: Fred Astaire, Cyd Charisse, Janis Paige, Peter Lorre, Jules Munshin, Joseph Buloff, George Tobias, Wim Sonneveld; **Prod Co**: Metro-Goldwyn-Mayer.

Sing as We Go
UK, 1934 – 80 mins
Basil Dean

Famously, born above a chip shop in Rochdale, Gracie Fields's down-to-earth, working-class Lancashire origins were integral to her persona and popularity: for the mass audience, she was 'one of us', 'our Gracie' – Britain's most popular 1930s female star. Like George Formby (Britain's most popular male star in the late 1930s/early 40s, with films like *Come on George!**), Fields came from music hall, and her films were partly unashamed vehicles for her music-hall skills – comic songs, impersonation, funny walks and other comic business. Her confidence and matriarchal instincts, however, contrasted sharply with Formby's humbler, more timid character. Fields's popularity, like Formby's, was also reflected in massive sales of records and sheet music.

Sing as We Go and *Look up and Laugh* (1935) differ from Fields's earlier films. Both were scripted by J. B. Priestley, an important popular leftist 1930s figure, and firmly rooted in Lancashire and the Depression. As *Sing as We Go* begins, the local textile mill closes; unemployed, Gracie heads to Blackpool – by pushbike – to look for work, and her (mis)adventures there, comic and otherwise, occupy most of the narrative. *Sing as We Go* and *Look up and Laugh* underplay class difference, but they stress co-operation, community and solidarity, especially among women; though Gracie belongs to the community, she is set somewhat apart by her charisma as an entertainer. Priestley (1934) noted Fields's 'shrewdness, homely simplicity, irony, fierce independence, an impish delight in mocking whatever is thought to be affected or pretentious', and Jeffrey Richards (1997) claims justifiably that 'Gracie was able to embody simultaneously Rochdale, Lancashire, Britain, the Empire, the working class, women and the people at large'. Fields's 1930s films (like Formby's) were shot at Ealing Studios, and their essential Britishness is foregrounded.

Unlike Jessie Matthews (see *Evergreen**), Fields was not conventionally glamorous. Her attractiveness derived from her humour,

Gracie Fields leads the workers back to work, 'Sing as We Go'

energy and common sense. In *Sing as We Go*, she loses the 'only chap I ever cared about' (John Loder, the mill-owner's son) to the more glamorous, younger Phyllis (Dorothy Hyson), whom Gracie has taken under her wing – but 'there's nowt to cry about', and Gracie's personal loss is subsumed in the triumphant reopening of the mill.

Fields's films are closer to conventional musicals than Formby's, including sometimes quite complex musical production numbers, covering her range of performance styles. The stirring 'Sing as We Go' opens the film, over documentary shots of factories and cotton production, but is halted by the mill's closure, only to be reprised at the end as Gracie leads the singing mill girls back to work. In 'Just a Catchy Little Tune', Gracie promotes a new song and the Blackpool crowd joins in. Fields's music-hall background comes to the fore in two fine comic songs, 'Thora' and 'My Little Bottom Drawer'. But she also included more 'straight' romantic standards, and 'Love, Wonderful Love', one of the film's highlights, sung to herself and to us rather than to or with some on-screen audience, is given a more lyrical treatment (though undercut by Stanley Holloway's comic version in the street outside). Taken together, 'Sing as We Go' and 'Love, Wonderful Love' embody different sides of the Fields persona – the optimistic, community-minded, boisterously vocal woman and the vulnerable, stoical, more private figure often disappointed in love – while the music-hall songs allow her temporarily to inhabit different personae.

Though she remained 'our Gracie', Fields's later films focused more on her role as an entertainer; she made several films in Hollywood and spent much of her later life in luxury on the isle of Capri. JH

Dir/Prod: Basil Dean; **Scr**: J. B. Priestley, Gordon Wellesley; **DOP**: Robert Martin (b&w); **Song Music/Lyrics**: Harry Parr Davies; Stephen Adams, Frederick Edward Weatherly; William Haines, Jimmy Harper; Leo Towers, Harry Leon; **Musical Dir**: Ernest Irving; **Art**: J. Elder Wills, Edward Carrick (uncredited); **Main Cast**: Gracie Fields, John Loder, Dorothy Hyson, Stanley Holloway, Frank Pettingell, Maire O'Neill, Norman Walker, Lawrence Grossmith; **Prod Co**: Associated Talking Pictures.

Singin' in the Rain
USA, 1952 – 103 mins
Gene Kelly, Stanley Donen

Almost as soon as elegant silent-movie star Don Lockwood (Gene Kelly) addresses the radio audience at the Hollywood premiere with which the film begins, our view as film spectators diverges from that of spectators and listeners in the world of the film. As Don delivers the studio version of his rise to fame, with its refrain of 'Dignity, dignity, always dignity!', we see not the refined upbringing he outlines but the reality – including his splendidly undignified song and dance double act ('Fit as a Fiddle') with Cosmo (Donald O'Connor) and his far from glamorous early exploits as a stuntman. This separation of the two audiences is part of the ingenious play on what is 'true' and 'false', 'authentic' and 'inauthentic' in entertainment that is so central to the pleasures of *Singin' in the Rain*'s sophisticated variation on the backstage musical.

Kelly and Donen enthusiastically embraced the possibilities of the affectionate satire of the arrival of 'talkies' in Hollywood devised by Adolph Green and Betty Comden, after they were tasked with writing a musical based on the song catalogue of Arthur Freed (a successful lyricist before becoming a producer) and Nacio Herb Brown. 'False' are the posturing, phoney star images and deceitful artifice of the film's Hollywood; 'true' are the values associated with the suppressed world of popular musical entertainment, expressed through much of the film in numbers that characters perform 'only', as it were, to us.

Don, encouraged by Cosmo, reconnects with his 'low' musical past, finds love and a new co-star in Cathy Selden (Debbie Reynolds), and between them they save the studio and expose the manipulations of Don's previous co-star, Lina Lamont (Jean Hagen). The film even contains not one but four versions of the backstage musical's familiar motif of an unknown performer's rise to stardom – the two variants of Don's story, that of Cathy and the 'Broadway Melody/Broadway Rhythm' ballet's narrative of an unknown hoofer's ascent to fame.

Along the way, the film plays exhilarating and reflexive, 'now you see it, now you don't', games with the artifice of film-making. Cumbersome early sound recording and elocution lessons ('Moses Supposes') are the source of wonderful comic business. Don relies on the technology of studio lights and a wind machine to romance Cathy in 'You Were Meant for Me', yet when Cyd Charisse's long veil flows out behind her in the ballet, no wind machine is to be seen. We see Cathy seamlessly dub Lina's voice when the disastrous talkie 'The Dueling Cavalier' is transformed into a musical, but at the film's premiere, when Lina mimes on stage to Cathy's voice, the deception is revealed to all, exposing the artifice and finally uniting the film audience with that in the world of the film, as Cathy is revealed as the 'real' star. (There is a further nice irony in the fact that Debbie Reynolds's singing voice was itself dubbed.)

No artifice is revealed, however, in the film's greatest numbers: Cosmo's frantic and brilliant athletic clowning in 'Make 'em Laugh', 'Good Morning', which finally unites the three principals in performance, and, of course, 'Singin' in the Rain' itself, are presented as triumphs of spontaneity. In Kelly's great solo, the Don Lockwood who was earlier recognised in the street by everyone has been transformed: he waves away his taxi and rapturously celebrates his love for Cathy by 'singing and dancing in the rain', unrecognised even by the policeman who finally interrupts his joyful splashing.

Comden and Green's stage adaptation of *Singin' in the Rain* ran for three years in London from 1983 and has since been revived a number of times. DP

Dir: Gene Kelly, Stanley Donen; **Prod**: Arthur Freed; **Scr**: Adolph Green, Betty Comden, suggested by the song 'Singin' in the Rain' by Nacio Herb Brown and Arthur Freed; **DOP**: Harold Rosson (John Alton) (colour); **Song Music/Lyrics**: Nacio Herb Brown/Arthur Freed; **Musical Dir**: Lennie Hayton; **Choreog**: Gene Kelly, Stanley Donen; **Art**: Cedric Gibbons, Randall Duell; **Main Cast**: Gene Kelly, Debbie Reynolds, Donald O'Connor, Jean Hagen, Millard Mitchell, Cyd Charisse; **Prod Co**: Metro-Goldwyn-Mayer.

Snow White and the Seven Dwarfs
USA, 1937 – 84 mins
David Hand

Snow White and the Seven Dwarfs is one of the great milestones of cinema history: Hollywood's first animated feature film and the first in colour anywhere in the world. It was instantly hailed as an extraordinary achievement by an industry that had derided what *Variety* called 'Disney's folly' when the film was being planned. Few apart from Walt Disney had believed that an animated feature could hold an audience, but the film was a huge box-office hit, rapidly recouping its very high production costs and going on to become one of the most profitable Hollywood movies of all time. It was in effect the film on which the Walt Disney empire was built.

There were significant technical challenges in producing a feature film using cel animation, in which every frame is separately painted and filmed. Disney had to extend his already well-established methods to produce increased detail and convincing movement of the human characters in space, as well as refining the multi-plane camera that was so crucial to achieving a vivid illusion of depth. Perhaps the greater challenges, however, were aesthetic, and the film creates an animated world unprecedented in the richness of its detail. Originally aiming for a more uniformly comic mode, the film-makers developed complementary forms of characterisation – the brilliantly inventive caricature of the dwarfs and the greater realism with which the archetypal figures of the other characters are realised. Songs that have since become almost universally familiar (the dwarfs' 'Hey Ho' and 'Whistle While You Work', and Snow White's 'Some Day My Prince Will Come', among others) were chosen to enhance character and develop the story, making the film a fully integrated musical.

Although the film simplifies the original narrative and transforms what happens to the wicked queen (no hot iron shoes here), in Disney's fairy-tale world evil is a genuine threat, vividly created in sequences

Snow White

some of which the British censor thought too disturbing for unaccompanied young children. The film creates a natural harmony between the goodness of Snow White and the little creatures of the woods, but goodness is frail and evil very powerful. The Prince is handsome yet ineffectual, absent most of the time but turning up to administer the decisive kiss (in the story, the piece of poisoned apple is dislodged from Snow White's throat when her glass coffin is being carried to the Prince's castle). Snow White is a perfect image of traditional femininity: beautiful and good, possessed of a remarkable range of domestic skills for a princess – but essentially passive and defenceless. The triumph of good is a precarious business.

From the outset, Disney saw the dwarfs as the main attraction of the tale in terms of the opportunities they offered for animation, and they are certainly the film's glory, richly comic individual creations that make up one of cinema's most memorable groups of men without women (their cousins inhabit many Westerns). Their scruffy self-sufficiency melts away, as it must in this fairy tale, when Snow White enters their world (even Grumpy finally thaws), but the sustained energy and wit with which they are animated powers much of the film. It is entirely appropriate that in this version of the tale, it is their pursuit of the Wicked Queen, up the mountains and through thunder and rain, that leads to her death. The Prince pales by comparison.

The film's great success initiated the long tradition of Disney animated features, including in the years following *Snow White*, *Pinocchio* (1940), *Dumbo* (1941) and *Bambi* (1942), as well as the more experimental *Fantasia* (1940). DP

Prod: Walt Disney; **Supervising Dir**: David Hand; **Sequence Dir**: Perce Pearce, William Cottrell, Larry Morey, Wilfred Jackson, Ben Sharpsteen; **Supervising Animators**: Hamilton Luske, Fred Moore, Vladimir Tytla, Norman Ferguson; **Story Adapt**: Ted Sears, Richard Creedon, Otto Englander, Dick Rickard, Earl Hurd, Merrill De Maris, Dorothy Ann Blank, Webb Smith, from Grimms' *Fairy Tales*; **Character Designers**: Albert Hurter, Joe Grant; **Song Music/Lyrics**: Frank Churchill/Larry Morey; **Score**: Leigh Harline, Paul Smith; **Voices**: Adrianna Caselotti, Harry Stockwell, Lucille La Verne, Moroni Olsen, Billy Gilbert, Pinto Colvig, Scotty Mattraw, Roy Atwell, Stuart Buchanan, Marian Darlington, James MacDonald; **Prod Co**: Walt Disney.

The Sound of Music
USA, 1965 – 173 mins
Robert Wise

The Sound of Music was Rodgers and Hammerstein's last musical – Oscar Hammerstein II died in 1960, the year after the show opened on Broadway. A considerable hit in New York and even more so in London, it was eclipsed by the unprecedented success of the film, which won five Academy Awards, including Best Picture and Best Director, and within a few years had become one of the top-grossing films ever made. It was the kind of success – of a big-budget, family-oriented movie – that Hollywood found impossible to repeat as the 1960s went on. Even forty-five years on from the film's release, the popularity of *The Sound of Music*, on stage and screen, seems inexhaustible.

Like Rodgers and Hammerstein's earlier shows, *The King and I* and *South Pacific*, *The Sound of Music* centres on the relationship between a young woman and a widower with children, although those shows' cross-cultural complexities give way in *The Sound of Music* to a more straightforward focus on traditional values in opposition to encroaching Nazism. Ernest Lehman's screenplay skilfully reworked the original – based on Maria von Trapp's 1949 memoir, *The Von Trapp Family Singers* (filmed in Germany as *Die Trapp-Familie*, 1956) – dropping some songs, moving others and tightening its structure. Robert Wise's eloquent use of locations creates an Austria that is simultaneously real and idealised, anchoring the action but intensifying the show's potent appeal to values of freedom, patriotism and family.

There is no ambivalence in *The Sound of Music*'s vision: no children like Tootie in *Meet Me in St. Louis** here. At the same time, the power of niceness has rarely been so effectively dramatised. Maria (Julie Andrews) is almost as magical in her effect as Mary Poppins, the spontaneity of her music and its associations with nature – evoked immediately as she sings 'The Sound of Music' – challenging the ritual formality of the abbey, bringing new life to the von Trapp children (in songs like 'My Favourite

Things' and 'Do Re Me'), as well as softening Captain von Trapp (Christopher Plummer)'s military style of child-rearing, and ultimately the patrician Captain himself. Yet neither music nor Maria is anarchic or really threatening to tradition. Maria may be a plain-speaking governess but the warmth and sincerity of Andrews's persona – and her very English middle-class voice – dissolve any potential class uneasiness; her music is resolutely cheerful and by teaching the children to sing, Maria makes music the heart of a revived and unified family life.

As the film goes on, music embraces the whole family but in the less spontaneous form of performance – the children sing 'The Sound of Music' to the Baroness (Eleanor Parker), the Captain sings 'Edelweiss' and the children perform 'So Long, Farewell' to the guests at the ball. 'Edelweiss' and the Austrian folk dance, the *Ländler*, which the Captain and Maria dance together, make the final links in the film's mythic cluster – from music to national tradition and to love, 'the unification', as Richard Dyer (1976/7) writes, 'of music and the world, of freedom and order'. Perhaps inevitably, given what has gone before, the film is at its most uneasy with the sexual attraction that love implies: in their one love scene, centring on 'Something Good', specially written by Richard Rodgers for the film, Maria and the Captain make a very unconvincing couple. But with marriage, the family is complete once more. Finally, though, niceness and traditional values have their limits: the von Trapp family singers perform at the Salzburg festival but then have to flee from Austria to escape the Nazis. DP

Dir/Prod: Robert Wise; **Scr**: Ernest Lehman, from the stage musical, book by Howard Lindsay and Russel Crouse; **DOP**: Ted McCord (colour); **Song Music/Lyrics**: Richard Rodgers/Oscar Hammerstein II; **Musical Dir**: Irwin Kostal; **Choreog**: Marc Breaux, Dee Dee Wood; **Art**: Boris Leven; **Main Cast**: Julie Andrews, Christopher Plummer, Eleanor Parker, Richard Haydn, Peggy Wood, Charmian Carr, Heather Menzies, Nicholas Hammond, Duane Chase, Angela Cartwright, Debbie Turner, Kym Karath; **Prod Co** 20th Century-Fox.

A Star Is Born
USA, 1954 – 175 mins
George Cukor

A Star Is Born is perhaps the most significant film in a development of the Hollywood musical during the mid-1950s away from the benign fantasies that had dominated the genre (see also, for instance, *It's Always Fair Weather**, *Love Me or Leave Me** and *Carousel**). Michael Wood (1975) associates this new mood with a loss of confidence in the metaphorical power of musical numbers to convey 'how it feels to be succeeding', whether in love, friendship or performance. We might also think of it in terms of melodrama increasingly invading what had been predominantly musical comedy, a shift – to use Deborah Thomas (2000)'s terms – from 'safe' to 'oppressive' fictional worlds, and from fantasies of 'happily ever after' to 'ever after' without the 'happily'. Indeed, Rick Altman (1987) notes the increasing number of musicals from 1954 onwards that focus on marriage, the terrain of Hollywood domestic melodrama, rather than on romance.

   A Star Is Born was George Cukor's first musical but also a return to his past – an adaptation of William Wellman's 1937 film that in turn derived from Cukor's *What Price Hollywood?* (1932). It was also Judy Garland's return to the screen, four years after her contract was suspended by MGM – a return initiated by Garland and her then husband, Sid Luft, who formed a production company, Transcona, specifically to make the film. Formally, it is in part a Hollywood-based backstage musical, tracing the familiar story of a rise to fame under the guidance of an established star – in outline not unlike that of *Singin' in the Rain*, a movie deliberately evoked at times in *A Star Is Born* (the Hollywood preview with which the film opens, Esther [Garland] splashing in puddles in 'Lose That Long Face'). But Esther's rise is followed by the alcoholic decline and suicide of her mentor and husband, Norman Maine (James Mason). This is not a world in which characters can happily burst into apparently spontaneous song and dance.

There are rumours that a print of Cukor's original version of the film still exists, but what is publicly available is a 1980s reconstruction – now digitally restored – that includes parts of the almost 30 minutes cut by Warner Bros. after the film opened. What remains is remarkable, despite the fragmented narrative of the long section from Esther and Norman's first encounter to Esther's transformation into Vicki Lester, Hollywood star. Garland gives a performance of great emotional breadth and depth. Her numbers range from the intensity of the long single take 'The Man Who Got Away' on the night Norman discovers her and her recording of 'What Am I Here For?', through those that evoke Garland's earlier life and career, such as the montage of various songs in the famous 'Born in a Trunk' sequence and the sound-stage performance of 'Lose That Long Face', to 'Somewhere There's a Someone', Esther's wonderful send-up for Norman of the production number she has been rehearsing. Dramatically, Garland is equally impressive, while Mason, in a very different register, gives a performance of characteristic skill and delicacy. George Cukor directs his cast brilliantly and also creates one of the most eloquent of early CinemaScope movies, staging, lighting and editing his scenes with a flexibility that belies the supposed technical limitations of the new process. Garland and Mason both won Golden Globes and were nominated for Academy Awards, but neither won the Oscar – Judy Garland, widely tipped to win, lost out to Grace Kelly for her role in *The Country Girl*. DP

Dir: George Cukor; **Prod**: Sidney Luft; **Scr**: Moss Hart, from the screenplay by Dorothy Parker, Alan Campbell, Robert Carson; **DOP**: Sam Leavitt (colour); **Song Lyrics/Music**: Harold Arlen/Ira Gershwin; Leonard Gershe ('Born in a Trunk'); **Musical Dir**: Ray Heindorf; **Choreog**: Richard Barstow, Eugene Loring; **Art**: Malcolm Bert, Irene Sharaff ('Born in a Trunk'); **Main Cast**: Judy Garland, James Mason, Jack Carson, Charles Bickford, Tom Noonan; **Prod Co**: Transcona/Warner Bros.

Stormy Weather
USA, 1943 – 78 mins
Andrew L. Stone

The all-black cast musicals *Cabin in the Sky** and *Stormy Weather* were
released within months of each other, and context is all-important.
The year 1943 saw the successful Broadway opening of Oscar
Hammerstein's all-black *Carmen Jones*; the National Association for the
Advancement of Colored People was pressurising Hollywood over its
images of African-Americans; and by then, thousands of black soldiers
were serving in the US armed forces. *Stormy Weather* opens with Bill
Williamson (Bill 'Bojangles' Robinson) remembering black soldiers
returning from Europe in 1918 and ends with an entertainment for black
servicemen about to be sent overseas.

A longish introduction establishes dancer Bill and sidekick Gabe
(Dooley Wilson) returning from World War I and meeting singer Selina
Rogers (Lena Horne); the backstage story follows Bill's and Selina's on–off
romance and rise to celebrity. But the plot is only a frame for a series of
song and dance performances – twenty or so in 78 minutes.
Fox proclaimed it 'a cavalcade of Negro entertainment', 'celebrating the
magnificent contribution of the colored race to the world of
entertainment during the past 25 years': the film features some of the
top African-American dancers, singers and musicians of the time, but it is
not altogether clear what the film wants to 'say' about black people.
On the one hand, several dances emphasise 'jungle' exoticism and 'dem
darkies do love to dance/have rhythm'. On the other hand, despite
censorship constraints, there is an unselfconsciously joyful lubricity about
the proceedings, particularly Fats Waller's wonderfully suggestive
performances of 'That Ain't Right' and 'Ain't Misbehavin', and
flamboyant bandleader Cab Calloway's scat vocals and dancing on
'Geechy Joe', 'My, My, Ain't that Somethin'' and 'The Jumpin' Jive'.

Both Horne and Robinson had some success in Hollywood, but in a
ghettoised way. Robinson was best known for partnering Shirley Temple,

in films like *The Littlest Rebel**. Horne both benefited and suffered from her 'sultry' beauty and light skin (she talked about being 'a sepia Hedy Lamarr'): her movie performances were often cameo songs which could be cut by distributors in the South (as with *Ziegfeld Follies**).

Horne (loaned by MGM to Fox, MGM's only real musical rival in the 1940s) provides lovely performances of 'Diga Diga Doo', 'There's No Two Ways about Love' and 'I Can't Give You Anything but Love', but (unsurprisingly) the film's highlight is the elaborate 'Stormy Weather' (Horne's career-long signature song), featuring Katherine Dunham and

Zoot-suited Cab Calloway performs 'Geechy Joe'

her dancers. Choreographer-dancer Dunham was an influential exponent of African-American modern American dance, and her dramatic ballet style here suggests considerable affinity with Gene Kelly's developing style (for example, in *Cover Girl**, made the following year). Curiously, co-star Robinson's 'educated feet' have fewer opportunities to shine. Robinson may have been one of the best tap dancers of the century – probably the equal of Fred Astaire, who paid homage to him in 'Bojangles of Harlem' in *Swing Time** – but he is less striking here than the Nicholas Brothers in their astonishing 'Jumpin' Jive' routine, which Astaire declared one of the most accomplished ever recorded on film.

Calloway and his male chorus appear in zoot suits towards the film's finale, reminding us that the release of *Cabin in the Sky* and *Stormy Weather* (April–July 1943) coincided with serious 'race riots' in Los Angeles (where they were known as the 'zoot suit riots'), Detroit, Harlem and elsewhere. No doubt this contributed to over half of US first-run theatres refusing to book *Stormy Weather*, though the film still managed to be relatively successful. JH

Dir: Andrew L. Stone; **Prod**: William LeBaron; **Scr**: Frederick Jackson, Ted Koehler, adapted by H. S. Kraft from an original story by Jerry Horwin; **DOP**: Leon Shamroy (b&w); **Song Music/Lyrics**: Jimmy McHugh/Dorothy Fields; Harold Arlen/Ted Koehler; Nat 'King' Cole/Irving Mills; Fats Waller, Harry Brooks/Andy Razaf; James P. Johnson/Irving Mills, Ted Koehler; Cab Calloway, *et al*.; **Musical Dir**: Emil Newman; **Choreog**: Clarence Robinson; **Art**: James Basevi, Joseph C. Wright; **Main Cast**: Lena Horne, Bill Robinson, Cab Calloway, Katherine Dunham, Fats Waller, Ada Brown, Dooley Wilson, the Nicholas Brothers; **Prod Co**: 20th Century-Fox.

Summer Holiday
USA, 1948 – 92 mins
Rouben Mamoulian

In 1945, Rouben Mamoulian had not directed a film for several years and no film musical since *High, Wide and Handsome* (1937), but his reputation on Broadway was at its peak, with his phenomenally successful productions of Rodgers and Hammerstein's groundbreaking musicals *Oklahoma!* (1943) (2,000+ performances) and *Carousel* (1945) (890 performances). MGM producer Arthur Freed managed to interest Mamoulian in a musical version of Eugene O'Neill's stage play *Ah, Wilderness!* (previously filmed by MGM in 1935). O'Neill was best known for weighty dramas, but *Ah, Wilderness!* was a generous account of a 1900s New England childhood (so bitterly dramatised in *Long Day's Journey into Night*). Set on the 4th of July, O'Neill's play was 'sort of wishing out loud … the way I would have *liked* my boyhood to have been' (quoted in Christine Dymkowski, 1995). *Summer Holiday* is as loving and utopian a celebration of early 1900s small-town America as other popular musicals from the 1940s and 50s like *Meet Me in St. Louis** (with which *Summer Holiday* shared some key personnel), *State Fair* (1945), *On Moonlight Bay* (1951) and the later *The Music Man**. These films of 'pastoral retreat' offer utopia as 'what we have – or had – or, more complicatedly, imagine ourselves having had as a prelude to imagining what we might have again in the future' (Babington and Evans, 1985), turning away from the wartime and postwar problems which mark the contemporaneous urban, dystopian film noir.

Mamoulian had in mind a 'musical play' which would translate O'Neill's dialogue 'into their musical equivalent of song and dance' (Fordin, 1975), with actors rather than established singers and dancers carrying the film. The opening ('Our Home Town'), like *Meet Me in St. Louis*, introduces us to the main characters – Nat Miller (Walter Huston), his wife Essie (Selena Royle), their children, notably Richard (played by Mickey Rooney as a pompous Andy Hardy), Uncle Sid (Frank Morgan) and cousin Lily (Agnes Moorehead) and Richard's girlfriend Muriel (Gloria DeHaven), their neighbourhood and home – but in song-cum-recitative, with rhyming dialogue (owing something to the opening of *Love Me Tonight**).

Ever ambitious, Mamoulian wanted 'a very narrow chromatic range – various degrees of yellow, beige and green' (Fordin, 1975), rather than MGM's usually more extravagant colours, and introduced self-conscious cutaways to recreated iconic American images (Grant Wood's 'Daughters of Revolution' and 'American Gothic') over the distant strains of Dannville High School's graduation ceremony. Richard's abortive tryst with chorus girl Belle (Marilyn Maxwell) experiments with subjective vision: as Richard becomes inebriated and aroused, Belle's dress changes from pastel pink to scarlet red – an intriguing idea that Freed was nevertheless probably right to dislike for its failure to differentiate sufficiently between subjective and objective vision. More conventional numbers work better, particularly the town picnic, in which the men drink ('It's Independence Day/Bottoms up and put the beer away!'), the women play genteel croquet and fuss over food and the dancing teenagers take us back to the opening melodic line.

As in other fundamentally utopian musicals like *Meet Me in St. Louis*, Dannville also has its dark side: in Uncle Sid's addiction to drink, the bar in the wrong part of town where Richard gets drunk and the sexual frustration that fuels his repressed resentments and urge to rebel.

Summer Holiday's release was delayed some eighteen months and met with limited critical and public acclaim. It went significantly over budget and made a considerable loss in initial release, which, with the film's lack of memorable standards, have made it a 'forgotten' MGM musical, but it deserves a place alongside better-known films. *Ah, Wilderness!* was later adapted for the stage as *Take Me Along*, with new songs and score by Robert Merrill. JH

Dir: Rouben Mamoulian; **Prod**: Arthur Freed; **Scr**: Irving Brecher, Jean Holloway, from screenplay by Frances Goodrich, Albert Hackett, based on Eugene O'Neill's stage play *Ah,*

Wilderness!; **DOP**: Charles Schoenbaum (colour); **Song Music/Lyrics**: Harry Warren/Ralph Blane; **Musical Dir**: Lennie Hayton; **Choreog**: Charles Walters; **Art**: Cedric Gibbons, Jack Martin Smith; **Main Cast**: Mickey Rooney, Gloria DeHaven, Walter Huston, Frank Morgan, Butch Jenkins, Marilyn Maxwell, Agnes Moorehead, Selena Royle; **Prod Co**: Metro-Goldwyn-Mayer.

Swing Time
USA, 1936 – 103 mins
George Stevens

Swing Time is a fitting conclusion to the main period of Astaire/Rogers musicals that began with their secondary roles in *Flying Down to Rio** and led to the five films in which they starred together between 1934 and 1936. After *Swing Time*, the number and rate of productions slowed: only three more were made in the later 1930s, one in each year between 1937 and 1939, a time during which Ginger Rogers developed an increasingly independent career. The film was the only one of the cycle directed by George Stevens, who later directed Rogers in *Vivacious Lady* (1938).

    Swing Time works variations on the previous films but also seems to play on the expectations generated by an Astaire/Rogers film. Again, their characters meet accidentally and Lucky (Astaire) pursues Penny (Rogers) after she finds him only too resistible. The first number, however, is held back until 30 minutes into the movie and is preceded by Lucky pretending to be a hopeless dancer when he follows Penny to the dance studio where she teaches. She sings 'Pick Yourself Up' to encourage her apparently inept student, but they end up demonstrating their perfect harmony as dance partners in a display of wonderful exuberance staged for Penny's boss (Eric Blore).

    The film repeats from *Top Hat** the threat of an unsuitable marriage for the Rogers character when she thinks Astaire is not available (though Georges Metaxa plays the bandleader, Romero, as an altogether more serious potential rival than Bettini in *Top Hat*). But in this film, the Astaire character also has an alternative partner – as the film opens, he is late for his wedding to Margaret (Betty Furness), whose furious, wealthy father only agrees to reschedule the ceremony if Lucky can make $25,000 in New York. It is this commitment (unknown to Penny) that inhibits Lucky in their relationship. Musical numbers, too, repeatedly evoke but undercut romantic unity in ways that vary from incongruity to something

darker. When Lucky sings 'The Way You Look Tonight' at the piano in Penny's apartment, she is drawn gradually from the bathroom where she is washing her hair; as he concludes the song and turns at her touch, he is confronted by Penny wreathed in shampoo. 'A Fine Romance' ('… with no kisses') is sung initially by Penny as a lament for Lucky's romantic reticence on their trip into the snow-covered country. 'Never Gonna Dance', which leads into their great dance number in the huge empty nightclub set, is an intense song of farewell to Penny and to his dancing life; the number ends with Penny slipping into the wings and Lucky left forlornly alone. These numbers are all woven into the narrative, yet at the same time they have the feeling of splendid set pieces, as though the film's world on this occasion constrains the transition from talking and walking into song and dance that felt so natural in *Top Hat*. Even more disconnected is the big show number, 'Bojangles of Harlem', Astaire's blackface homage to the great black dancer Bill 'Bojangles' Robinson (see *The Littlest Rebel**, *Stormy Weather**).

The threat of alternative marriages is sustained almost to the end but is dissolved in a burst of laughter that begins with Margaret admitting that she too is in love with someone else, and spreads through the final minutes, embracing all the main characters until even the unfortunate Romero joins in. Laughter sweeps away all obstacles as if to declare – though perhaps rather too assertively to carry conviction – that it is after all a benign world. DP

Dir: George Stevens; **Prod**: Pandro S. Berman; **Scr**: Howard Lindsay, Allan Scott, from Erwin Gelsey's story; **DOP**: David Abel (b&w); **Song Music/Lyrics**: Jerome Kern/Dorothy Fields; **Musical Dir**: Nathaniel Shilkret; **Choreog**: Hermes Pan, Fred Astaire (uncredited); **Art**: Van Nest Polglase, Carroll Clark (Silver Sandal set by John Harkrider); **Main Cast**: Fred Astaire, Ginger Rogers, Victor Moore, Helen Broderick, Georges Metaxa, Eric Blore, Betty Furness; **Prod Co**: RKO.

(*Opposite page*) Ginger Rogers, Fred Astaire, 'Pick Yourself Up'

Top Hat
USA, 1935 – 101 mins
Mark Sandrich

Top Hat was the third of the eight RKO musicals in which Fred Astaire and Ginger Rogers starred between 1933 and 1939. The narrative pattern for the cycle was well established by the time *Top Hat* was made: a movement from initial conflict, through challenge and misunderstanding, via increasing compatibility in performance, to a final unity confirmed in dance. *Top Hat* is particularly reminiscent of *The Gay Divorcee** (Dwight Taylor, author of the stage show on which that film was based, was one of the writers) and key supporting players are reassembled from the earlier cast, but its specific combination of script, design and performances, together with the brilliance of Irving Berlin's songs (in his first film musical) and the choreography of Astaire and Hermes Pan, make it the most memorable of the Astaire–Rogers films.

In *Top Hat*'s luxurious European settings, we are at the furthest remove in the series from Depression America, but while the characters are at ease in the privileged world, European formality and pretension are challenged by the American energy and informality associated with Astaire's and Rogers' star images, even when – as so often – they are costumed in the most elegant evening dress. So the film opens with Jerry (Astaire), a professional dancer, disturbing the repressive silence of London's Thackeray Club with an explosive burst of tap dancing. Although some numbers in these films form parts of shows, central to the pleasure of the whole cycle is the way in which energy finds apparently spontaneous expression off stage in song and dance. In the hotel suite of his friend Horace (Edward Everett Horton), Jerry celebrates his footloose life in the number 'No Strings', moving smoothly from speech to song and appearing to improvise a dance that draws on whatever is at hand in the room. Inadvertently, he also wakes Dale (Rogers) in the room below and their relationship begins characteristically in attraction on his side but annoyance on hers. Later, sheltering from the

rain in a bandstand, Dale responds to Jerry's attempt to romance her ('Isn't This a Lovely Day (to Be Caught in the Rain)?') by engaging in ironic challenge – Arlene Croce (1972) named these numbers 'challenge dances' – first echoing his steps and moving through pleasurable competition to become an equal partner as they dance in perfect synchronisation.

Soon, however, comic misunderstandings intervene. When the action moves to Venice, represented by the elegant splendour and artifice of the Big White Set designed by Van Nest Polglase and his collaborators, Dale believes Jerry to be Horace, husband of her friend Madge (Helen Broderick). Dale dances 'Cheek to Cheek' – perhaps the most intensely romantic of all Astaire/Rogers numbers – with Jerry, still thinking he is a married man and that Madge is encouraging their relationship ('Well, if Madge doesn't care, I certainly don't'). Before the truth can be revealed, however, the film takes us through an elaborately comic play on couples and coupling. Jerry and Horace are booked into the bridal suite; Madge becomes caught up in the misunderstandings and gives Horace a black eye; the disillusioned Dale marries the foppish dress designer, Beddini (Erik Rhodes); Horace and his manservant, Bates (Eric Blore), continue to act like a bickering couple; Jerry still believes Dale is married when she sings 'The Piccolino' and they join in the film's huge concluding production number. Only when Bates reveals that he impersonated a priest and Dale and Beddini are not really married is everything resolved, and Jerry and Dale can be definitively united in a joyous final burst of dance. DP

Dir: Mark Sandrich; **Prod**: Pandro S. Berman; **Scr**: Dwight Taylor, Allan Scott, from Dwight Taylor's story; **DOP**: David Abel (b&w); **Song Music/Lyrics**: Irving Berlin; **Musical Dir**: Max Steiner; **Choreog**: Hermes Pan, Fred Astaire (uncredited); **Art**: Van Nest Polglase, Carroll Clark; **Main Cast**: Fred Astaire, Ginger Rogers, Edward Everett Horton, Helen Broderick, Erik Rhodes, Eric Blore; **Prod Co**: RKO.

True Stories
USA, 1986 – 90 mins
David Byrne

True Stories is one of the more arresting and adventurous efforts of the past thirty or so years to incorporate popular music into some form of musical film. David Byrne and Talking Heads were one of the most distinctive popular music sounds to emerge in the 1970s, and their concert film *Stop Making Sense* (directed by Jonathan Demme, 1984), one of the best (and most commercially successful) concert movies, offers a fine record of their work.

As its opening caption says, *True Stories* (based on supposedly true stories Byrne had encountered) is 'a film about a bunch of people in Virgil, Texas'. Virgil is a fictional composite of several real Texas towns – typical but, in its very typicality, unique and extraordinary. The film's brief montage of Texan history, culminating in the computer industry which provides Virgil's economic base and the mall which has taken over from the town square as communal centre, is very insightful, but Byrne is specially interested in the ordinary/eccentric characters who people the town and the music that runs through their lives: the climax of the film is Virgil's talent show for the sesquicentennial celebration of its 'specialness'. The quirky characters include Louis Fyne (John Goodman), driven by desire for matrimony, the woman who never gets out of bed (Swoosie Kurtz), the Lying Woman (Jo Harvey Allen), and the town's visionary Earl Culver (Spalding Gray) and his wife Kay (Annie McEnroe), who communicate only via their children. Of course, *True Stories* is unashamedly a showcase for Byrne's eclectic musical tastes, from the frenetic all shapes, sizes and races karaoke of 'Wild, Wild Life', to the gospel-tinged 'Puzzling Evidence' and the Hispanic rhythms of 'Soy de Tejas'. But Byrne also does simple: one of the most intriguing musical sequences, 'Hey Now', features a group of children (and a goat) singing and making music with bits of wood and metal as they hop through a building site.

True Stories shares some of the affection for small-town life of musicals like *Summer Holiday** or *The Music Man** but though resolutely set in the present rather than some idealised early twentieth century, it nevertheless conjures an imaginary landscape saturated by media images ('We Live in the City of Dreams'). In other ways, it could be related to the disenchantment of Robert Altman's *Nashville**: one of the film's final numbers, 'People Like Us' ('We don't want freedom/We don't want justice/We just want someone to love') recalls *Nashville*'s 'It Don't Worry Me'. The narrator figure (Byrne himself, dressed up in Western suit and stetson and driving around in a red convertible) is so deadpan and noncommittal that it is not always clear what we are meant to make of his observations: contemplating a sequence of identical, featureless brick houses perched next to scrubby prairie, Byrne philosophises, typically, 'Look at this. Who can say it isn't beautiful? Sky. Bricks. Who do you think lives there? Four-car garage. Hope. Fear. Excitement. Satisfaction.' Much of the pleasure of the film, in fact, arises from Byrne's and photographer Ed Lachman's iconic imagery of freeways, malls, gas stations and standardised, anonymous buildings. The film has a particularly American feel, familiar from the Western, for the town's precarious existence in the middle of the prairie, what Earl calls 'the edge of the civilised world'. JH

Dir: David Byrne; **Prod**: Gary Kurfirst, Edward R. Pressman; **Scr**: David Byrne, Beth Henley, Stephen Tobolowsky; **DOP**: Ed Lachman (colour); **Song Music/Lyrics**: David Byrne; **Choreog**: Dee McCandless, Gene Menger; **Art**: Barbara Ling; **Main Cast**: David Byrne, John Goodman, Spalding Gray, Swoosie Kurtz, Alix Elias, Annie McEnroe, Jo Harvey Allen; **Prod Co**: Warner Bros.

Viktor und Viktoria
Germany, 1933 – 102 mins
Reinhold Schünzel

Viktor und Viktoria, the top German box-office hit of 1933, was one of
several German films trying to challenge the dominance of Hollywood,
drawing on both Hollywood models and German theatrical traditions,
whether the fairy-tale operetta splendour of *Der Kongress tanzt** or the
contemporary backstage Weimar cabaret culture of *Viktor und Viktoria*.
Viktor (Hermann Thimig), a splendid creation, is a camp, hammy actor
unable to find work except (secretly) as a female impersonator (Viktoria).
Susanne (Renate Müller) is a sweet young woman seeking theatrical
work. Fate throws them together and Viktor, struck down with a heavy
cold, prevails on Susanne to dress up as a man and stand in for Viktor as
Viktoria. A resounding success, Susanne is pressured into continuing
living as a man to perform as Viktoria on stage. Gender confusion and

Hermann Thimig, Renate Müller

complications occur when socialites Robert (Adolf Wohlbrück, later
known as Anton Walbrook), Ellinor (Hilde Hildebrand) and Douglas (Fritz
Odemar) all 'fall for' – indeed, lust after – 'Viktor'. Not far below the
surface is an attraction to their own sex, even after Robert discovers,
accidentally, that 'Viktor' is in fact a woman, and although, naturally
enough, gender order is restored at the end.

Unsurprisingly, the story lends itself to much comic business, from
the slapstick antics of Viktor preparing for a duel, to screwball play with
gender identity in scenes where Susanne, as Viktor, practises how to
drink, walk and sit on a bar stool 'like a man', or is subjected by Robert –
in a kind of 'punishment' for her gender transgression – to various male
rituals, including a barbershop shave. Much of the film's charm, however,
comes from its inventive use of sound, its rhyming dialogue (as in
Rouben Mamoulian's *Love Me Tonight**) merging into spoken song and,
occasionally, into actual song, notably 'Von einem Tag in Frühling klopfs
das Glück an Deine Tür' ('One Day in Spring Luck Will Knock at Your
Door'), and its many gags based on sound, used as punctuation and
mimicry. Like *Der Kongress tanzt*, *Viktor und Viktoria* is equally inventive
in its use of the mobile camera and long takes.

As was common for films aiming at international markets before
dubbing was widely accepted, *Viktor und Viktoria* was made
simultaneously in a French version, *Georges et Georgette*, and the film's
intriguing premise has led to several remakes. *First a Girl* (directed by
Victor Saville, 1935) was a somewhat less gender-challenging British
version, to suit Jessie Matthews's persona (see *Evergreen**); Karl Anton
directed a German remake in 1957. *Victor/Victoria* (1982), scripted and
directed by Blake Edwards (with music by Henry Mancini and lyrics by
Leslie Bricusse), profited from greater openness about gender issues:
Robert Preston in the Victor role is openly gay and more play is made of
James Garner's attraction to Julie Andrews-as-Victor-as-Victoria ('I don't
care if you are a man' – 'I'm not a man' – 'I still don't care').
Though Edwards rewrote much of the story (relocated to 1930s 'Gay
Paree'), more long-winded than the economical original, the film owes a

more significant debt to the 1933 film than the buried end credit suggests. *Victor/Victoria*'s commercial success led to a 1995 Broadway adaptation, also starring Andrews (adapted for television, also 1995).

Reinhold Schünzel acted in numerous German films between 1916 and 1931 (including *Die Dreigroschenoper**) and directed many between 1920 and 1937 before leaving in 1937 for Hollywood, where he both directed and acted (for example, in *Hangmen Also Die!*, 1943, and *Notorious*, 1946) until 1953. JH

Dir/Scr: Reinhold Schünzel; **Prod**: Erich Pommer, Eduard Kubat, Alfred Zeisler; **DOP**: Konstantin Irmen-Tschet (b&w); **Music**: Franz Doelle, Bruno Balz; **Choreog**: Sabine Ress; **Art**: Benno von Arent, Artur Günther; **Main Cast**: Renate Müller, Hermann Thimig, Hilde Hildebrand, Friedel Pisetta, Fritz Odemar, Aribert Wäscher, Adolf Wohlbrück (Anton Walbrook); **Prod Co**: Universum-Film (UFA).

Volga-Volga
USSR, 1938 – 104 mins
Grigori Aleksandrov

Grigori Aleksandrov collaborated with Sergei Eisenstein on his major 1920s films *Strike* (1925), *Battleship Potemkin* (1925), *October* (1928) and *The Old and the New* (1929) (as well as on *¡Que viva Mexico!*, 1932). It might therefore look curious that Aleksandrov became best known in the 1930s for a series of musical comedies, notably *Vesyole rebyata* (*Moscow Laughs*, or *Jolly Fellows*, 1934), *Tsirk* (*Circus*, 1936) and *Volga-Volga*, all starring the very popular Lyubov Orlova (who became Aleksandrov's partner). Of course, the very idea of musical comedies being made in the period of the Stalinist 'terror' and the Moscow trials can appear problematic or paradoxical. But the context is clear enough: when Boris Shumyatsky was appointed head of the state cinema organisation Soyuzkino in 1930, he set out to encourage a 'cinema for the millions' that would propagate Soviet policies while entertaining popular audiences. 'Socialist realist' films like *Chapayev* (1934), *We from Kronstadt* (1936) and the Maxim Gorky trilogy (1935–8) may be the best-known results outside of Russia, but the Aleksandrov–Orlova musicals found great favour with audiences.

At the heart of *Volga-Volga* is the on–off romance between accordion-playing postal worker Strelka Petrova (Orlova) and music conductor Aloysha (Andrei Tutyshkin). The culture clash they represent – communal, amateur music and dancing vs. official 'classical' music – comes to a head when local bureaucrat Byvalov (Igor Ilyinsky, who formerly worked with Meyerhold), in charge of the local musical instrument factory but in fact work-shy, self-important and only interested in self-advancement, is instructed to send contestants to the People's Art Olympiad in Moscow. Despite the frenzy of local music-making and dance which Strelka stages at his every turn, Byvalov insists that 'a water-carrier can't be an artist' and joins Aloysha and his orchestra on the riverboat that will take them down the Volga to

Andrei Tutyshkin, Lyubov Orlova

Moscow. The talented villagers set off separately and a comic race ensues, interspersed with songs and dances. Naturally, the two groups (and Strelka and Aloysha) come together, uniting around Strelka's (ultimately prize-winning) song about the Volga river; Byvalov continues to be a (comic) thorn in their side and claims all the credit but is ultimately ridiculed.

The film is full of good-natured knockabout fun, sometimes reminiscent of the Marx Brothers (as when a trio of cooks dance with knives and other kitchen implements), with much falling off boats into the water as well as plenty of life-affirming numbers. The film reserves its barbs for Byvalov, and ends with the main actors turning to the camera, before taking their bow, to tell us that they made the film to demonstrate the power of laughter and show us how to rid ourselves of obstructive blockheads like Byvalov. As Maya Turovskaya (1993) argues, Byvalov is less satirised than rendered as a buffoon. She records that the film was made in chaotic conditions, its personnel prone to disappearing for political reasons. Others have detected oblique comic references to the paranoid political climate of the time. No doubt the film's sentimental attachment to the talent and good humour of ordinary people, and its critical presentation of officialdom, endeared it to popular audiences, and maybe this was why Stalin liked it too. *Volga-Volga* was reputed to be Stalin's favourite film, and he presented a copy to President Roosevelt. A shortened, dubbed version was shown in Britain in the 1940s. JH

Dir: Grigori Aleksandrov; **Prod**: not known; **Scr**: Nikolay Erdman, Vladimir Nilsen, Mikhail Volpin; **DOP**: Vladimir Nilsen, Boris Petrov (b&w); **Music**: Isaak Dunayevsky; **Choreog**: G. Shakhovskaya; **Art**: Georgi Grivstov, M. Karyakin; **Main Cast**: Igor Ilyinsky, Lyubov Orlova, Pavel Olenev, Andrei Tutyshkin, Sergei Antimonov; **Prod Co**: Mosfilm.

West Side Story
USA, 1961 – 153 mins
Robert Wise, Jerome Robbins

In 1957, the year *West Side Story* opened on Broadway, Fred Astaire (in *Silk Stockings** and *Funny Face**) and Gene Kelly (in *Les Girls*) starred in their last major Hollywood musicals. The year before, Elvis Presley had made his first movie, *Love Me Tender*, and Hollywood began to exploit the new phenomenon of rock and roll (see *The Girl Can't Help It**). *West Side Story* was very much of this transitional moment. Jerome Robbins had first approached Leonard Bernstein and Arthur Laurents in 1949 to collaborate on a musical based on *Romeo and Juliet*, but only in 1954 did New York street gangs become the focus and the ethnic identities of the two sides change from Catholics and Jews to Anglos and Puerto Ricans. It became Broadway's first major musical about teenagers, innovative in its setting among Manhattan's West Side gangs, its treatment of inner-city racial tensions and its versatile young cast, who were all required to sing, dance and act.

Several reviewers were caught up in the excitement of Bernstein's music ('one of his nervous, flaring scores that capture the shrill beat of life in the streets' – *New York Times*) and Robbins's choreography ('the most savage, restless, electrifying dance patterns we've been exposed to in a dozen seasons' – *New York Herald Tribune*). In a Broadway context that included two exceptional hits, *My Fair Lady* (2,717 performances) and *The Music Man* (1,375), the show ran for a handsome 732 performances before touring. Fours year later, however, the screen adaptation was successful on an altogether larger scale.

The film is at its most impressive in the ensemble numbers. Jerome Robbins's direction and choreography had been crucial to the show, and he and Robert Wise started the film as co-directors. Robbins had no film experience and was fired when his perfectionism led to schedule and budget overruns, but his choreography remained. In its only sequence shot on location, the action begins (after the famous aerial approach across Manhattan) with a long, choreographed 'Prologue', the rhythmic finger-clicking of the Jets gradually leading into dance as they take to the streets, the music increasing in tempo when they encounter their Puerto Rican rivals, the Sharks. It is an exhilarating opening and the rest of the film is powered by Robbins's other dance sequences, such as 'Dance at the Gym', 'America' and 'Cool', which respond to the dramatic contexts and challenging rhythms of Bernstein's music with hard-edged, often explosive choreography and are danced by an outstanding cast led by Russ Tamblyn, Rita Moreno and George Chakiris.

Less effective is the romance between Maria (Natalie Wood) and Tony (Richard Beymer). They sing the film's most familiar melodies ('Maria', 'Tonight', 'I Feel Pretty', 'There's a Place for Us' – though both Beymer and Wood were dubbed), but it is a challenge for both film and performers that until the story's last movements, the characters (especially Tony) have little to do except fall in love. They are the tragic centre of the drama, but most of the action and energy are elsewhere. It is revealing that their love-at-first-sight romance is accompanied by clumsy optical effects – blurred or darkened backgrounds, heightened colour, dimmed lighting – as though to make up in rhetorical enhancement for what is dramatically lacking. There is certainly little sexual chemistry between Wood and Beymer, although the role of Tony, in particular, would be challenging for anyone.

The film was greeted rapturously. It became the second most successful release of the year and was awarded a remarkable ten Oscars from its eleven nominations, including Best Film and Best Director – still the record for a film musical. DP

Dir: Robert Wise, Jerome Robbins; **Prod**: Robert Wise; **Scr**: Ernest Lehman, from the musical play, book by Arthur Laurents; **DOP**: Daniel L. Fapp (colour); **Song Music/Lyrics**: Leonard Bernstein/Stephen Sondheim; **Musical Dir**: Johnny Green, Saul Chaplin; **Choreog**: Jerome Robbins; **Art**: Boris Leven; **Main Cast**: Natalie Wood, Richard Beymer, Russ Tamblyn, George Chakiris, Rita Moreno; **Prod Co**: United Artists.

The Wizard of Oz
USA, 1939 – 101 mins
Victor Fleming

The Wizard of Oz is probably the best known of all children's films.
Its popularity grew with re-releases in 1949 and 1954 and increased with
TV screenings from the mid-1950s, until it achieved an unparalleled
status both as a family favourite and a cultural reference point.

At the time, though, it was a risky project. In the 1930s, as Hugh
Fordin (1975) puts it, 'fantasies didn't play well', and they were also
expensive. It was the enormous success of Walt Disney's *Snow White and
the Seven Dwarfs** that encouraged MGM to make a new film version of
L. Frank Baum's hugely popular tales of Oz (there had been a stage
musical as early as 1903, and two silent movies). MGM committed major
resources to the challenge of visualising the world of Oz, and it is a
tribute to the studio's creative team that the film is unscarred by a
production process that involved four directors – Richard Thorpe, George
Cukor and King Vidor, in addition to Victor Fleming. It seems remarkable
now that there was also uncertainty over who should play Dorothy:
Shirley Temple and Deanna Durbin were considered before sixteen-year-
old Judy Garland was given her first starring role. That Garland was cast
was due to the insistence of associate producer Arthur Freed, shortly to
become head of a team at MGM ('the Freed unit') that created the most
outstanding run of musicals in Hollywood history. Freed also recruited
Harold Arlen and E. Y. 'Yip' Harburg, whose songs were so crucial to the
film's success.

The film works powerful variations on the familiar motif of a child
being magically transported from home to a world of wonders, with its
competing pulls of security and adventure. Here, the vibrant Technicolor
of Oz is framed by the black and white of a bleak rural Kansas where
Dorothy is persecuted by the vindictive Miss Gulch (Margaret Hamilton),
largely ignored by her overworked and ineffectual aunt and uncle, and
sings longingly of 'Somewhere over the Rainbow'. When Dorothy and

her dog, Toto, are whirled up by a tornado, she finds herself in a world – brilliantly realised by MGM's designers and Harold Rosson's Technicolor photography – that appears in every way the opposite of Kansas. It becomes a place where, as she journeys to the Emerald City to ask the Wizard how to return home, she must confront and overcome fear and danger, but finds companionship and even love that has no equivalent there, from unlikely new friends, the Scarecrow (Ray Bolger), the Tin Man (Jack Haley) and the Cowardly Lion (Bert Lahr). Yet, oddly, it is a place where these friends, as well as the Wizard (Frank Morgan) and the Wicked Witch of the West (Margaret Hamilton), are characters from Kansas in strange new guises.

As she prepares to leave Oz, Dorothy is distressed at deserting her friends, yet desperate to return home. When she does so, repeating 'There's no place like home' and clicking the heels of her ruby slippers, the Technicolor glory of Oz gives way to the black and white of an unchanged Kansas. Dorothy wakes, disorientated, in her bedroom: unlike in Baum's stories, Oz has been a dream. With the weight of the film behind it, Judy Garland's tremulous delivery of the final line ('Oh Aunty Em, there's no place like home') makes it feel more like a plea than an affirmation.

An African-American stage version, *The Wiz*, opened in 1973 and was filmed, starring Diana Ross, in 1978. The story and film also inspired the stage hit *Wicked* (2003). DP

Dir: Victor Fleming; **Prod**: Mervyn LeRoy; **Scr**: Noel Langley, Florence Ryerson, Edgar Allan Woolf, from L. Frank Baum's novel *The Wonderful Wizard of Oz*; **DOP**: Harold Rosson (colour); **Song Music/Lyrics**: Harold Arlen/E. Y. Harburg; **Musical Dir**: Herbert Stothart (Roger Edens); **Choreog**: Bobby Connolly; **Art**: Cedric Gibbons, William A. Horning; **Main Cast**: Judy Garland, Frank Morgan, Ray Bolger, Bert Lahr, Jack Haley, Margaret Hamilton, Billie Burke, Charley Grapewin, Clara Blandick; **Prod Co**: Metro-Goldwyn-Mayer.

Yankee Doodle Dandy
USA, 1942 – 126 mins
Michael Curtiz

The framing story of *Yankee Doodle Dandy* has George M. Cohan (James Cagney) receiving a summons to the White House on the Broadway opening night of *I'd Rather Be Right*, in which he impersonates President Roosevelt. It is in conversation with the President (Capt. Jack Young) that Cohan starts to reminisce and the film's main narrative – an extended flashback – begins with Cohan's birth on 4 July 'sixty years ago'.

The film went into production just as Pearl Harbor was attacked and it opened, to great acclaim, on Memorial Day 1942. A biopic based on the life of the writer of songs such as 'Yankee Doodle Dandy', 'The Grand Old Flag' and 'Over There', with its interwoven themes of individual success, the importance of family and the celebration of national identity, could hardly have been more apposite, and the potential of the film to capture the patriotic fervour of the moment was very much in the company's mind as production went on. Indeed, the film ends with Cohan leaving the White House after receiving the Congressional Medal of Honor from the President and joining, unrecognised, in the singing of 'Over There' as troops in battledress march past.

Biopics invariably run into problems of remaining reasonably true to the life, respecting areas of sensitivity for the subject or his/her family, and yet developing a script that works dramatically. As correspondence reveals, there were acute difficulties in negotiating with Cohan, who retained right of refusal over the script for *Yankee Doodle Dandy* and insisted on limiting reference to his private life. At the same time, after the first section of the film, which showed George's early life and the family vaudeville act, 'The Four Cohans', the writers struggled to find a dramatic focus in Cohan's life during the period of his major success, from 1904 to about 1920, when he had hit after hit on Broadway (Behlmer, 1985). A partial solution to both problems was to introduce a fictitious wife, Mary (Joan Leslie), to provide a romantic focus alongside the rise to fame (Cohan's two marriages had ended in divorce).

Even so, like most biopics (see also *Love Me or Leave Me**), the film is inevitably episodic, with several montage sequences enabling elliptical treatment of theatre tours, the succession of hit show titles, the various numbers in a show, and so on. That the film is so successful is certainly due in part to Michael Curtiz's direction of a generally excellent cast, and to the combination of talents that went into design, choreography and staging that closely followed accounts of numbers in the original shows. Most of all, though, the film depends on Cagney's extraordinary performance as Cohan, a role he considered his best and for which he won his only Best Actor Academy Award. His staccato, rhythmic speaking of songs apparently pays homage to Cohan's style, but there is no sense of impersonation in the performance overall. Cagney had begun his career as a hoofer in vaudeville, and his eccentric dance style – straight-legged, high-energy strutting, toe turns and tap – in numbers like 'Yankee Doodle Dandy', 'Give My Regards to Broadway' and 'Strictly off the Record' make one wish he had made more musicals. Cagney played Cohan once more, in *The Seven Little Foys* (1955), and a musical, *George M!*, based on Cohan's life and starring Joel Grey, opened on Broadway in 1968. DP

Dir: Michael Curtiz; **Prod**: Hal B. Wallis, William Cagney; **Scr**: Robert Buckner, Edmund Joseph; **DOP**: James Wong Howe (b&w); **Song Lyrics/Music**: George M. Cohan; **Musical Dir**: Leo F. Forbstein; **Choreog**: LeRoy Prinz, Seymour Felix, John Boyle; **Art**: Carl Jules Weyl; **Main Cast**: James Cagney, Joan Leslie, Walter Huston, Jeanne Cagney, Rosemary DeCamp, Richard Whorf, Irene Manning, George Tobias, Capt. Jack Young; **Prod Co**: Warner Bros.

You and Me
USA, 1938 – 90 mins
Fritz Lang

You and Me is a semi-musical directed by Fritz Lang, inspired by Bertolt
Brecht and with music by Kurt Weill, co-authors of *Die Dreigroschenoper**
(film version 1931). As Lang put it: 'there's no question that Brecht was
most responsible for *You and Me* … He invented the epic theatre and
something else – *Lehrstück* – a play that teaches something … I wanted
to make a picture that teaches something in an entertaining way, with
songs' (Bogdanovich, 1967). Lang made the film shortly after *Fury* (1936)
and *You Only Live Once* (1937), and *You and Me* is a companion piece to
those films. It shares their proto-noir visuals and a crime story – as well
the spunky innocence of Sylvia Sidney – but, as a semi-romantic comedy
with a (more or less) happy ending, it replaces their pessimism with some
optimism, despite its underlying bitterness about ordinary people's life
chances. The story involves the ups, downs and misunderstandings in the
courtship and marriage of two ex-convicts, Joe (George Raft) and Helen
(Sidney), who work in a department store whose owner, Morris (Harry
Carey), believes in giving ex-cons a second chance. Joe, who has worked
out his probation, has come clean about his past but Helen, still on
probation, is unable to; her probation terms forbid her from marrying,
so complications arise when they tie the knot on impulse. Joe, helped by
the casting of Raft, is a complex character, bitter, jealous and not wholly
reconciled to the straight life.

Weill abandoned the project halfway through filming, and the film
ended up with only three production numbers. However, those numbers
suggest that the film was intended to be more of a musical than a
comedy-drama with a couple of songs, and their oblique relationship to
the narrative suggests a more episodic structure. Certainly, they show a
very bold approach to musical conventions. The first number, preceding
the start of the story and sung/chanted by an off-screen voice, sets the
social context: 'You Cannot Get Something for Nothing', a montage of

formally arranged shots of consumer goods and activities and shots of a cash register, critiques a society which encourages people to consume products and where everything has its price. (This opening number is balanced, at the film's conclusion, by the – non-musical – sequence in which Helen demonstrates to the ex-cons that 'crime does not pay' – a bourgeois-liberal argument/message, but one that relates to the situation of workers under capitalism.) During their courtship, Helen and Joe go to a nightclub, where a singer (Carol Paige) sings 'The Right Guy for Me', a relatively conventional number articulating Helen's feelings, although, unusually, the performance is intercut with stylised images embodying her fantasy of Joe as a misunderstood, isolated figure. 'Stick to the Mob', in which the reconvened gang, waiting for Joe, engages in a communal nostalgic evocation of life in jail, is the film's most radical formal invention, replacing music with rhythmic diegetic sounds and vocal chanting, much of it addressed straight to camera. When Joe joins them, he takes up the rhythms and speaks in rhyming couplets. Unsurprisingly, this extraordinary 'number' baffled critics and audiences.

You and Me failed at the box office and Lang himself reckoned the film a failure, but Tom Gunning (2000) claims it as 'Lang's most experimental film and one of his most fascinating, a film in need of rediscovery and re-evaluation'. JH

Dir/Prod: Fritz Lang; **Scr**: Virginia Van Upp, from a story by Norman Krasna; **DOP**: Charles Lang (b&w); **Song Music/Lyrics**: Kurt Weill/Sam Coslow; **Musical Dir**: Boris Morros; **Art**: Hans Dreier, Ernest Fegté; **Main Cast**: Sylvia Sidney, George Raft, Robert Cummings, Barton MacLane, Harry Carey; **Prod Co**: Paramount.

Ziegfeld Follies
USA, 1946 – 115 mins
Vincente Minnelli *et al*.

For over fifty years before sound cinema, vaudeville, revues, variety shows and music halls – all offering a varied repertoire of acts, from singing, dancing and comic sketches to acrobatics, juggling and animal acts – were the most popular entertainments. Impresario Florenz Ziegfeld's lavish *Follies* (named after Paris's Folies Bergère) ran almost every year from 1907 to the early 1930s. In the early sound years, many films tried the 'variety' format (Warners' *Show of Shows*, MGM's *Hollywood Revue of 1929*, Fox's *Movietone Follies*, *Paramount on Parade*, for example, all 1929–30), but the revue format collapsed in popularity in both film and theatre (resurfacing later in television). Like operetta, 'musical comedy' films became more story-based, with integrated song and dance – as had begun to happen in theatre shows like Ziegfeld's 1927 *Show Boat* – although often enough, 'story' was a flimsy pretext for, essentially, a collection of numbers (see, for example, *Anchors Aweigh**).

One basic musical question – how do the song and dance sequences relate to the story? – does not arise with *Ziegfeld Follies*, despite a prologue in which Ziegfeld (William Powell, reprising his role from MGM's biopic *The Great Ziegfeld*, 1936), housed in heaven alongside Shakespeare and Barnum, wonders what a *Follies* would look like now. *Ziegfeld Follies* is simply a sequence of separate song and dance numbers and sketches, by different directors, or, as MGM put it, 'the greatest assemblage of celebrated talent ever to appear in one show on stage or screen'. MGM's stars and extravagant spectacle made it the natural inheritor of Ziegfeld's theatrical legacy, and the film is faithful to his formula: 'high' and 'low' song and dance (Verdi as well as popular standards, ballet as well as ballroom and tap), comedy sketches, a 'water ballet' and, naturally, lots of 'girls' (perhaps the ultimate *raison d'être* of Ziegfeld's shows).

The comedy sketches – Keenan Wynn, Victor Moore and Edward Arnold, Fanny Brice, Red Skelton – now look dated, although many 1946 reviewers considered them the film's highlights. For contemporary tastes, the highlights are clearly Fred Astaire's three big dance numbers directed by Vincente Minnelli. Astaire and Lucille Bremer (like Judy Garland, fresh from *Meet Me in St. Louis**) dance together in the 'dance story' 'This Heart of Mine', with Astaire as a raffish gentleman jewel thief trying to rob Bremer but falling in love instead, and the 'dramatic pantomime' 'Limehouse Blues', in which poor Chinaman Astaire dreams of courting exotic Bremer. Bremer proves a good partner for Astaire (here and in Minnelli's *Yolanda and the Thief*, 1945), and Metro's designers provide highly stylised sets: 'Limehouse Blues' places the scarlet-clad dancers against garish purple and yellow. Astaire is as virtuoso as ever but looks more comfortable in his only ever appearance with Gene Kelly (fresh from *Cover Girl**), in 'The Babbitt and the Bromide': their good-humoured rivalry, in a more 'hoofer'-type dance routine, is superb, Astaire's effortless elegance contrasting with Kelly's more muscular, athletic style. Similarly fresh is Garland's funny, sexy 'A Great Lady Has an Interview'. The appeal of swimming star Esther Williams's 'water ballet' now looks unfathomable, but she was for several years MGM's top box-office attraction: other than novelty value, her main appeal for 1940s/50s audiences (male at least) must surely have been her state of relative undress.

The film ends with soprano Kathryn Grayson's 'There's Beauty Everywhere', the epitome of MGM 'art', but more interesting is Lena Horne (recently starred in *Stormy Weather**) singing 'Love': Horne apparently hated MGM's setting for the song (two black women fighting over a man in a West Indian bar), but the song became permanently associated with the singer. JH

Dir: Vincente Minnelli, *et al*.; **Prod**: Arthur Freed; **Scr**: Lemuel Ayers, Robert Lewis, *et al*.; **DOP**: George Folsey, Charles Rosher (colour); **Song Music/Lyrics**: Harry Warren/Arthur Freed; George Gershwin/Ira Gershwin; Roger Edens/Arthur Freed, Earl K. Brent, Kay

Thompson, *et al*.; **Musical Dir**: Roger Edens/Lennie Hayton; **Choreog**: Robert Alton; **Art**: Cedric Gibbons, Merrill Pye, Jack Martin Smith; **Main Cast**: Fred Astaire, Gene Kelly, William Powell, Cyd Charisse, Lucille Ball, Virginia O'Brien, Lucille Bremer, Esther Williams, Keenan Wynn, James Melton, Marion Bell, Victor Moore, Edward Arnold, Fanny Brice, Lena Horne, Red Skelton, Judy Garland, Kathryn Grayson; **Prod Co**: Metro-Goldwyn-Mayer.

Zouzou
France, 1934 – 92 mins
Marc Allégret

Zouzou is one of only two sound films showcasing the talents of the legendary black performer Josephine Baker (the other is *Princesse Tam Tam*, 1935, directed by Edmond T. Gréville), though her famously erotic dance routines had featured in several silent films. After singing and dancing in Harlem in the 1920s, Baker achieved spectacular success and lasting stardom in Paris, where she encountered levels of racial tolerance and equality unimaginable in the US, thus avoiding the fate of contemporaries like talented black dancer Bill Robinson (see *The Littlest Rebel**, *Stormy Weather**), relegated to minor movie roles and little mainstream attention. In *Zouzou*, her character's race is barely a live issue, and the Southern stereotypes of all-black musicals like *Hallelujah!** are wholly absent.

　The narrative premise of *Zouzou* is that the mulatto Zouzou (Baker) and white Jean (Jean Gabin), orphans of different parentage, are brought up as brother and sister. Later, in Paris, Jean gets a job as a lighting technician in a theatre, while Zouzou works in a laundry. The free-spirited Zouzou – we see her releasing some caged birds – and Jean are very close, but Zouzou has a more than sisterly interest in Jean, who falls in love with Zouzou's best friend at the laundry, Claire (Yvette Lebon). All this brings together two major narrative strands: the love triangle and the theatre's struggle to put on a show, centred on the unreliable (and untalented) lead female singer, inevitably replaced by Zouzou (who we have seen leading an impromptu song in the laundry). When Jean is arrested and imprisoned for a murder he did not commit, Zouzou takes the lead at the theatre to pay the costs of fighting his case and freeing him.

　Zouzou is a romantic comedy, with screwball elements, combined with a rather end-loaded backstage musical modelled on Hollywood films like *42nd Street** and *Gold Diggers of 1933**, down to extravagant production numbers which take up much of the final third of the film. One number discovers a crowd of girls in a giant bed; another creates the effect of water from a bridge pouring down over the chorus girls; like Busby Berkeley numbers, both far exceed the physical limitations of the theatre stage. Baker is the main interest here (though co-star Gabin, earlier a music-hall singer and not yet a major star, is given a song, 'Viens, Fifine', and is already very much the Gabin persona). As well as her song in the laundry, Zouzou, in a skimpy, sparkling playsuit, performs some of the gymnastic dance movements Baker was famous for, shown in part in shadow form, as she helps Jean position a light; though these movements are 'private', the producer sees them and wants her for the show. Baker performs several numbers in the show itself, including 'Pour moi, il n'y a qu'un seul homme à Paris' and, most notably, 'Haiti', sung while she perches, almost naked, in a gilded cage. Though Baker benefited from racial tolerance in France, this did not mean that she was entirely free from racial stereotyping: her character's lack of inhibition and her exotic eroticism are surely related to her skin colour. It is certainly striking that the film's final image is of Zouzou, having lost Jean to Claire, in her gilded cage – a star but (rather un-Hollywood-like) romantically unfulfilled. JH

Dir: Marc Allégret; **Prod**: Arys Nissotti; **Scr**: Carlo Rim, from the novel by G. Abatino; **DOP**: Boris Kaufman, Michel Kelber, Jacques Mercanton, Louis Née (b&w); **Music**: Alain Romans, Vincent Scotto, Georges Van Parys; **Choreog**: Floyd du Pont; **Art**: Lazare Meerson, Alexandre Trauner; **Main Cast**: Josephine Baker, Jean Gabin, Pierre Larquey, Yvette Lebon, Illa Meery; **Prod Co**: Les Films H. Roussillon.

References

Altman, Rick (ed.), *Genre: the Musical: a Reader* (London, Boston & Henley: Routledge & Kegan Paul, 1981).

——, *The American Musical* (Bloomington & Indianapolis: Indiana University Press, 1987).

Assayas, Olivier, 'The Best Music on Screen', *Sight & Sound*, September 2004.

Babington, Bruce, and Peter William Evans, *Blue Skies and Silver Linings: Aspects of the Hollywood Musical* (Manchester & Dover, NH: Manchester University Press, 1985).

Behlmer, Rudy, *Inside Warner Bros. (1935–1951)* (New York: Viking Penguin, 1985).

Bogdanovich, Peter, *Fritz Lang in America* (London: Studio Vista, 1967).

Britton, Andrew, '*Meet Me in St. Louis*: Smith, or the Ambiguities', *Australian Journal of Screen Theory* (Kensington, New South Wales), no. 3, 1977; reprinted in Britton, *Britton on Film* (Detroit, MI: Wayne State University Press, 2009).

Clair, René, 'The Art of Sound' (1929), <www.lavender.fortunecity.com/hawkslane/575/art-of-sound.htm> (accessed 25 January 2011).

Claus, Horst, and Anne Jäckel, '*Der Kongress Tanzt*: UFA's Blockbuster Filmoperette for the World Market', in Bill Marshall and Robynn Stilwell (eds), *Musicals: Hollywood and Beyond* (Exeter & Portland, OR: Intellect Books, 2000).

Cohan, Steven (ed.), *Hollywood Musicals, the Film Reader* (London & New York: Routledge, 2002).

Cook, Pam, *Baz Luhrmann* (London: BFI, 2010).

Croce, Arlene, *The Fred Astaire and Ginger Rogers Book* (New York: Outerbridge & Lazard/E. P. Dutton, 1972; London: W. H. Allen, 1972).

Dyer, Richard, '*The Sound of Music*', *Movie*, no. 23, Winter 1976/7.

——, 'Entertainment and Utopia', *Movie*, no. 24, Spring 1977; reprinted in Altman (ed.), *Genre: the Musical*, and in Cohan (ed.), *Hollywood Musicals*.

———, 'Is *Car Wash* a Musical?', in Manthia Diawara (ed.), *Black American Cinema: Aesthetics and Spectatorship* (New York: Routledge, 1993).

Dymkowski, Christine, Introduction to the play, in Eugene O'Neill, *Ah, Wilderness!* (London: Royal National Theatre and Nick Hern Books, 1995).

Elsaesser, Thomas, 'Vincente Minnelli', *Brighton Film Review*, nos. 15 (December 1969) and 18 (March 1970); reprinted in Altman (ed.), *Genre: the Musical*.

Feuer, Jane, *The Hollywood Musical* (London & Basingstoke: Macmillan, 1982).

Fordin, Hugh, *The World of Entertainment: Hollywood's Greatest Musicals* (New York: Doubleday, 1975); reprinted as *M-G-M's Greatest Musicals: The Arthur Freed Unit* (New York: Da Capo Press, 1996).

Fowler, Cathy, 'Harnessing Visibility: The Attractions of Chantal Akerman's *Golden Eighties*', in Bill Marshall and Robynn Stilwell (eds), *Musicals: Hollywood and Beyond* (Exeter & Porrtland, OR: Intellect Books, 2000).

Fujiwara, Chris, *The World and Its Double: The Life and Work of Otto Preminger* (New York: Faber and Faber, 2008).

Glitre, Kathrina, *Hollywood Romantic Comedy: States of the Union, 1934–1965* (Manchester: Manchester University Press, 2006).

Godard, Jean-Luc, 'Hollywood or Bust', *Cahiers du cinéma*, no. 73, July 1957, translated in Tom Milne (ed.), *Godard on Godard* (London: Secker and Warburg, 1972); reprinted as *On Godard* (New York: Da Capo Press, 1986).

Gunning, Tom, *The Films of Fritz Lang: Allegories of Vision and Modernity* (London: BFI, 2000).

Kemp, Peter H., 'Love Me Tonight', *Senses of Cinema*, no. 32, July 2004.

Lippe, Richard, '*New York, New York* and the Hollywood Musical', *Movie*, no. 31/2, Winter 1986.

Macnab, Geoffrey, *Searching for Stars* (London & New York: Cassell, 2000).

Mamber, Stephen, *Cinema Verite in America: Studies in Uncontrolled Documentary* (Cambridge, MA, and London: MIT Press, 1974).

Merck, Mandy, 'Travesty on the Old Frontier', in J. Clarke, D. Simmonds and M. Merck, *Move over Misconceptions: Doris Day Reappraised* (BFI Dossier no. 4) (London: BFI, 1980).

Miller, Scott, 'Inside *Grease*: Background and Analysis' (2006–7), <www.newlinetheatre.com/greasechapter.html> (accessed 2 November 2010).

Milne, Tom, *Mamoulian* (London: Thames & Hudson, in association with *Sight & Sound*, 1969; reprinted Basingstoke: Palgrave Macmillan, 2010).

Minnelli, Vincente, *I Remember It Well* (New York: Doubleday, 1974).

Morcom, Anna, 'Tapping the Mass Market: The Commercial Life of Hindi Film Songs', in Sangita Gopal and Sujata Moorti (eds), *Global Hollywood: Travels of Hindi Song and Dance* (Minneapolis & London: University of Minnesota Press, 2008).

Mulvey, Laura, '*Gentlemen Prefer Blondes*: Anita Loos/Howard Hawks/Marilyn Monroe', in Jim Hillier and Peter Wollen (eds), *Howard Hawks: American Artist* (London: BFI, 1996).

Naremore, James, *The Films of Vincente Minnelli* (Cambridge: Cambridge University Press, 1993).

Neale, Steve, *Genre and Hollywood* (London & New York: Routledge, 2000).

Preistley, J. B., *English Journey* (London: Heinemann, in association with Victor Gollancz, 1934).

Ratnam, Mani, Interview (*The Hindu*, 12 April 2002), <www.hinduonnet.com/thehindu/fr/2002/04/12/stories/2002041201050100.htm> (accessed 25 January 2011).

Rayns, Tony, '*Opera Jawa*', *Sight & Sound*, September 2007.

Richards, Jeffrey, *Films and British National Identity: From Dickens to Dad's Army* (Manchester & New York: Manchester University Press, 1997).

Rosenbaum, Jonathan, 'Not the Same Old Song and Dance', *Chicago Reader*, 26 November 1998; reprinted in booklet accompanying BFI DVD edition of *Les Demoiselles de Rochefort* (2008).

Roth, Mark, 'Some Warners Musicals and the Spirit of the New Deal', in Altman (ed.), *Genre: the Musical*.

Sarris, Andrew (ed.), *Hollywood Voices* (London: Secker & Warburg, 1971).

Thomas, Deborah, *Beyond Genre* (Moffat: Cameron and Hollis, 2000).

Turovskaya, Maya, 'The Strange Case of the Making of *Volga, Volga*', in Andrew Horton (ed.), *Inside Soviet Film Satire* (Cambridge & New York: Cambridge University Press, 1993).

Vincendeau, Ginette, '*Pas sur la bouche*', *Sight & Sound*, May 2004.

Williams, Alan, *Republic of Images: A History of French Filmmaking* (Cambridge, MA, & London: Harvard University Press, 1992).

Wood, Michael, *America in the Movies* (New York: Columbia University Press, 1975).

Wood, Robin, *Personal Views* (London: Gordon Fraser, 1972); reprinted as *Personal Views: Explorations in Film*

(Detroit, MI: Wayne State University Press, 2006).

——, 'Art and Ideology: Notes on *Silk Stockings*', in Altman (ed.), *Genre: the Musical*.

——, 'Ideology, Genre, Auteur: *Shadow of a Doubt*', reprinted in Wood, *Hitchcock's Films Revisited* (New York: Columbia University Press, 1989).

Further Reading

Altman, Rick (ed.), *Genre: the Musical: a Reader* (London, Boston & Henley: Routledge & Kegan Paul, 1981).

——, *The American Musical* (Bloomington & Indianapolis: Indiana University Press, 1987).

Babington, Bruce, and Peter William Evans, *Blue Skies and Silver Linings: Aspects of the Hollywood Musical* (Manchester & Dover, NH: Manchester University Press, 1985).

Barrios, Richard, *A Song in the Dark: The Birth of the Musical Film* (Oxford & New York: Oxford University Press, 1995).

Baxter, Joan, *Television Musicals* (Jefferson, NC: McFarland, 1997).

Bilderback, Willis, *The Caveman and the Machine: An Analysis of the American Musical Film, 1929–1935* (Saarbrücken: VDM Verlag, 2009).

Billman, Larry, *Film Choreographers and Dance Directors* (Jefferson, NC: McFarland, 1997).

Cohan, Steven (ed.), *Hollywood Musicals, the Film Reader* (London & New York: Routledge, 2002).

—— (ed.), *The Sound of Musicals* (Basingstoke: Palgrave Macmillan, 2010).

Conrich, Ian, and Estella Tincknell (eds), *Film's Musical Moments* (Edinburgh: Edinburgh University Press, 2006).

Creekmur, Corey K., and Linda Y. Mokdad (eds), *The International Film Musical* (Edinburgh: Edinburgh University Press, forthcoming 2012).

Crenshaw, Marshall, *Hollywood Rock: The Ultimate Guide to Rock 'n' Roll in the Movies* (New York: HarperCollins, 1994).

Croce, Arlene, *The Fred Astaire and Ginger Rogers Book* (New York: Outerbridge & Lazard/E. P. Dutton, 1972; London: W. H. Allen, 1972).

Donnelly, K. J., *Pop Music in British Cinema* (London: BFI, 2001).

——, *British Film Music and Film Musicals* (Basingstoke: Palgrave Macmillan, 2007).

Dunne, Michael, *American Film Musical Themes and Forms* (Jefferson, NC: McFarland, 2004).

Dyer, Richard, 'Entertainment and Utopia', *Movie*, no. 24, Spring 1977; reprinted in Altman (ed.), *Genre: the Musical*, and in Cohan (ed.), *Hollywood Musicals*.

——, *Only Entertainment* (New York & London: Routledge, 2nd edition, 2002).

Evans, Peter William, *Top Hat* (Chichester: Wiley-Blackwell, 2010).

Everett, William A., and Paul R. Laird (eds), *The Cambridge Companion to the Musical* (Cambridge: Cambridge University Press, 2002).

Feuer, Jane, *The Hollywood Musical* (London & Basingstoke: Macmillan, 1982).

Fordin, Hugh, *The World of Entertainment: Hollywood's Greatest Musicals* (New York: Doubleday, 1975); reprinted as *M-G-M's Greatest Musicals: The Arthur Freed Unit* (New York: Da Capo Press, 1996).

Frank, Gerold, *Judy* (New York: HarperCollins, 1975/Da Capo Press, 1999).

Gallafent, Ed, *Astaire and Rogers* (Moffat: Cameron Books, 2000; New York: Columbia University Press, 2002).

Gopal, Sangita, and Sujata Moorti (eds), *Global Hollywood: Travels of Hindi Song and Dance* (Minneapolis & London: University of Minnesota Press, 2008).

Green, Stanley, *Encyclopedia of the Musical Film* (Oxford & New York: Oxford University Press, 1981).

——, and Burt Goldblatt, *Starring Fred Astaire* (New York: Dodd, Mead, 1973/Doubleday, 1977; London: W. H. Allen, 1974).

——, and Barry Monush, *Hollywood Musicals Year by Year* (New York: Applause, 3rd revised edition, 2010).

Hemming, Roy, *The Melody Lingers On: The Great Songwriters and Their Movie Musicals* (New York: Newmarket Press, 1987).

Herzog, Amy, *Dreams of Difference, Songs of the Same: The Musical Moment in Film* (Minneapolis: University of Minnesota Press, 2009).

Hirschorn, Clive, *Gene Kelly: A Biography* (Washington, DC: Regnery, 1974).

——, *The Hollywood Musical* (New York: Crown, 1981).

Hischak, Thomas, *The American Film Musical Song Encyclopedia* (Westport, CT: Greenwood Press, 1999).

——, *Film It with Music: An Encyclopedic Guide to the American Movie Musical* (Westport, CT: Greenwood Press, 2001).

Hischak, Thomas S., *American Plays and Musicals on Screen* (Jefferson, NC: McFarland, 2005).

——, *The Oxford Companion to the American Musical: Theatre, Film, and Television* (Oxford & New York: Oxford University Press, 2008).

Hyam, Hannah, *Fred and Ginger: The Astaire–Rogers Partnership 1934–1938* (Brighton [UK]: Pen Press, 2007).

Knapp, Raymond, *The American Musical and the Formation of National Identity* (Princeton, NJ, & London: Princeton University Press, 2008).

——, *The American Musical and the Performance of Personal Identity* (Princeton, NJ, & London: Princeton University Press, 2009).

Knight, Arthur, *Disintegrating the Musical: Black Performance and American Musical Film* (Durham, NC, & London: Duke University Press, 2002).

Kobal, John, *Gotta Sing, Gotta Dance: A Pictorial History of Film Musicals* (London: Hamlyn, 2nd edition, 1983).

Larkin, Colin (ed.), *The Virgin Encyclopedia of Stage and Film Musicals* (London: Virgin Books, 1999).

Macnab, Geoffrey, *Searching for Stars* (London & New York: Cassell, 2000).

Marshall, Bill, and Robynn Stilwell (eds), *Musicals: Hollywood and Beyond* (Exeter & Portland, OR: Intellect Books, 2000).

Mast, Gerald, *Can't Help Singin': The American Musical on Stage and Screen* (Woodstock, NY: Overlook Press, 1987).

Milne, Tom, *Mamoulian* (London: Thames & Hudson, in association with *Sight & Sound*, 1969).

Minnelli, Vincente, *I Remember It Well* (New York: Doubleday, 1974).

Mordden, Ethan, *The Hollywood Musical* (New York: St Martin's Press, 1981).

Muir, John Kenneth, *Singing a New Tune: The Rebirth of the Modern Film Musical* (New York: Applause, 2005).

Mundy, John, *Popular Music on Screen: From Hollywood Musical to Music Video* (Manchester: Manchester University Press, 1999).

——, *The British Musical Film* (Manchester: Manchester University Press, 2007).

Naremore, James, *The Films of Vincente Minnelli* (Cambridge: Cambridge University Press, 1993).

Parish, James Robert, and Michael K. Pitts, *The Great Hollywood Musical Pictures* (Jefferson, NC: McFarland, 1992).

Parkinson, David, *The Rough Guide to Film Musicals* (London & New York: Rough Guides/Penguin Books, 2007).

Romney, Jonathan, and Adrian Wootton (eds), *Celluloid Jukebox: Popular Music and the Movies from the 50s* (London: BFI, 1996).

Roth, Mark, 'Some Warners Musicals and the Spirit of the New Deal', in Altman (ed.), *Genre: the Musical*.

Sandahl, Linda J., *Rock Films: A Viewer's Guide to Three Decades of Musicals, Concerts, Documentaries and Soundtracks 1955–1986* (New York: Facts on File, 1987).

Smith, Susan, *The Musical: Race, Gender and Performance* (London: Wallflower Press, 2005).

Telotte, J. P., 'The New Hollywood Musical: From *Saturday Night Fever* to *Footloose*', in Steve Neale (ed.), *Genre and Contemporary Hollywood* (London: BFI, 2002).

Wood, Michael, *America in the Movies* (New York: Columbia University Press, 1975).

Index

Credits and Appendices have not been indexed. Page numbers in **bold** denote the principal entry for a selected film; those in *italic* denote illustrations

List of Illustrations

While considerable effort has been made to correctly identify the copyright holders this has not been possible in all cases. We apologise for any apparent negligence and any omissions or corrections brought to our attention will be remedied in any future editions.

The Band Wagon, Loew's Incorporated; *Cabin in the Sky*, © Loew's Incorporated; *Cover Girl*, © Columbia Pictures Corporation; *Easter Parade*, Loew's Incorporated/Metro-Goldwyn-Mayer; *Footlight Parade*, Warner Bros.; *Funny Face*, Paramount Pictures; *Gentlemen Prefer Blondes*, © Twentieth Century-Fox Film Corporation; *Gold Diggers of 1933*, Warner Bros.; *A Hard Day's Night*, Proscenium Films Ltd/United Artists; *The Jazz Singer*, Vitaphone Corporation; *The Littlest Rebel*, Twentieth Century-Fox Film Corporation; *Love Me or Leave Me*, Loew's Incorporated/Metro-Goldwyn-Mayer; *Love Me Tonight*, © Paramount Publix Corporation; *Meet Me in St. Louis*, Loew's Incorporated/Metro-Goldwyn-Mayer; *The Merry Widow*, Metro-Goldwyn-Mayer Corporation; *The Music Man*, © Warner Bros.; *Naughty Marietta*, Metro-Goldwyn-Mayer Corporation; *New York, New York*, Chartoff-Winkler Productions; *One from the Heart*, © Zoetrope Studios; *On the Town*, © Loew's Incorporated; *The Pajama Game*, Warner Bros.; *Pakeezah*, Mahal Pictures; *Les Parapluies de Cherbourg*, Parc Film/Madeleine Films/Beta Film; *The Pirate*, © Loew's Incorporated; *Pyaasa*, Guru Dutt Films Private Ltd; *Seven Brides for Seven Brothers*, © Loew's Incorporated; *Show Boat*, Universal Productions; *Shree 420*, R. K. Films; *Sing as We Go!*, Associated Talking Pictures; *Snow White and the Seven Dwarfs*, Walt Disney Productions; *Stormy Weather*, Twentieth Century-Fox Film Corporation; *Swing Time*, RKO Radio Pictures; *Top Hat*, RKO Radio Pictures; *Viktor und Viktoria*, UFA; *Volga-Volga*, Mosfilm.